HOWL

BY ALLEN GINSBERG

Poetry

Collected Poems, *1947–1980*. 1984.

Howl and Other Poems. 1956.
Kaddish and Other Poems. 1961.
Empty Mirror, Early Poems. 1961.
Reality Sandwiches. 1963.
Angkor Wat. 1968.
Planet News. 1968.
Airplane Dreams. 1969.
The Gates of Wrath, Rhymed Poems. *1948–51*. 1972.
The Fall of America, Poems of These States. 1973.
Iron Horse. 1973.
First Blues. 1975.
Mind Breaths, Poems. *1971–76*. 1978.
Poems All Over the Place, Mostly '70s. 1978.
Plutonian Ode, Poems *1977–1980*. 1982.
White Shroud, Poems *1980–1985*. 1986.

Prose

The Yage Letters (w/William S. Burroughs). 1963.
Indian Journals. 1970.
Gay Sunshine Interview (w/Allen Young). 1974.
Allen Verbatim: Lectures on Poetry, Politics, Consciousness (Gordon Ball, ed.). 1974.
Chicago Trial Testimony, 1975.
To Eberhart from Ginsberg. 1976.
Journals Early Fifties Early Sixties (Gordon Ball, ed.). 1977.
As Ever: Collected Correspondence Allen Ginsberg & Neal Cassady (Barry Gifford, ed.). 1977.
Composed on the Tongue (Literary Conversations *1967–1977*). 1980.
Straight Hearts Delight, Love Poems and Selected Letters *1947–1980*, w/Peter Orlovsky
    (Winston Leyland, ed.). 1980.

ALLEN GINSBERG

HOWL

ORIGINAL DRAFT FACSIMILE, TRANSCRIPT

& VARIANT VERSIONS, FULLY ANNOTATED BY AUTHOR,

WITH CONTEMPORANEOUS CORRESPONDENCE, ACCOUNT OF FIRST

PUBLIC READING, LEGAL SKIRMISHES, PRECURSOR TEXTS

& BIBLIOGRAPHY

*"For the nightly Visitor is at the window of the impenitent,
while I sing a psalm of my own composing."*

Edited by Barry Miles

HARPER & ROW, PUBLISHERS, New York

*Cambridge, Philadelphia, San Francisco, Washington
London, Mexico City, São Paulo, Singapore, Sydney*

Copyright acknowledgments follow the Index.

Howl was originally published in 1956
by City Lights Books, San Francisco, CA.

FIRST EDITION

Designer: *Sidney Feinberg*

Library of Congress Cataloging-in-Publication Data

Ginsberg, Allen, 1926–

   Howl : original draft facsimile, transcript & variant versions, fully anno-
tated by author with contemporaneous correspondence, account of first
public reading, legal skirmishes, precursor texts & bibliography.

   Rev. ed. of: Howl, and other poems. 1956.

   Bibliography: p.

   Includes index.

   1. Ginsberg, Allen, 1926–   . Howl, and other
poems—Manuscripts—Facsimiles. 2. Ginsberg, Allen,
1926–   —Technique. I. Miles, Barry, 1943–   .
II. Ginsberg, Allen, 1926–   . Howl, and other poems.
III. Title.

PS3513.I74H6 1986   811'.54   86–45105

ISBN 0–06–015628–7   86 87 88 89 90 10 9 8 7 6 5 4 3 2 1

ISBN 0–06–015651–1 (limited)

To
Lawrence Ferlinghetti
Poet
Editor, Publisher and Defender of "Howl"
in gratitude for his comradeship over three decades

Missing all our appointments
and turning up unshaven
years later
old cigarette papers
stuck to our pants
leaves in our hair.

Contents

ILLUSTRATIONS

Contemporaneous Photographs & Images Relevant to HOWL

(Above) 1010 Montgomery Street San Francisco, author's room facing back to fireplace, Summer 1955. Robert La Vigne's watercolors on wall; bed bureau, Bach & clock, checkered blanket over alley window. *Photo by A.G.*

(Below) Same furnished room facing front street window shade, La Vigne's gesso portrait of Orlovsky on floor. Part I *Howl* written on desk typewriter, corner left, same month photo taken. *Photo by A.G.*

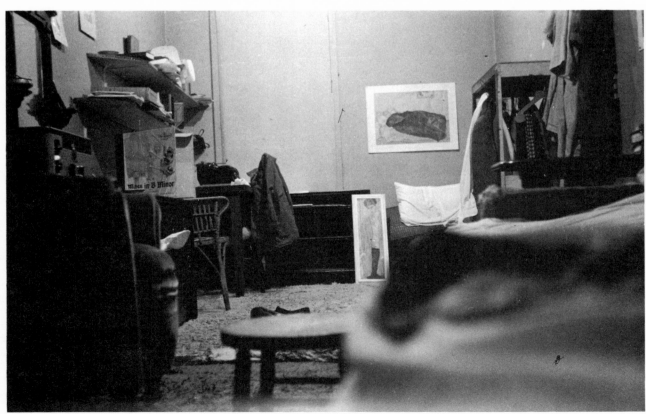

Author's Preface: Reader's Guide

Since this work is not done posthumously, I've had the liberty to annotate each verse regarding appropriate cultural references which few critics have examined (especially to Christopher Smart's "Jubilate Agno," Cézanne's aesthetics and Schwitters' sound poems). I've lived with and enjoyed Howl for three decades, it has become a social and poetical landmark, notorious at worst illuminative at best, more recently translated for understanding hitherto forbidden to the public in Eastern Europe, the Soviet Union and China. It seems helpful in this fourth decade of the poem's use to clarify its literary background and historical implications as well as its author's intentions. Few poets have enjoyed the opportunity to expound their celebrated texts. Usually it is the lamplit study of an academic scholar, as with Mr. J. Livingston Lowes' hard interesting work on Coleridge's "Rime." Wordsworth essayed explanations of his editions. Whitman early and appreciatively critiqued his own *Leaves* with modest anonymity for a generally hostile or indifferent literary society. Later, for a more sympathetic public, he expounded its purport through several prefaces unique in comprehension of his own appointments and disappointments. Still I've ventured my intelligence, neither modest nor immodest, for the general public, poetry lovers, scholars, breakthrough artists and future generations of inspired youths.

The appeal in "Howl" is to the secret or hermetic tradition of art "justifying" or "making up for" defeat in worldly life, to the acknowledgment of an

> "Unworldly love
> that has no hope
>   of the world
>   and that
> cannot change the world
> to its delight—"*

after desolation

> "as if the earth under our feet
> were
> an excrement of some sky
>
> and we degraded prisoners
> destined
> to hunger until we eat filth"†

Thus William Carlos Williams appealed to the "imagination" of art to reveal our deepest natural ground: love, hopeless yet permanently present in the heart, unalterable. ("Love is not love / Which alters when it alteration finds.") The unworldly love hypostatized as comradeship through thick and thin with Carl Solomon rose out of primordial filial loyalty to my mother, then in distress. Where mother love conflicts with social facade, the die is cast from antiquity in favor of sympathy.

Blocked by appearances, love comes through in the free play of the imagination, a world of art, the field of space where Appearance—natural recognition of social tragedy & world failure—shows lesser sentience than original compassionate expansiveness of heart.

It is in the poem, as W.C.W. says, that we reconstruct the world lost. The end

---

* William Carlos Williams, "Rain," in *The Collected Earlier Poems* (New York: New Directions, 1966), p. 76.

† Williams, "To Elsie," ibid., pp. 271–2.

verses of Part I hypothesize various arts that reconstruct our original *"petite sensation"* of *"Pater Omnipotens Aeterne Deus."* The classic art tactics catalogued there suggest a shrewd humor that protects our unobstructed sympathy from chaos. The matter is in objective acknowledgment of emotion.

"Howl" was written in a furnished room at 1010 Montgomery, a few houses up from where the street meets Broadway, in North Beach, and continues down a few steep blocks into San Francisco's financial district. I had weeks earlier quit work as a minor market research executive, had moved in with new-met friend Peter Orlovsky, but as he returned to Long Island to visit his family over the summer, I was alone. I had the leisure of unemployment compensation for six months ahead, had concluded a longish period of psychotherapeutic consultation, enjoyed occasional visits from Neal Cassady, decade-old friend, now brakeman on Southern Pacific Railroad, and maintained energetic correspondence with Jack Kerouac in Long Island and William Burroughs in Tanger.

I had recently dreamt of the late Joan Burroughs, a sympathetic encounter with her spirit. She inquired the living fate of our friends. I wrote the dream as a poem ("Dream Record: June 8, 1955"), about which in a few days Kenneth Rexroth, an elder in this literary city, wrote me he thought was stilted & somewhat academic. A week later, I sat idly at my desk by the first-floor window facing Montgomery Street's slope to gay Broadway—only a few blocks from City Lights literary paperback bookshop. I had a secondhand typewriter, some cheap scratch paper. I began typing, not with the idea of writing a formal poem, but stating my imaginative sympathies, whatever they were worth. As my loves were impractical and my thoughts relatively unworldly, I had nothing to gain, only the pleasure of enjoying on paper those sympathies most intimate to myself and most awkward in the great world of family, formal education, business and current literature.

What I wrote that afternoon, printed here in facsimile, was not conceived as a poem to publish. It stands now as the first section of "Howl." Later parts were written in San Francisco, and in a garden cottage in Berkeley over the next few months, with the idea of completing a poem.

In publishing "Howl," I was curious to leave behind after my generation an emotional time bomb that would continue exploding in U.S. consciousness in case our military-industrial-nationalist complex solidified into a repressive police bureaucracy. As a sidelight, I thought to disseminate a poem so strong that a clean Saxon four-letter word might enter high school anthologies permanently and deflate tendencies toward authoritarian strong-arming (evident in later-'50s neoconservative attacks on Kerouac's heartfelt prose and Burrough's poetic humor).

This facsimile edition is a "How to" book, a handbook for composition of one kind of expansive poetry: its process, basic sorting and judgment, revision, transposition of artful choices. Some interpretations, obvious to old-dog poet-teacher-critic, may unbewilder folk who think they can't understand "poetic inspiration." A ground of common sense is exposed in first draft, a path of re-composition is mapped in orderly detail, the stages and associations leading to finished text are laid bare. For writers interested in open form or long-line verse, annotations provide a key to ordinary writing activity, dissolving mystery's veil of private allusion, or author's subjective assumptions of common reference.

Detailed contents pages provide reader with a map through these leaves of manuscript, persons, decades of anecdote & gossip, aesthetic theory, familiar epistles, noble attacks & sympathies, notable literary moments, poetic arrests, trials & judgment, spiritual breaths, and books & images indexed for posterity.

Pleased with this *Howl*, I remain

Your yet living servant, etc.

The author,

Allen Ginsberg

May 17, 1986

A Note on the Manuscript

The manuscript of "Howl" is on standard typing paper, as reproduced here. Part I and possibly Part III were composed directly on the typewriter. The first drafts of Part II and Part IV were composed in holograph, with all subsequent drafts of all parts composed on the typewriter. "Howl" Part I was written early in August 1955 (before August 16th), at 1010 Montgomery Street, San Francisco. The first three lines and the last four of Part II were written on, or shortly before August 24th, in San Francisco, while the middle section of the poem was composed at 1624 Milvia Street, Berkeley. Ginsberg moved to Milvia Street on September 1st, 1955 and first met Gary Snyder on September 8th,* who was present in the cottage when draft five of Part II was being composed. It therefore seems likely that the middle section of Part II dates from late September, 1955. Part IV, or "Footnote to Howl" cannot be accurately dated. Part I was the only section regarded by Ginsberg as sufficiently complete to be read in public at the time of the Six Gallery reading on October 7, 1955. Ginsberg continued to make minor changes to all sections of the poem right up until the time of publication and many of the later drafts reproduced here date from the winter of 1955–56 and the following spring.

As soon as he had made a clean copy from the original manuscript of "Howl," Part I, Ginsberg sent the first six pages to Jack Kerouac, who was living in Mexico City. The seventh page was retained ("I probably didn't send it because it was so messy") and was kept among the author's papers. On August 30, 1955, Kerouac sent the manuscript on to John Clellon Holmes in New York City. Holmes writes:

"Sometime in the mid-50's, certainly over a year before the City Lights edition, Jack Kerouac wrote me a newsy letter from San Francisco,† enclosing an early draft of 'Howl.' It was such a cross-hatch of emendations and inkings-out that it was hard to get any coherent idea of its accumulating power. But power it had, even then, and when Richard Eberhart reported to the *New York Times* on the Six Gallery Reading‡ a little later (one of the first East Coast notices of the ferment going on in Frisco just then), he mentioned the poem as the ultimate event of the evening. This early draft proved different than the final version, but having no address to which to return it, I filed it away, and forgot it. Years later, in the late 70's, I discovered it in a box of old papers in Saybrook, Conn. That fall, back in Arkansas for my annual teaching gig, I finally returned it to Allen, not without some reluctance, knowing its value, but in memory of those early *samizdat* days when mss. criss-crossed the country, friend to friend, seeking a readership the circumstances in the culture then denied us." (January 18, 1986.)

The other drafts of "Howl," together with the drafts of the later parts, were all stored in a trunk at Ginsberg's father's house in Paterson, New Jersey, when Ginsberg and Peter Orlovsky departed for Europe in March 1957. The manuscript remained there until March 12, 1969, when all of Ginsberg's papers were deposited at the Special Collections department of the Butler Library of Columbia University.

Holmes returned the first six pages of "Howl," Part I, to Ginsberg in July 1980, and they were placed in a bank vault for safekeeping. These pages were reunited with the final, seventh, page in the fall of 1985, when I examined all the extant manuscripts in preparation for this volume.

---

* *Kerouac* by Ann Charters, New York, Warner Books, 1973, 1974, p. 239.

† Kerouac left Mexico City for San Francisco on September 9, 1955, so if the annotation on the first page of the original manuscript is correct, and Holmes received the manuscript from Kerouac in August, it must have been sent from Mexico.

‡ See Appendix II.

The manuscripts were in no particular order, and it took Ginsberg and myself some time to agree to an exact chronology of folios, particularly for the drafts of "Howl," Part II, where the second folio of each draft was sometimes difficult to identify. Some of the drafts were accompanied by carbon copies, and these, together with a number of drafts that showed only slight development of the text, have been excluded from this volume.

There are a number of other variants of the text available. Ginsberg sent copies of the manuscript in its various stages to a number of his friends and acquaintances, and many of these drafts are now in the libraries of universities and other specialized collections. Two different drafts, similar but not identical to the drafts included here, are in the William Carlos Williams collection at Yale. Other drafts are no longer extant. An early clean typed copy, taken from the heavily annotated first draft reproduced here, was given to Sheila Boucher as a gift in exchange for retyping first versions. This draft, which included a number of major revisions, was lost shortly afterward.

BARRY MILES

HOWL: FINAL TEXT, 1986

Howl

For Carl Solomon

I

1 I saw the best minds of my generation destroyed by madness, starving hysterical naked,
 dragging themselves through the negro streets at dawn looking for an angry fix,
 angelheaded hipsters burning for the ancient heavenly connection to the starry dynamo in the
  machinery of night,
 who poverty and tatters and hollow-eyed and high sat up smoking in the supernatural darkness of
  cold-water flats floating across the tops of cities contemplating jazz,
5 who bared their brains to Heaven under the El and saw Mohammedan angels staggering on tenement
  roofs illuminated,
 who passed through universities with radiant cool eyes hallucinating Arkansas and Blake-light tragedy
  among the scholars of war,
 who were expelled from the academies for crazy & publishing obscene odes on the windows of the
  skull,
 who cowered in unshaven rooms in underwear, burning their money in wastebaskets and listening
  to the Terror through the wall,
 who got busted in their pubic beards returning through Laredo with a belt of marijuana for New York,
10 who ate fire in paint hotels or drank turpentine in Paradise Alley, death, or purgatoried their torsos
  night after night
 with dreams, with drugs, with waking nightmares, alcohol and cock and endless balls,
 incomparable blind streets of shuddering cloud and lightning in the mind leaping toward poles of
  Canada & Paterson, illuminating all the motionless world of Time between,
 Peyote solidities of halls, backyard green tree cemetery dawns, wine drunkenness over the roof-
  tops, storefront boroughs of teahead joyride neon blinking traffic light, sun and moon and tree
  vibrations in the roaring winter dusks of Brooklyn, ashcan rantings and kind king light of mind,
 who chained themselves to subways for the endless ride from Battery to holy Bronx on benzedrine
  until the noise of wheels and children brought them down shuddering mouth-wracked and
  battered bleak of brain all drained of brilliance in the drear light of Zoo,
15 who sank all night in submarine light of Bickford's floated out and sat through the stale beer after-
  noon in desolate Fugazzi's, listening to the crack of doom on the hydrogen jukebox,
 who talked continuously seventy hours from park to pad to bar to Bellevue to museum to the
  Brooklyn Bridge,
 a lost battalion of platonic conversationalists jumping down the stoops off fire escapes off windowsills
  off Empire State out of the moon,
 yacketayakking screaming vomiting whispering facts and memories and anecdotes and eyeball kicks
  and shocks of hospitals and jails and wars,
 whole intellects disgorged in total recall for seven days and nights with brilliant eyes, meat for the
  Synagogue cast on the pavement,
20 who vanished into nowhere Zen New Jersey leaving a trail of ambiguous picture postcards of Atlantic
  City Hall,
 suffering Eastern sweats and Tangerian bone-grindings and migraines of China under junk-withdrawal
  in Newark's bleak furnished room,
 who wandered around and around at midnight in the railroad yard wondering where to go, and went,
  leaving no broken hearts,
 who lit cigarettes in boxcars boxcars boxcars racketing through snow toward lonesome farms in
  grandfather night,

who studied Plotinus Poe St. John of the Cross telepathy and bop kabbalah because the cosmos instinctively vibrated at their feet in Kansas,

who loned it through the streets of Idaho seeking visionary indian angels who were visionary indian angels,

who thought they were only mad when Baltimore gleamed in supernatural ecstasy,

who jumped in limousines with the Chinaman of Oklahoma on the impulse of winter midnight streetlight smalltown rain,

who lounged hungry and lonesome through Houston seeking jazz or sex or soup, and followed the brilliant Spaniard to converse about America and Eternity, a hopeless task, and so took ship to Africa,

who disappeared into the volcanoes of Mexico leaving behind nothing but the shadow of dungarees and the lava and ash of poetry scattered in fireplace Chicago,

who reappeared on the West Coast investigating the FBI in beards and shorts with big pacifist eyes sexy in their dark skin passing out incomprehensible leaflets,

who burned cigarette holes in their arms protesting the narcotic tobacco haze of Capitalism,

who distributed Supercommunist pamphlets in Union Square weeping and undressing while the sirens of Los Alamos wailed them down, and wailed down Wall, and the Staten Island ferry also wailed,

who broke down crying in white gymnasiums naked and trembling before the machinery of other skeletons,

who bit detectives in the neck and shrieked with delight in policecars for committing no crime but their own wild cooking pederasty and intoxication,

who howled on their knees in the subway and were dragged off the roof waving genitals and manuscripts,

who let themselves be fucked in the ass by saintly motorcyclists, and screamed with joy,

who blew and were blown by those human seraphim, the sailors, caresses of Atlantic and Caribbean love,

who balled in the morning in the evenings in rosegardens and the grass of public parks and cemeteries scattering their semen freely to whomever come who may,

who hiccuped endlessly trying to giggle but wound up with a sob behind a partition in a Turkish Bath when the blond & naked angel came to pierce them with a sword,

who lost their loveboys to the three old shrews of fate the one eyed shrew of the heterosexual dollar the one eyed shrew that winks out of the womb and the one eyed shrew that does nothing but sit on her ass and snip the intellectual golden threads of the craftsman's loom,

who copulated ecstatic and insatiate with a bottle of beer a sweetheart a package of cigarettes a candle and fell off the bed, and continued along the floor and down the hall and ended fainting on the wall with a vision of ultimate cunt and come eluding the last gyzym of consciousness,

who sweetened the snatches of a million girls trembling in the sunset, and were red eyed in the morning but prepared to sweeten the snatch of the sunrise, flashing buttocks under barns and naked in the lake,

who went out whoring through Colorado in myriad stolen night-cars, N.C., secret hero of these poems, cocksman and Adonis of Denver—joy to the memory of his innumerable lays of girls in empty lots & diner backyards, moviehouses' rickety rows, on mountaintops in caves or with gaunt waitresses in familiar roadside lonely petticoat upliftings & especially secret gas-station solipsisms of johns, & hometown alleys too,

who faded out in vast sordid movies, were shifted in dreams, woke on a sudden Manhattan, and picked themselves up out of basements hungover with heartless Tokay and horrors of Third Avenue iron dreams & stumbled to unemployment offices,

who walked all night with their shoes full of blood on the snowbank docks waiting for a door in the East River to open to a room full of steam-heat and opium,

who created great suicidal dramas on the apartment cliff-banks of the Hudson under the wartime blue
   floodlight of the moon & their heads shall be crowned with laurel in oblivion,

who ate the lamb stew of the imagination or digested the crab at the muddy bottom of the rivers of
   Bowery,

who wept at the romance of the streets with their pushcarts full of onions and bad music,

who sat in boxes breathing in the darkness under the bridge, and rose up to build harpsichords in
   their lofts,

50 who coughed on the sixth floor of Harlem crowned with flame under the tubercular sky surrounded
   by orange crates of theology,

who scribbled all night rocking and rolling over lofty incantations which in the yellow morning were
   stanzas of gibberish,

who cooked rotten animals lung heart feet tail borsht & tortillas dreaming of the pure vegetable
   kingdom,

who plunged themselves under meat trucks looking for an egg,

who threw their watches off the roof to cast their ballot for Eternity outside of Time, & alarm clocks
   fell on their heads every day for the next decade,

55 who cut their wrists three times successively unsuccessfully, gave up and were forced to open antique
   stores where they thought they were growing old and cried,

who were burned alive in their innocent flannel suits on Madison Avenue amid blasts of leaden verse
   & the tanked-up clatter of the iron regiments of fashion & the nitroglycerine shrieks of the
   fairies of advertising & the mustard gas of sinister intelligent editors, or were run down by the
   drunken taxicabs of Absolute Reality,

who jumped off the Brooklyn Bridge this actually happened and walked away unknown and forgotten
   into the ghostly daze of Chinatown soup alleyways & firetrucks, not even one free beer,

who sang out of their windows in despair, fell out of the subway window, jumped in the filthy Passaic,
   leaped on negroes, cried all over the street, danced on broken wineglasses barefoot smashed
   phonograph records of nostalgic European 1930s German jazz finished the whiskey and threw up
   groaning into the bloody toilet, moans in their ears and the blast of colossal steamwhistles,

who barreled down the highways of the past journeying to each other's hotrod-Golgotha jail-solitude
   watch or Birmingham jazz incarnation,

60 who drove crosscountry seventytwo hours to find out if I had a vision or you had a vision or he had a
   vision to find out Eternity,

who journeyed to Denver, who died in Denver, who came back to Denver & waited in vain, who
   watched over Denver & brooded & loned in Denver and finally went away to find out the
   Time, & now Denver is lonesome for her heroes,

who fell on their knees in hopeless cathedrals praying for each other's salvation and light and breasts,
   until the soul illuminated its hair for a second,

who crashed through their minds in jail waiting for impossible criminals with golden heads and the
   charm of reality in their hearts who sang sweet blues to Alcatraz,

who retired to Mexico to cultivate a habit, or Rocky Mount to tender Buddha or Tangiers to boys or
   Southern Pacific to the black locomotive or Harvard to Narcissus to Woodlawn to the
   daisychain or grave,

65 who demanded sanity trials accusing the radio of hypnotism & were left with their insanity & their
   hands & a hung jury,

who threw potato salad at CCNY lecturers on Dadaism and subsequently presented themselves on the
   granite steps of the madhouse with shaven heads and harlequin speech of suicide, demanding
   instantaneous lobotomy,

and who were given instead the concrete void of insulin Metrazol electricity hydrotherapy psycho-
   therapy pingpong & amnesia,

who in humorless protest overturned only one symbolic pingpong table, resting briefly in catatonia,

returning years later truly bald except for a wig of blood, and tears and fingers, to the visible madman
doom of the wards of the madtowns of the East,

70 Pilgrim State's Rockland's and Greystone's foetid halls, bickering with the echoes of the soul, rocking
and rolling in the midnight solitude-bench dolmen-realms of love, dream of life a nightmare,
bodies turned to stone as heavy as the moon,

with mother finally ******, and the last fantastic book flung out of the tenement window, and the
last door closed at 4 A.M. and the last telephone slammed at the wall in reply and the last fur-
nished room emptied down to the last piece of mental furniture, a yellow paper rose twisted
on a wire hanger in the closet, and even that imaginary, nothing but a hopeful little bit of
hallucination—

ah, Carl, while you are not safe I am not safe, and now you're really in the total animal soup of time—

and who therefore ran through the icy streets obsessed with a sudden flash of the alchemy of the use
of the ellipsis catalog a variable measure and the vibrating plane,

who dreamt and made incarnate gaps in Time & Space through images juxtaposed, and trapped the
archangel of the soul between 2 visual images and joined the elemental verbs and set the noun
and dash of consciousness together jumping with sensation of Pater Omnipotens Aeterne Deus

75 to recreate the syntax and measure of poor human prose and stand before you speechless and in-
telligent and shaking with shame, rejected yet confessing out the soul to conform to the
rhythm of thought in his naked and endless head,

the madman bum and angel beat in Time, unknown, yet putting down here what might be left to say
in time come after death,

and rose reincarnate in the ghostly clothes of jazz in the goldhorn shadow of the band and blew the
suffering of America's naked mind for love into an eli eli lamma lamma sabacthani saxophone
cry that shivered the cities down to the last radio

with the absolute heart of the poem of life butchered out of their own bodies good to eat a thousand
years.

II

What sphinx of cement and aluminum bashed open their skulls and ate up their brains and imagination?

80 Moloch! Solitude! Filth! Ugliness! Ashcans and unobtainable dollars! Children screaming under the
stairways! Boys sobbing in armies! Old men weeping in the parks!

Moloch! Moloch! Nightmare of Moloch! Moloch the loveless! Mental Moloch! Moloch the heavy
judger of men!

Moloch the incomprehensible prison! Moloch the crossbone soulless jailhouse and Congress of sor-
rows! Moloch whose buildings are judgment! Moloch the vast stone of war! Moloch the
stunned governments!

Moloch whose mind is pure machinery! Moloch whose blood is running money! Moloch whose
fingers are ten armies! Moloch whose breast is a cannibal dynamo! Moloch whose ear is a
smoking tomb!

Moloch whose eyes are a thousand blind windows! Moloch whose skyscrapers stand in the long streets
like endless Jehovahs! Moloch whose factories dream and croak in the fog! Moloch whose
smokestacks and antennae crown the cities!

85 Moloch whose love is endless oil and stone! Moloch whose soul is electricity and banks! Moloch whose
poverty is the specter of genius! Moloch whose fate is a cloud of sexless hydrogen! Moloch
whose name is the Mind!

Moloch in whom I sit lonely! Moloch in whom I dream Angels! Crazy in Moloch! Cocksucker in
Moloch! Lacklove and manless in Moloch!

Moloch who entered my soul early! Moloch in whom I am a consciousness without a body! Moloch
who frightened me out of my natural ecstasy! Moloch whom I abandon! Wake up in
Moloch! Light streaming out of the sky!

Moloch! Moloch! Robot apartments! invisible suburbs! skeleton treasuries! blind capitals! demonic industries! spectral nations! invincible madhouses! granite cocks! monstrous bombs!

They broke their backs lifting Moloch to Heaven! Pavements, trees, radios, tons! lifting the city to Heaven which exists and is everywhere about us!

90 Visions! omens! hallucinations! miracles! ecstasies! gone down the American river!

Dreams! adorations! illuminations! religions! the whole boatload of sensitive bullshit!

Breakthroughs! over the river! flips and crucifixions! gone down the flood! Highs! Epiphanies! Despairs! Ten years' animal screams and suicides! Minds! New loves! Mad generation! down on the rocks of Time!

Real holy laughter in the river! They saw it all! the wild eyes! the holy yells! They bade farewell! They jumped off the roof! to solitude! waving! carrying flowers! Down to the river! into the street!

III

Carl Solomon! I'm with you in Rockland
        where you're madder than I am
95 I'm with you in Rockland
        where you must feel very strange
I'm with you in Rockland
        where you imitate the shade of my mother
I'm with you in Rockland
        where you've murdered your twelve secretaries
I'm with you in Rockland
        where you laugh at this invisible humor
I'm with you in Rockland
        where we are great writers on the same dreadful typewriter
100 I'm with you in Rockland
        where your condition has become serious and is reported on the radio
I'm with you in Rockland
        where the faculties of the skull no longer admit the worms of the senses
I'm with you in Rockland
        where you drink the tea of the breasts of the spinsters of Utica
I'm with you in Rockland
        where you pun on the bodies of your nurses the harpies of the Bronx
I'm with you in Rockland
        where you scream in a straightjacket that you're losing the game of the actual pingpong of the abyss
105 I'm with you in Rockland
        where you bang on the catatonic piano the soul is innocent and immortal it should never die ungodly in an armed madhouse
I'm with you in Rockland
        where fifty more shocks will never return your soul to its body again from its pilgrimage to a cross in the void
I'm with you in Rockland
        where you accuse your doctors of insanity and plot the Hebrew socialist revolution against the fascist national Golgotha
I'm with you in Rockland
        where you will split the heavens of Long Island and resurrect your living human Jesus from the superhuman tomb

I'm with you in Rockland
> where there are twentyfive thousand mad comrades all together singing the final stanzas of the Internationale

110 I'm with you in Rockland
> where we hug and kiss the United States under our bedsheets the United States that coughs all night and won't let us sleep

I'm with you in Rockland
> where we wake up electrified out of the coma by our own souls' airplanes roaring over the roof they've come to drop angelic bombs the hospital illuminates itself imaginary walls collapse O skinny legions run outside O starry-spangled shock of mercy the eternal war is here O victory forget your underwear we're free

I'm with you in Rockland
> in my dreams you walk dripping from a sea-journey on the highway across America in tears to the door of my cottage in the Western night

San Francisco, 1955–1956

Footnote to Howl

Holy! Holy! Holy! Holy! Holy! Holy! Holy! Holy! Holy! Holy! Holy! Holy! Holy! Holy! Holy!
The world is holy! The soul is holy! The skin is holy! The nose is holy! The tongue and cock and hand and asshole holy!

115 Everything is holy! everybody's holy! everywhere is holy! everyday is in eternity! Everyman's an angel!
The bum's as holy as the seraphim! the madman is holy as you my soul are holy!
The typewriter is holy the poem is holy the voice is holy the hearers are holy the ecstasy is holy!
Holy Peter holy Allen holy Solomon holy Lucien holy Kerouac holy Huncke holy Burroughs holy Cassady holy the unknown buggered and suffering beggars holy the hideous human angels!
Holy my mother in the insane asylum! Holy the cocks of the grandfathers of Kansas!

120 Holy the groaning saxophone! Holy the bop apocalypse! Holy the jazzbands marijuana hipsters peace peyote pipes & drums!
Holy the solitudes of skyscrapers and pavements! Holy the cafeterias filled with the millions! Holy the mysterious rivers of tears under the streets!
Holy the lone juggernaut! Holy the vast lamb of the middleclass! Holy the crazy shepherds of rebellion! Who digs Los Angeles IS Los Angeles!
Holy New York Holy San Francisco Holy Peoria & Seattle Holy Paris Holy Tangiers Holy Moscow Holy Istanbul!
Holy time in eternity holy eternity in time holy the clocks in space holy the fourth dimension holy the fifth International holy the Angel in Moloch!

125 Holy the sea holy the desert holy the railroad holy the locomotive holy the visions holy the hallucinations holy the miracles holy the eyeball holy the abyss!
Holy forgiveness! mercy! charity! faith! Holy! Ours! bodies! suffering! magnanimity!
Holy the supernatural extra brilliant intelligent kindness of the soul!

Berkeley, 1955

HOWL: FOR CARL SOLOMON

Original Drafts: Selected Facsimiles and Transcripts

Guide to Original Manuscripts, Part I

Facsimile of Manuscripts of HOWL, Part I (Drafts 1–5)

Guide to Original Manuscripts, Part II

Facsimile of Manuscripts of HOWL, Part II (Drafts 1–18)

Guide to Original Manuscripts, Part III

Facsimile of Manuscripts of HOWL, Part III (Drafts 1–5)

Guide to Original Manuscripts, Part IV (Footnote)

Facsimile of Manuscripts of HOWL, Part IV (Drafts 1–7)

Note to the Reader

Facing several facsimiles of the early typescript drafts of "Howl" are pages of transcription which use a two-color format to illuminate the poet's creative process. Ginsberg's pencil deletions and additions to the poem appear in red in the transcription, while his typed changes in the manuscript are indicated in black on the transcription pages.

Guide to Original Manuscripts, Part I

Draft 1: Alphabetic marginalia (A, B, C, D in author's handscript, left) were made to sort out groups of lines in thematic order; verses or single-motif sections "hooked" into each other, linked by my own associations or external logic; these were assembled together physically in later typescript drafts.

Page 1 of original ms. Part I has relative integrity of progression. Note that first page's verse line breaks down under weight of associations and extended breath (see note, verse 42); the original intention was to build on the triadic ladder form established by W. C. Williams, imitated by the author in "Sakyamuni Coming Out from the Mountain," and a tetradic verse variant in "The Green Automobile," both 1953.*

Lines marked "A" (page 2, original draft) seemed to proceed from or around New York, as page 4, "expelled from colleges" returns to N.Y. Columbia University & Madison Avenue, impressions of late '40s. Page 4 "A" lines also revolve around Columbia University, Lower East Side, & my own York Avenue apartment, 1948.

"B" verses continue N.Y. theme, but relate to the break of life between the womb of college days & the shock & alienation entering the world, making a crippled living outside of family & academic shelter—this motif accounting vocational failure or re-adjustment, leaving the city, or nervous breakdown, typical post-college crisis.

"C" groups together personal apocalypsis, estrangement, breakthrough to social solitude, disaster or triumph, mixed illumination and/or madness, travel, unthinkable dramas, comedies & tragedies of maturation—arrest, hospitalization, outcast status—degradation and transcendence (see "late C"—"Who stood before you speechless").

"D" verses conjoin images of practical transformation of self-defeat & social ignominy into conscious illumination via artworks for Eternity, "Calling the Great Call" of candor and actuality: "alchemy of the use of the [ellipsis]" (haiku), "catalogue" (Whitman), "a relative measure [the meter]" (W. C. Williams), the "vibrating plane" (Cézanne).

Crossouts (single line or x-cancellation) indicate either (1) rejection of a verse or (2) completed shift of a verse to its agglomerate motif group of verses.

Drafts 2–5: Successive drafts rearrange and rehook the verses into their appropriate groups; some further refine rhythm, syntax or diction to create an even and elastic flow verse to verse (as exampled by Smart). These revisions condense the syntax into solid blocks or "chains of flashing images," and eliminate words that embarrass by inaccuracy or impractical "idiot compassion"; thus "starving mystical naked" was changed to "starving hysterical naked." More in Annotations.

---

* Allen Ginsberg, *Collected Poems 1947–1980* (New York: Harper & Row, 1984).

sent by Kerouac to me
aug. 30, 1955
JCH

mystical

I saw the best minds of my generation
        generation destroyed by madness
dragging   starving, mystical, naked,
who dragged themselves thru the angry streets at
        dawn looking for a negro fix
who poverty and tatters and fantastic minds
        sat up all night in lofts
                contemplating jazz,
who bared their brains to heaven under the El
        and saw Mohammedan angels staggering
                on tenement roofs illuminated,
who sat in rooms naked and unshaven
        listening to the Terror through the wall,
who burned their money in wastebaskets
        amid the rubbish of unread Bronx manifestos,
who got busted in their beards returning
        through the border with a belt
                of marihuana for New York,
who loned it through the streets of Idaho
        seeking visionary indian angels
                who were visionary indian angels,
who passed through universities
        with radiant cool eyes hallucinating
drowsy   anarchy & Blake-light tragedy
                among the post-war cynical scholars,
who burned in the hells of poetry   turpentine + paint
        whose apartments flared up in the joyous fires
                of their heavenly brains,
who purgatoried their bodies night after night
        with dreams, with drugs, with waking nightmeares,
                alchohol and cock and endless balls,
Peyotl solidities of the halls, backyard cemetary mornings,
        wine drunkeness over the rooftops, teahed red light
                districts, sun and moon and tree vibrations
                in the roaring dusks of winter
                        winter dusks of Brooklyn,
who chained themselves to subways for an endless ride
        from Battery to holy Bronx until the noise
                of wheels and children brought them down
                trembling wide eyed on Benzadrine shuddering
                mouth-racked and brilliant brained
                        in the drear light of Zoo,
who mopped all night in desolate Bickfords
        or   listening to the crack of doom
        el   on the hydrogen jukebox,
who talked continuously seventy hours from park
        to pad to bar to Bellevue to museum
                to Long Island to
the Brooklyn Bridge, a lost batallion of platonic
        conversationalists jumping down the stoops
Everybody+   vomiting out their facts and anecdotes
                memories and eyeball kicks and shocks
                of hospitals and jails and wars,
who vanished into the Jersies of the New Jersies of amnesia
        posting cryptic picture postcards
                of Belmar City Hall and last years sharks,
who suffering sweats and bone grindings and migraines
        of junk-witdrawel in Newark's bleak frnisjed room,

and bleak of brained
all

brained
of brilliance

[*in John Clellon Holmes' holograph*]
sent by Kerouac to me
Aug. 30, 1955
JCH

1

I saw the best minds of my generation
generation destroyed by madness
starving, ~~mystical,~~ naked,   hysterical

dragging ——————— ~~who dragged~~ themselves thru the angry streets at
dawn looking for a negro fix
who poverty and tatters and fantastic minds
sat up all night in lofts
contemplating jazz,
who bared their brains to heaven under the El
and saw Mohammedan angels staggering
on tenement roofs illuminated,

5

who sat in rooms naked and unshaven
listening to the Terror through the wall,
who burned their money in wastebaskets
amid the rubbish of unread Bronx manifestos,
who got busted in their beards returning
through the border with a belt
of marihuana for New York,
who loned it through the streets of Idaho
seeking visionary indian angels
who were visionary indian angels,
who passed through universities
with radiant cool eyes hallucinating

Arkansaw ————————————— ~~anarchy~~ & Blake-light tragedy
among the post-war ~~cynical~~ scholars,

10

s ——— who burned in the hell|of ~~poetry & paint~~ ——————— turpentine & paint
whose apartments flared up in the joyous fires
of their heavenly brains,
who purgatoried their bodies night after night
with dreams, with drugs, with waking nightmeares,
alchohol and cock and endless balls,
Peyotl solidities of the halls, backyard cemetary mornings,
wine drunkeness over the rooftops, teahed red light

flying / districts,|sun and moon and tree vibrations
in the roaring ~~dusks of winter~~
winter dusks of Brooklyn,
who chained themselves to subways for an endless ride

& batter - ~~thru~~ from Battery to holy Bronx until the noise
and bleak ~~of~~ brained of wheels and children brought them down
all ~~trembling~~ wide eyed on Benzadrine shuddering
drained of brilliance ————————— mouth-racked and brilliant brained
in the drear light of Zoo,
who mopped all night in desolate Bickfords

or ed listening to the crack of doom
on the hydrogen jukebox, ——— in the stale beer bars

15

who talked continuously seventy hours from park   of third avenue,
to pad to bar to Bellevue to museum
to Long Island to
the Brooklyn Bridge, a lost batallion of platonic
conversationalists jumping down the stoops ——————— off fire escape

Screaming & ————————— vomiting ~~out~~ their facts and anecdotes   off Empire ~~State bldg,~~
—memories and eyeball kicks and shocks   ~~& off the Empire State~~
of hospitals and jails and wars,   & off the moon
who vanished into ~~the Jersies of~~ the New Jersies of amnesia
posting cryptic picture postcards
of Belmar City Hall and last years sharks

ing ~~who~~ suffered sweats and bone grindings and migraines ——————— of Tangier
in ——————— ~~of~~ junk-witdrawel ~~in~~ Newark's bleak frnisjed room,   under

who studied ~~Gnostisffxand~~ ~~Reichxandxorganax~~ Kaballa and ~~Fxkxx~~ Fludd and ~~Vico~~
                                                  Kaballa *Vico*
        ~~and~~ telepathy & jazz because the cosmos
                    instinctively vibrated at their feet in Kansas,
who let themselves be fucked in the ass
        by saintly motorcyclists, and screamed with joy,
who ~~blew and~~ were blown by those human angels, the sailors,
        caresses of Atlantic ~~andx~~Carribean love,
who copulated all weekend exstatic and insatiate
        with a bottle of beer, and fell off the bed,
        and continued along the floor and down the hall
                    and ended fainting on the wall
                    with a vision of ultimate cunt and come
        hopeless   eluding the ~~~~ of consciousness;
who fell on their knees in ~~Catxhxx~~ Cathedrals praying
        for each other's salvation & light & breasts,
who burned on highways journying night to each others
        hot-rod golgotha ~~er~~ jail solitude watch
                    or Burmingham jazz incarnation, *incarnate*
waiting, watching, thinking blind or nude or pointed *we leaned back*
        staring at the sky eternity behind the ~~rooftops~~
                    and television treetop naked ~~heights,~~ *lights,*
where the stars wheeled ~~inxthexnightxxandxhxxxxnx~~
                    in the ball of heaven~~,~~ *~~+~~ heaven,*
        and the solid light of sun revolved ~~in their hair~~
                    and the soul illuminated itself
                    for a few brightened seconds & ~~light~~ *the rays*
                    of ancient years fell through the air,
who picked themselves up out of alleys hungover
        with heartless Tokay & horrors of iron,
                    theirand stumbled to unemployment offices,
who fell out of/windows in dispair, or drowned
        their heads in ~~xx~~ vomit in the toilet,
                    moans in their ears and blast of steamwhistles,
who screamed on all fours in the subway, and were dragged
        off the roof waving genitals and manuscripts,
who howled with delight in the police cars for committing
        no crime but their own ~~intoxixationx~~ wild cooking
                    ~~fuxking~~ pederasty & intoxication,
who passed out leaflets to themselves weeping and naked
        in Union Square ~~during~~ while atomic sirens wailed
                    them down, and wailed down ~~the city,~~
who plunged themselves under meat trucks looking for ~~an~~ egg,
        who jumped off the Brooklyn Bridge
                    and walked away unknown and forgotten
                    into the ~~daxaxand~~ ghostly daze of Chinatown
                    soup ~~knxxk~~ alleyways & firetrucks,
who painted their pictures ~~snxbarixqxand~~ ~~wxapping~~ fishpaper
        in their unhappiness ~~and~~ knowledge,
who burned cigarette holes in their arms
        protesting the ~~naxeoticx~~ tobacco of capitalism,
                    narcotiv   haze
who drove crosscountry in 72 hours to find out if I
        had a vision or you had a vision or he *who*
                    had ~~illumination yet,~~ to find out the ~~future,~~
who journeyed to Denver, who died in Denver again, who
        waited in Denver, watched and went away, to find
                    out the ~~past~~ *future finally* finally

Kaballa ——————————————————————— Kaballa and Fuldd Fludd and Vico   Vico
                    who studied Gurdjieff and Reich and orgones
                    and telepathy & jazz because the cosmos
                          instinctively vibrated at their feet in Kansas,
                    who let themselves be fucked in the ass

20
                          by saintly motorcyclists, and screamed with joy,
                    who blew and were blown by those human angels, the sailors,   in
                          caresses of Atlantic and Carribean love,
                    who copulated all weekend exstatic and insatiate
                          with a bottle of beer, and fell off the bed,
                          and continued along the floor and down the hall
                                and ended fainting on the wall,
                                with a vision of ultimate cunt and come

A   hopeless   eluding the end of consciousness;   last
                    who fell on their knees in Catebd Cathedrals praying
                          for each other's salvation & light & breasts,
                    who burned on highways journeying night to each others   nite

A 25   hot-rod golgotha or jail solitude watch
                                or Burmingham jazz incarnation, ——————— incarceration
                    waiting, watching, thinking blind or nude or pointed ——— up leaned back   cocks
on their arms on rooftops ——— staring at the sky eternity behind the rooftops
                                and television treetop naked heights ——————————— lights,
nite   where the stars wheeled in the night, and heaven
stood still in the height   in the ball of heaven ——————— & height,
        over their hair   and the solid light of sun revolved in their hair
                                and the soul illuminated itself
                                for a few brightened seconds & light ——————— the rays
                                of ancient years fell through the air,
                    who picked themselves up out of alleys hungover
                          with heartless Tokay & horrors of iron,
                                and stumbled to unemployment offices,

A   their   who fell out of windows in dispair, or drowned
                          their heads in vm vomit in the toilet,   their own
                          moans in their ears and blast of steamwhistles,
                    who screamed on all fours in the subway, and were dragged
                          off the roof waving genitals and manuscripts,
                    who howled with delight in the police cars for committing

30   no crime but their own intoxication, wild cooking
                                fucking pederasty & intoxication,

A   who passed out leaflets to themselves weeping and naked
                          in Union Square during while atomic sirens wailed
                                them down, and wailed down the city, ——— Bronx—Wall St

A   & the whole of Bronx—
                    who plunged themselves under meat trucks looking for an egg,   a gold bad
                          who jumped off the Brooklyn Bridge
                          and walked away unknown and forgotten
                          into the daze and ghostly daze of Chinatown
                          soup truck alleyways & firetrucks,
                    who painted their pictures on burlap and wrapping fishpaper
                          in their unhappiness and knowledge, ——————— Subtlety, & Craft,
                    who burned cigarette holes in their arms
narcotiv   protesting the narcotic tobacco of capitalism,   haze
35   who drove crosscountry in 72 hours to find out if I
                          had a vision or you had a vision or he ——————— yet
A   a vision   had illumination yet, to find out the future, ——— Past Present
                    who journeyed to Denver, who died in Denver again, who
                          waited in Denver, watched and went awayx, to find   finally
future   out the past ——————— finally
                                to find out the past (Huston)

                                                HOWL, PART I: DRAFT I   15

who   bit detectives in the neck and climbed ~~xxx watertanks~~
        ~~xkaxzmxkaskaxkz~~ green smokestacks & flaming watertanks
flew   and flew up intoheaven x with their screams,
who ~~xkxmbkxd xx~~ out of cars ~~upxkxxxdxxxxxkkxxkxxxkk~~
        ~~hyxxxxxkkxxfx xixxxxkyxxxxx~~ in one shoe upside down
        on Utopia Bulovard with the hyena ~~xxkkzxfxxkpxxxx~~
        ~~xkxxx~~sirens of eternity wailing in the void,
who stumbled by billboards with 6 cents and broken glasses on
        ~~xxxxx~~ bloody nose and stomach full of ~~guilt metaphysixx~~
                        wind &   ~~kxxxxx xkikfrigk~~
                and metaphysical lightning blasting through
                                        the icy skull,
who broke down crying in white gymnasiums naked   other
        and trembling before the machinery x of ~~xxxkxxxxx~~
                                        skeleton**s**,
who disappeared intoMexican volcanos leaving ~~bxhixx~~
        nothing but the ~~xxxdx~~ shadow of dungarees
                and the lava and ashe~~xxxfxxkxxx~~ poetry
                scattered in the fireplace~~x~~ of Chicago;
who sat years after ~~xxkkxxxkxxxxkxkxxxkxxxxx~~ bickering
        their own echoes in the madtowns of the east,
                rocking in the minight solitude bench~~xxx~~ dolmen

rolling &
                realms of love, Rocklands and Greystones, foetid
                hasseling with imaginary ghouls ~~in xxxkxx~~ halls,
                ~~xxx~~ tangled in the shrouds & straightjackets
of mental rage   aching for their ancestors, laughing in
                        ~~xxxkxxxxxxxfxxxxxxx~~
                eclipse~~x~~ until their bodies
                turn to stone as heavy as the moon,
                        and noone gave them a fuck,
who demanded sanity trial~~s~~ accusing the radio ofhypnotism,
        & were left with ~~hxxxxjxxxxx~~ their insanity ~~xxxkxxxx~~
                and their   hands and a hung jury,
who ran thru icy streets obsessed with a sudden flash
alchemy of the   of the use of the ellipse, the catalogue ~~x~~
                the meter and vibrating plane,
who dreamt and made incarnate gaps in time and space
        showin   through images juxtaposed and ~~pigxxxkx xxxx~~blocks of
pigments ~~xkxxkxx fxxxxkxxxxkxxxxxx~~ ~~xx~~ a flat dimension,
~~shifting~~ back in forth in front of
                and lost their loveboys to the three old shrews of fate
        ~~xxx~~ the one eyed shrew of the heterosexual dollar,
                the one eyed shrew that winks out of the womb
                & the oneeyed shrew that does nothing
                        but sit on her ass and snip (the golden)
                ~~xxxxkxxxxdxxxfxxkxxxxkkxxxxxxxxxxxx~~
                intellectual thread of the ~~kxxxx~~
                        craftsman's loom,

who threw potato salad at dadaist lecturers at CCNY &
        subsequently presented themselves on the granite steps
        of madhoused with shaven heads ~~dxxxxdkxgx~~ and
        harlequin speech of ~~xxkxxdxxx xxxxxxx~~suicide,
                demanding instantaneous lobotomies,
        and who were given the concrete void of ~~xxxxx~~ insulen
        metrosol electricity hydrotherapy psychotherapy
        occupational therapy ~~x~~pingpong & amnesia
                and who in protest ~~xxx~~ overturned one
                symbolic pingpong table,

   flew

who bit detectives in the neck and climbed ~~wae watertanks~~
~~the smokestack~~ green smokestacks ———————————— ~~& flaming watertanks~~
and flew up intoheaven ~~a~~ with their screams,
who ~~stumbled~~ on out of cars ~~upside down with the wil[d]~~
~~hyena wail of~~ ~~siren hyena~~ in one shoe upside down
on Utopia Bulovard with the hyena ~~wail of sirens~~
~~the~~ sirens of eternity wailing in the void,

wind &

who stumbled by billboards with 6 cents and broken glasses
~~and a~~ bloody nose and stomach full of ~~guilt metaphysics~~ on ~~terror shit~~fright
and metaphysical lightning blasting through
the icy skull,
who broke down crying in white gymnasiums naked
and trembling before the machinery ~~f~~ of ~~their own~~ ———————— other
who disappeared into Mexican volcanos leaving ~~behind~~ ———————— skeletons,
nothing but the ~~hsade~~ shadow of dungarees
and the lava and ashes ~~of their~~ poetry
scattered in the fireplaces of Chicago;

rolling & ————————————

en

of mental rage ————————————

who sat years after ~~talking to their shades~~ bickering
their own echoes in the madtowns of the east,
rocking in the minight solitude bench~~es~~ ———————— dolmen
realms of love, Rocklands and Greystones,
hasseling with imaginary ghouls ~~in halls,~~ ———————— foetid halls,
~~and~~ tangled in the shrouds & straightjackets
aching for their ancestors, laughing in
~~in the last forgotten~~
eclips~~es~~ until their bodies
turn to stone as heavy as the moon,
and noone gave them a fuck,
who demanded sanity trial~~ds~~ accusing the radio ofhypnotism,
& were left with ~~hung juries~~ their insanity ~~on their~~
and their ———————— hands and a hung jury,

alchemy of the ————————————

who ran thru icy streets obsessed with a sudden flash
of the use of the ellipse, the catalogue ~~&~~
the meter and vibrating plane,

who dreamt and made incarnate gaps in time and space
through images juxtaposed and ~~pigments shot~~blocks of

shoving ————————————

pigments ~~slipping forward and backward on~~ a flat dimension,
shifting back in forth in front of   space
and lost their loveboys to the three old shrews of fate
and the one eyed shrew of the heterosexual dollar,
~~and~~ the one eyed shrew that winks out of the womb
& the oneeyed shrew that does nothing
but sit on her ass and snip (the golden) intellectual
~~the threads of the intellectual loom~~
intellectual thread of the ~~loom~~
craftsman's loom,
who threw potato salad at dadaist lecturers at CCNY &
subsequently presented themselves on the granite steps

of madhouses with shaven heads ~~demanding~~ and
harlequin speech of ~~suicide,~~ ———————— ~~modern~~ suicide,
demanding instantaneous lobotomies,

instead

and who were given the concrete void of ~~shock~~ insulen
metrosol electricity hydrotherapy psychotherapy
occupational therapy ~~&~~ pingpong & amnesia

humorless
tabletennis

and who in protest ~~only~~ overturned one   only
symbolic ~~pingpong~~ table, giggling ~~humorlessly~~
homosexually,

```
              megnetic                of the wards
        returning to the/xxxx reality/wards years later  truly bald,
 theib own      xith blood on their hanxx xhxxx fingers & tears
              sfzxxxkkxzfxxxxxxxxxxxxxxxxfdxxxxxxxx
              xf self-delivered truth's final lobotomy,
                        to
        and a heartfull of Time, & the bleak xxxxxxxx uncle-lawyer
              xf unxxxxxxxxxxxxxxxxxxdxxxxxxxxx tve
              scream of imaginary Society blasting his eardrums
           ixtha greek chorus of thxxxxxxxxxxxxxxxxxxxxxxxx
                        visible madman doom,

                    own
        with his/mother finally fucked & the last book burned
        on the windowsill & the last prosepoem covered with anal
          as    xxxxxxzxixx xxxxe Apocalypse fob ofte   i       slime
        & published to xhx xxxxxxx multitudinous rats of the
                        sewer xxxxxxxxx
                        & the last door closed at four AM and the last
 hopeless      xxxxxx  companion flown West and the last
                        telephone slammed dxxxxxxxxxxx at the wall
                        in reply and the last furnished room
              emptied      haxxd toxxxxxxxxxxxxx the last piece of
              cxxxxxxxxxxxxxxxx mental furnature
                        a yellow paper rose twisted on
                              a wire hanger, in the closet,
                        and even akixthat imaginary,
                 nothing but a hopeful little hallucination,
                              bit of


        ah Carl Solomon, while you are not safe none of us are safe--
        for now    xxx you'xre really in the trouble of all Time,


        who were expelled from colleges for printing obscene odes in the dust
              of the sexless xxxxxxxxxf windows of men's dormatories
              and burned alive in bloody flannel suits of innocence
              oxzxxxxxxxxxxxxxxxxxxxxxxxx
              cannon xxxxxxx  bestsellers
              amid the xxx blasts/and schrapbels afxxxx of leaden verse
              and nitroglycerine  shrieks of fairies
                 and mustard gas of sinister intelligent xxxxxxx
                                   editors

              xxxxxxxxxxxxxxxxxxxxxxxxxxxxxxxx
              and the subconscous grxxxxxx bloops of the hand grenades
 of the xxxxxxxxxx zoxxxxxxxxxxxxxxxshock corps of advertising
              pxxxxxxxxxxxxxxxxxxxxxxxxx
              with xhx explosions of pseudobulshit xxxxxxx
                    their
 charred xxx up     undeniable reality  annotating the
              xxxxxxx margins of hix flesh with xxxxxxxxx
                        the
              xxxxxxxxxxxxxxxxxxxxxxxxxx jellied petroleum
        sfzxxxxxx of their xxxxxxxxxxbrains.

 who lounged hungry and lonesome thru Huston seeking
              xxxxxxx jazz or soup; & ate candy for six days
              and followed the brilliant SPaniard
                        to converse about America & Eternity
 a hopeless task,
```

megnetic   returning to the ~~grey~~ reality wards years later truly bald,   of the wards

their own ——————————————————— ~~with~~ blood on their ~~hands elbows~~ fingers & tears   hands, all

        ~~of truth's final lobotomy selfdelivered~~

to   ~~of~~ self-delivered| truth's final lobotomy,

     and a heartfull of Time, & the bleak ~~screams~~ uncle-lawyer

     ~~of uncles and lawyers and doctors and~~

     scream of imaginary Society blasting ~~his~~ eardrums   the

with a ——————————————————— greek chorus of ~~the dd doom of visible madmen,~~ visible madman doom,

own   with his|mother finally fucked & the last book burned

     on the window sill & the last prosepoem covered with anal ——————— slime

     as ~~covered with to be~~ Apocalypse ~~for~~ ———————————— of the

     & published to ~~the sewers multitudinous~~ rats of| the   in

     sewer ~~system,~~

     & the last door closed at four AM and the last

hopeless   ~~inept~~ ——————————— companion flown West and the last

     telephone slammed ~~down in reply~~ at the wall

      in reply and the last furnished room

emptied ——————————————————⌋ ~~bared to~~furnished ~~with~~ the last piece of

     ~~consciousness,~~ a mental furnature

     a yellow paper rose twisted on

      a wire hanger, in the closet,

     and even ~~all~~ that imaginary,

   nothing but a hopeful little|hallucination,   bit of

  ah Carl Solomon, while you are not safe none of us are safe—

     for now ~~and~~ you're really in the trouble of all Time,

  who were expelled from colleges for printing obscene odes in the dust

     of the sexless ~~windows of~~ windows of men's dormatories

     and burned alive in bloody flannel suits of innocence

     ~~on the stake of their innocense~~

cannon ———————————————————— ~~in the~~

     amid the ~~gas~~ blasts|and schrapbels ~~of the~~ of leaden verse   bestsellers

     and nitroglycerine shrieks of fairies

     and mustard gas of sinister intelligent ~~manners~~ ————— editors

     ~~with an eye nervous on the ball~~

     and the subconscous ~~grenades~~ bloops of the hand grenades

    of the ~~& explosions of pseudobulshit~~ shock corps of advertising

     ~~pseudobullshit advertising~~

their   with| ~~the~~ explosions of pseudobulshit ~~sex and~~

      undeniable reality annotating the

the   charred ~~out~~ up nervous margins of|his flesh with ~~competent~~

     ~~editorial liquid petroleum~~ jellied petroleum

     ~~of their~~ of their ~~competent~~ brains.

  who lounged hungry and lonesome thru Huston seeking

     ~~love or~~ jazz or soup; and ate candy for six days

     and followed the brilliant SPaniard

      to converse about America & Eternity

    a hopeless task,

C

50

A

B

Who   cut out each others hearts on the banks of the Hudson
         xxxif lifexxxxx a drama on a great lost stage
              under the searxhxlxxhxxxxxlxghxx fixxxlxghxxxxxxx
                   crimson fixxxlamp of the moon,
                                      streetlamp
    who digested xxxxxxxxxxxxxxxxxxxxxxxxxxxxxxxxxxxxx rotten
              animals lung heart feet tail borsht and tortillas
              dreaming of the pure vegetable kingdom,
       who wept at the romance of the xxxxxxxxlxxfxxxxxxxxxxxxxx
              pushcart streets full of onions and bad music,
         who coughed up celluloid balls in Harlem with their lungs
              full of sixth floors of skyxz tuburcular sky
              and orange crates of theology,
         who wandered all night x with their shoes full of blood
              on the snowbanks of East River looking for the door
in the river xxxxxxxxdoor to open on a roomfull of steamheat
              and opium, picking his scabs saying who is my
              friend? cherries
           whopondered his xxx xxxxxxxx in longchamps waiting to
              kidnap a xxxxxxxxxxxxxxxxxxxxxxxxxxx
                   axxxxxxxxxxxxxxxxxxxxxxxxxxxxxx an overcoat
                   on a coat hanger, apparition of a week's rent,
         who wandered in bryant park digging the color of the negro of
                   the skyx evening sky,
         who cut their wrists three times xxxxxxxxxxx xxxxxxxxxxxx
                   xxxxxxxxxxxxxx successively and were forced to
                   xxxxxxxxxxxxxxxxxxxxxx where they xxxxxxxxxx cried,
              open antique stores
         who threw their watches out of the windows in the ballot of
                   far eternity and were presented with alarm clocks
                   daily for the next ten years,
         who retired to mexico to cultivate sex or Rocky Mount to Buddha
                   or Exxxxxxxxxxxx Southern Pacific to the black
                   Locomotive or harvard to narcissus to Woodlawn
                   to the grave to cultivate a final dxxxxxxxxxxxx
                   daisychain of blue, all Poe,

                                                      with
         who hiscouped endlessly trying to giggle but wound up in a sob
                   behind a partition in a turkish bath when the blond
              & naked angelsx came to pierce them with the sword
Who   xxxxxxxxxxxxxxxxxxxxxxxxxxxxxxxx& sat in boxes breathing
                   in the darkness under the bridge, and rose up to
                   build harpsichers in their lofts,
         who rose xxxxxxxxxxxx in the xxx goldhorn shadow of the band
in clothes of   and blew sixxxxxx up a saxophone cry that shivered
music   the cities down to the last radio xxxxxxxxxxx
                   xxxxxxxxxxxxxxxxxxxxxxxxxxxxxxxxxxxxxxxx whith a
                   lament for the blue/jelly of the xxxxxx Time,
                                      sad
         who died eating the octpus of their own imagination,
                   but it was autohypnosis all along & they wound up
                   eating xxxxxxxxx at the muddy bottom of the rivers
                   of Bowery, crabs or lamb xxxx stew in paradise,

A   Who cut out each others hearts on the banks of the Hudson
                   ~~as if~~ lifes~~were~~ a drama on a great lost stage
                      under the search~~light~~the moonlight ~~floodlight moon,~~

A   crimson ~~floodlamp~~ of the moon,
                           streetlamp
              who digested ~~lung stw and hearts and feet and tails~~ rotten
                      animals lung heart feet tail borsht and tortillas
                      dreaming of the pure vegetable kingdom,
             who wept at the romance of the ~~street full of py pushcarts~~
                      pushcart streets full of onions and bad music,

A 55   who coughed up celluloid balls in Harlem with their lungs
                      full of sixth floors of ~~sky~~ tuburcular sky
                      and orange crates of theology,
             who wandered all night ~~i~~ with their shoes full of blood
                      on the snowbanks of East River looking for the door
        in the river   ~~a glass~~ door to open on a roomfull of steamheat
                      and opium, picking his scabs saying who is my
                          friend?

A   cherries   whopondered his ~~eye icecream~~ in longchamps waiting to
                    kidnap a ~~russian overcoat the apparition~~
                        ~~an apartment in the apparition of~~ an overcoat

A   on a coat hanger,* apparition of a week's rent
             who wandered in bryant park digging the color of the negro of
                      the ~~sky~~ evening sky,
             who cut their wrists three times ~~successively unsuccessfulz~~

B   ~~and were forced~~ successively and were forced to
                    ~~go into another industry~~ where they ~~had to cry~~ cried,
                    open antique stores

60   who threw their watches out of the windows in the ballot of
B fall on their heads ———— ~~for~~ eternity and were ~~presented~~ with alarm clocks   stoned   had
                    daily for the next ten years,
             who retired to mexico to cultivate sex or Rocky Mount to Buddha

B   or ~~Frisco to the~~ Southern Pacific to the black
                    Locomotive or harvard to narcissus to Woodlawn
                    to the grave to cultivate a final ~~daisy, blue,~~
                    daisychain ~~of blue,~~ all Poe,
             who hiscicuped endlessly trying to giggle but wound up ~~in~~ a sob   with
                    behind a partition in a turkish bath when the blond
              & naked angels came to pierce them with the sword
  Who ———————— ~~who built harpsichords in lofts,~~ & sat in boxes breathing
                    in the darkness under the bridge, and rose to   up
                    build harpsichors in their lofts,

D in clothes of music ———— who rose ~~to the stand~~ in the ~~gl~~ goldhorn shadow of the band
                    and blew ~~sinsiter~~ up a saxophone cry that shivered
                    the cities down to the last radio ~~and dressed~~
                    ~~the high schools up in clothes of music,~~ whith a
65 last ————————————— lament for the blue jelly of ~~the world~~ Time,   ~~sad~~
             who died eating the octpus of their own imagination,
                    but it was autohypnosis all along & they wound up
                    eating ~~Lamb Stew~~ at the muddy bottom of the rivers
                    of Bowery, crabs or lamb ~~stwe~~ stew in paradise,

---

* [*in Jack Kerouac's holograph*] *Garver: "No coathangers in L' champs"*

                        cigarettes
Who lit ~~xxxxxxx~~ in boxcars boxcars boxcars racketing ~~xxxxxxxxx~~
        ~~xxxxxxxxxxxxxxxxxx~~   through snow toward lonesome ~~nights~~
        ~~xxxxxxxxxxxxxxxxx~~ farms in ~~xxxxxxxxxxxxxx~~ in ~~xxxx~~
        grandfather night,

who jumped in cars with chinamen on the impulse of winter midnight
        ~~xxxxxxxxxxxxxxx~~ smalltown ~~xxxx~~ smalltown streetlight rain,
                                        sidestreet
who took off their clothes on the/corner and wandered into groceries
        ~~xxxxxxxxxxxxxxxxxx~~ ~~xxxxxxxxxxxxxxxxxxxx~~ inquiring
        Milky Way?

who walked around and around in the railroad station wondering where
        to go, and went, leaving no broken hearts, and returned six
        weeks later ~~XX~~

                                                                growing
who limped ~~xxxxxxxxxx~~ over the city hills with half a mustache on
        ~~xxxxxxxxxx~~   the sinister side of the lip, ~~xx~~ ~~xxxxxxxxxxxx~~
~~xxxxxxxxxxxxxxxxxxxxxxxxxxxxxxxxxxxxxxxxxxxxxxxxxxxxxxxxxx~~
        his passion to absurd to inscribe, ~~xxxxxxxxxxxxxxxx~~ he said
        ~~xxxx~~ looking for an example of baroque architecture

        carrying ~~xxxxxxxxxxx~~ ~~xxxxxxxxxx~~ Butler's Analogy

who wandered around the ~~xxx~~ windy streets carrying Butlers analogy
        looking for an example of Butler's analogy
        ~~xxxxxxxx~~ rapidly
who/translated the Songs of Maldoror ~~xxxxxx~~ and threw himself
        on the mercy of Alchoholics Anonymous,
or
who appeared on the west coast in beards and shorts with big
        pacifist eyes ~~xxxxxx~~ sexy in their dark skin, passing
        out ~~xxxxxxx~~ incomprehensable ~~xxxxxxxxx~~ leaflets
                        reading   want ads
who investigated the FBI by ~~xxxxxx~~ spenglerian ~~xxxxxxxxxx~~ on Peyotl,

who read ~~xxxxxxxxxxxxxxxxxxxxxxxxxxxxxxxxxxxxxxxxxxxxxxxxxxxxx~~
        Genet ~~xxxxxxx~~ Spengler Dostoievsky ~~xxxxxxxxxxxx~~ Rimbaud
        ~~xxxxx~~ Louis Ferdinand Celine Proust Wolfe Whitman Buddha
        Ginsberg Kerouac Burroughs & Neal Cassady, I name them all,
        except ~~xxxxx~~ Carr who ~~xxxxxxxxxxxxxxxxxxxxxxxxxxxxx~~
        ~~xxxxxxxxxxxxxxxx~~ got psychoanalysed and took to journalism
        so they must have read him ~~xxxxxxxx~~ too anyway.
                        while
who sweetened the cunt ~~xx x~~ a million girls trembling in the sunset,
        and ~~xxxxxxxxx~~ were ~~xxxxxxxx~~ ~~xxx~~ red eyed in the morning
        but prepared to sweeten the sunrise, wearing their skin
        naked in the alleys ~~with the~~ flash of buttocks ~~xxx~~ by
        doorways

who didnt have enough time to speak among themselves of love

who crashed thru their minds in jail and waited for impossible
                                                        heads
        criminals, hipsters with angelic ~~minds~~ and no ~~xxxx~~ worries,
        poets with ~~xxxxxxx~~ sensibility and the charm of reality in
        their hearts who sang sweet blues to the ~~xxxxxxxxx~~
        their lawyers.

cigarettes

Who lit ~~matches~~ in boxcars boxcars boxcars racketing ~~toward the~~
~~lonesome apocalypse~~   through snow toward lonesome ~~nights~~
~~on granfathers farm,~~ farms in ~~gradfather night~~ in ~~the~~
grandfather night,
who jumped in cars with chinamen on the impulese of winter midnight
~~streetlight rain~~ smalltown ~~rain~~   smalltown streetlight rain,
who took off their clothes on the corner and wandered into groceries   sidestreet
~~on the   sidestreet asking for the Milky way,~~ inquiring
Milky Way?
who walked around and around in the railroad station wondering where
to go, and went, leaving no broken hearts, and returned six
weeks later ~~to~~
who limped ~~around the~~   over the city hills with half a mustache on   growing
~~the   his sinsi~~   the sinister side of the lip, ~~up expert amateur~~
~~of~~ in baroque architecture, looking for a church to look at
his passion to absurd to inscribe, ~~namely he was actually~~ he said
~~only~~ looking for an example of baroque architecture
carrying ~~a volume of Isaac Watts~~ Butler's Analogy
who wandered around the ~~su~~ windy streets carrying Butlers analogy
looking for an example of Butler's analogy

~~rapidly~~   rapidly

who translated the Songs of Maldoror ~~rapidly~~ and threw himself
on the mercy of Alchoholics Anonymous,

or

who appeared   on the west coast in beards and shorts with big
pacifist eyes ~~and were~~ sexy in their dark skin, passing
out ~~leaflets~~ incomprehensable propaganda   leaflets

reading

who investigated the FBI by ~~reding~~ spenglerian ~~newspapers~~ on Peyotl,   want ads
who read ~~Marx Spengler Antonin Artaud Gne Gneet Genet Gurjieff~~
Genet ~~Gurjieff~~ Spengler Dostoievsky ~~Antonin Artaud~~   Rimbaud
~~Wolfe~~ Louis Ferdinand Celine Proust Wolfe Whitman Buddha
Ginsberg Kerouac Burroughs & Neal Cassady, I name them all,
except ~~Lucien~~ Carr who ~~took to journalism so they must~~
~~have read himm too~~ got psychoanalysed and took to journalism
so they must have read him ~~anyway~~   too anyway.

while

who sweetened the cunt ~~of t~~ a million girls trembling in the sunset,
and ~~by sunrise~~   were ~~readyed   rea~~ red eyed in the morning
but prepared to sweeten the sunrise, wearing their skin

or   and

~~barns~~ — barns   ing

naked in the alleys ~~with the~~ flash ~~of~~ buttocks ~~in by~~   [indecipherable]
~~doorways~~   under
who didnt have enough time to speak among themselves of love
who crashed thru their minds in jail and waited for impossible

heads

criminals, hipsters with angelic ~~minds~~ and no ~~care~~ worries,
poets with ~~hophead~~ sensibility and the charm of reality in
their hearts who sang sweet blues to the ~~jau~~   jailers
~~their~~ lawyers.

70

D

Early
C

75

who translated lonesome Catullus into personal talk
            thru time across the ruinx of Siemsx thm a continent,
            and set down now xxxx what might be left to say
            anew xftxrzxxxxdxxthz in time after death,

who recreated syntax & structure of prose
            to conform to the rhythm of thought
                  in xxxxxxxxx naked and endless head,
                  his
                  archangelx of   visual
who trapped the zxxxxxxxxxxxxxxxxxxxxxxxxx soul between 2/images,
      &   xxxxxxxxxxxxxxxxxxxxxx
joined   xxxxxxlemental verbs   and   of consciou
            and set the noun xxxxxxxxxxxxxxxx dash/ together s
            jumping with xxxxxxxxxxxxxxx sensation
                  of   zxxxx Cezanne's
            pater omnipotens aeterna deus,
                  the father-thought of all.
            out of the
who invented xxx angels xxxx flesh and xxx blood of lovers,
            and the angelic consciousness
                  out of the rhetoric & xxxxxx secret cackle
                  of poor human xxxxx xxxxxxxx xxxxx poetry
who rejected the moral imagination of xxxxxxxx the wierd xxxxxxx
            academies of abstract prose and offered the ancient
            xxxxxxxxxxxxxxxxxxxxxxxxxxxxxxxxxxxxxxxxxxxxxxxx
            xxxxabsolute heart of the poem of life
                  butchered/from their own xxxxxxx xxxxxxxxxxx
                        out   bodies
            and good to eat a thousand years,
                  posessing xxxxxxxx xxx wisdom of real meat,
                        thenergy   &
            so   accept no substitutex, xxxxxxxxxx
                  xxx   for the true heart of the folk
                        naked   gasping original
            with all its xxxxxxxxx blood & xxxxxx xxxx
            unconditioned beat on the page

who stood before you speechless & intelligent and shaking with shame
            who were yourselves, your own xxx souls' confessions,
                  your miseries incarnate in madman xxx bum & angel
                  preaching neither acceptance nor rejection
            neither man nor god,   xxxxxxx
                  reality or imagination:xxx xxxx xxxx
                        xxxxxxxxxxxxxxxxxxxxxxx   saying
      xxxxxxxxxxxxxxxxxxxxxxxxxxxxxx xxxxxxxxxxxxxxxxxx.

      Ixxxxxx xxx suffering of love is naked mind.

who   love   naked
                  Dyamerica the xxxx mind & suffer love

Late C

who ate pigeon clampzxgeth xxxxxxx snails
      Borsht & tortillas. & save money

who wept xxxxx romace of the streets
      xxxx Dr Cheapxxxxx & xxx pxdxxxxxfull of onionz cheap
                                                      music,

D

D   80

D

       who translated lonesome Catullus into personal talk
          thru time across the ruins ~~of Sirmie, the~~ a continent,
          and set down now ~~anew~~ what might be left to say
           anew ~~after our death,~~ in time after death,
       who recreated syntax & structure of prose
          to conform to the rhythm of thought

his
               in ~~the neaked~~ naked and endless head,
archangels of   who trapped ~~the invisible sensations of the~~ soul between 2 images,   visual
     &   ~~&in theelements of verbs~~
     joined   ~~in the~~ elemental verbs

D

and
of — ~~like~~ Cezanne's   and set the noun ~~and adjective and~~ dash together s ness   of consciou
           jumping with ~~objective chemestry~~ sensation
          pater omnipotens aeterna deus,
           the father-thought of all.

out of the   who invented ~~the~~ angels ~~from~~ flesh and ~~be~~ blood of lovers,
          and the angelic consciousness

D

          out of the rhetoric & ~~cackle~~ secret cackle
          of poor human ~~prose academic prose~~ poetry
       who rejected the moral imagination of ~~academy~~ the wierd ~~academy~~
         academies of abstract prose and offered the ancient
          ~~a platter of dead cats, christmas livers~~
          ~~the~~ absolute heart of the poem of life

out
          butchered from their own ~~bodies imagination~~ ———— bodies

D

          and good to eat a thousand years,
thenergy   posessiog ~~forver & the~~ wisdom of real meat,   &
       so accept no substitute ~~m, it's ther,~~
          for   ———— for the true heart of the folk
naked   with all its ~~fantastic~~ blood & ~~naked beat~~ ———— gasping original
         unconditioned beat on the page
      who stood before you speechless & intelligent and shaking with shame
        who were yourselves, your own ~~sol~~ souls' confessions,
         your miseries incarnate in madman ~~and~~ bum & angel

Late C

         preaching neither acceptance nor rejection
         neither man nor god,
         reality or imagination: ~~not even love~~ ———— ~~but only~~
         ~~which is but naked mind.~~ ———— saying
      ~~the suffering of love, which is but naked mind.~~

~~my~~ love   ~~I think~~ The suffering ~~of love~~ is naked mind.
     who   In America the ~~naked~~ mind to suffer love   naked
               [hereon all holograph]

Who ate pigliver clamspaghetti lung stew snails
     borsht & tortillas to save money
Who wept at the romance of the streets
  ~~with its cheap music~~ & ~~piles~~ pushcarts full of onions & cheap music,

STROPHES

"I saw the best mind of my generation destroyed by madness, starving, hysterical, naked, ~~angel headed hopeless~~
     wandering around the negro streets at dawn looking for an angry fix, *angelheaded hipsters looking for the shuddering connection between the wheels + wires of the machine the Night*
     who poverty and tatters and ~~fantastic~~ *hollow* eyed and high sat up all night in the supernatural darkness of cold water flats floating across the tops of cities contemplating jjazz,
     who sat in rooms in underwear unshaven burning their dollars in wastebaskets listening to the Terror through the wall,
     who bared their brains to Heaven under the El and saw Mohhamedan angels staggering on tenement roofs illuminated,
     who chained themselves to subways for an endless ride from Battery to Holy Bronx until the noise of wheels and children brought them down shuddering mouth-racked and battered bleak of brain on Benzedrine all drained of brilliance in the drear light of Zoo, *in desolate Fugazzis bar*
     who ~~stood~~ in the stale ~~bars of morning~~ afternoon listening to the crack of doom on the hydrogen jukebox,
     who talked continuously seventy hours from park to pad to bar to Bellevue to museum to ~~saloon~~ to Brooklyn Bridge,
     a lost battalion of platonic conversationalists jumping off the stoops off windowsills off empire states out of the moon
     yackatayaking screaming vomiting whispering facts and memories and anecdotes and eyeball kicks and shocks of hospitals and jjails and wars,
     who lounged hungry and lonesome in Huston seeking Jazz or soup,
     who lit cigarettes in boxcars boxcars boxcars racketing thru snow toward lonesome farms in grandfather night,
     who studied Vico Fludd telepathy and bop kaballa because the cosmos instinctively vibrated at their feet in Kansas,
     who loned it through the streets of Idaho seeking visionary indian angels who were visionary indian angels,
     who jumped in cars with the Chinaman on the impulse of winter midnight streetlight smalltown rain,
     who disappeared into the volcanos of Mexico leaving behind nothing but the shadow of dungarees and the lava and ash of poetry in fireplace Chicago,
     who broke down crying in white gymnaseums naked and trembling before the machinery of other skeletons,
     who screamed on all fours in the subway and were dragged off the roof waving genitals and manuscripts,
     who let themselves be fucked in the ass by saintly motorcyclist and howled with joy,
     who blew and were blown by those human angels the sailors, caresses of atlantic and carribean love,
     who hiccuped endlessly trying to giggle but wound up with a sob when the blond and naked seraph emerged ~~from~~ the partition in a turkish bath to pierce them with a sword, *Celine*

Numbers mark lines (not verses) wherefrom less legible excisions and revisions are set in print.—A.G.

2: **Angel headed hipster** [canceled]
4: **Angelheaded hipsters looking for the shuddering connection between the wheels & wires of the machine of the Night**

5: hollow-
16: sat . . . in desolate Fugazzi's bar
19: ["saloon" canceled] . . . the
46: behind

who bit detectives in the neck and shrieked with delight in
policecars for committing no crime but their own wild cooking
pederasty and intoxication,

who copulated extatic and insatiate with a package of cigarettes
a sweetheart a bottle of beer and a candle, and fell off the bed,
and continued along the floor and down the hall and ended fainting
on the wall a vision of ultimate jazz eluding the last come of
consciousness,

who ate the lamb stew of the imagination or digested the crab
at the muddy bottom of the rivers of Bowery,

who digested rotten animals lung heart feet tail borsht and
tortillas dreaming of the pure vegetable kingdom,

who plunged themselves under meat trucks looking for an egg,
and wept at the romance of the streets with their pushcarts full of
onions and bad music,

who walked allnight with shoes full of blood on the snowbank
docks waiting for a door in the East River to open to a roomfull
of steamheat and opium,

who fell on their knees in cathedrals praying for eachothers'
salvation and light and breasts until the soul illuminated its hair
for a second,

who drove crosscountry seventytwo hours to find out if I had a
vision or you had a vision or he had a vision to find out the
present,

who journeyed to Denver who died in Denver who watched and waited
and came back and went away from Denver to find out the future,

who left for Tangiers to cultivate sex or Rocky Mount to Buddha
or southern Pacific to the black locomotive or Harvard to narcissus
to Woodlawn to the grave to daisychain,

who crashed through their minds in jail waiting for impossible
criminals with golden heads and the charm of reality in their hearts
who sang sweet blues to Alcatraz,

who threw potato salad at doctors of dadaism and subsequently
presented themselves on the granite steps of the madhouse with
shaven heads and harlequin speech of suicide demanding instant-
aneous lobotomy,

and who were given instead the concrete void of insulen metrasol
electricity hydrotherapy psychotherapy occupational therapy pingpong
& amnesia,

and who in humorless protest overturned only one symbolic
pingpong table and rested briefly in catatonia,

and who returned later truly bald with ▓▓▓ mother finally fucked
and the last door closed and the last telephone slammed at the wall
in reply and the last furnished room emptied down to the last piece
of mental furnature, a yellow paper rose twisted on a wire hangar in
the closet, and even that imaginary, nothing but a hopeful little bit
of hallucination,

--Ah, Carl, while you are not safe none of us are safe for now
your'e really in the total soup of Time,--

who stood before you speechless and intelligent and shaking
with shame rejected yet confessing out the soul of his naked and
endless head the madman bum and angel beat in time unknown yet
putting down what might be left to say in time come after death,

and rose reincarnate in the clothes of ghostly jjazz in the
goldhorn shadow of the band and blew the suffering of America's
naked mind for love into a saxophone cry that shivered the cities
down to the last radio

with the absolute heart of the poem of life butchered out of
~~their own bodies~~ good to eat a thousand years.

human y

their own bodies,

I   Howl For Carl Solomon

I saw the best minds of my generation destroyed by madness, /starving,
     hysterical, naked,
dragging themselves through the negro streets at dawn looking /for an
     angry fix,
angelheaded hipsters exploring for the ancient shuddering connection
     between the wires and the wheels of the dynamo of night,
who, poverty and tatters and hollow-eyed and high sat up in the super-
     natural darkness of coldwater flats /floating across the tops
     of cities contemplating jazz,
who bared their brains to heaven under the El and saw mohammedan
     angels staggering on tenement roofs illuminated,
who sat in rooms in underwear unshaven burning their money in waste-
     baskets amid the rubbish of memorable Berkeley manifestos
     listening to the Terror through the wall,
who got busted in their beards returning through Laredo with a belt
     of marijuana for New York,
who passed through universities with radiant cool eyes hallucinating
     Arkansas and Blake-light tragedy among the scholars of war,
who burned in hells of turpentine in Paradise Alley or purgatoried
     their torsos night after night
with dreams, with drugs, with waking nightmares, alchohol and cock
     and endless balls,
incomparable blind streets of shuddering cloud and lightning (in the mind)
     leaping toward poles of Canada and Paterson, illuminating
     all the motionless world of Time between,
peyote solidities of halls, backyard green tree cemetary dawns, wine
     drunkenness over the rooftops, boroughs of teahead neon green
     and blinking traffic light, sun and moon and tree vibrations
     in the roaring winter dusks of Brooklyn, ashcan rantings and
     kind king light of mind,
who chained themselves to subways for the endless ride from Battery
     to holy Bronx on benzedrine until the noise of wheels and children
     brought them down shuddering mouth-wracked and battered bleak
     of brain all drained of brilliance in the drear light of Zoo,
who moped all night in submarine Bickford's and returned to sit /all thru
     the stale morning in desolate Fugazzi's ~~war~~ listening to the crack
     of doom on the hydrogen jukebox,
who talked continuously seventy ~~two~~ hours from park to pad to bar to
     Bellevue to museum to the Brooklyn Bridge,
yackata yakking screaming vomiting whispering facts and memories and
     anecdotes and eyeball kicks and shocks of hospitals and jails /and war,
a lost battalion of platonic conversationalists jumping down the stoops
     off fire-escapes ~~and~~ windowsills off Empire State out of the moon,
who vanished into nowhere Zen New Jersey leaving a trail of ambiguous
     picture postcards of Atlantic Cryptic Hall,
suffering Eastern sweats and Tangerian bonegrindings and migraines
     of China under junk-withdrawall in Newark's bleak furnished room,
who lounged hungry and lonesome through Huston seeking Jazz or /soup,
     and followed the brilliant ~~Mexican~~ to converse about /America and
     Eternity, a hopeless task, and so took ship /to Africa,
who ~~sneaked through~~ the railroad yard wondering where /to go, and went,
     leaving no broken hearts,
who lit cigarettes in boxcars boxcars boxcars racketing through snow
     toward lonesome farms in grandfather night,
who studied Vico Fludd telepathy and bop kaballa because the cosmos
     instinctively vibrated at their feet in Kansas,
            Stumbling in the aisles of Kansas

wandered around & around in

5: searching   36: the   48: sex or   51: wandered around & around in
7: smoking   43: off   49: Spaniard   56: Stumbling in the aisles of Kansas

who loned it through the streets of Idaho seeking visionary indian angels
who were visionary indian angels,
~~who didn't have enough time to speak among themselves of love, who didn't have time to smoke their dark cigars,~~
who jumped in cars with the Chinaman ~~on~~ the impulse of winter
midnight streetlight smalltown rain,
who disappeared into the volcanos of Mexico leaving behind nothing _scattered_
but the shadow of dungarees and the lava and ash of poetry in
fireplace Chicago,
who reappeared on the West Coast investigating the FBI in beards and
shorts with big pacifist eyes sexy in their dark skin passing out
incomprehensible leaflets,
who limped penniless over city hills with half a moustache hanging on
the sinister lip looking for an example of baroque architecture
and spent hours in the bathroom washing their few nickles with
a Buffalo toothbrush,
who broke down crying in white gymnasiums naked and trembling before
the machinery of other skeletons,
who burned cigarette holes in their arms protesting the narcotic
tobacco haze of capitalism,
who passed out supercommunist leaflets in Union Square weeping and
undressing, while the sirens of Los Alamos wailed them down,
and wailed down Wall, and the Staten Island ferry also wailed,
who screamed on all fours in the subway, and were dragged off the roof
waving genitals and manuscripts,
who bit detectives in the neck and shrieked with delight in particulars
in policecars for committing no crime but their own wild
cooking pederasty and intoxication,
who let themselves be fucked in the ass by saintly motorcyclists,
and screamed with joy,
who blew and were blown by these human seraphs, the sailors,
caresses of Atlantic and Carribean love,
who hiccuped endlessly trying to giggle but wound up with a sob
behind a partition in a Turkish bath when the blonde and naked
angel came to pierce them with the sword,
who lost their loveboys to the three old shrews of fate, the one-eyed
shrew of the heterosexual dollar, the one-eyed shrew that winks
out of the womb and the one-eyed shrew that does nothing
but sit on her ass and snip the intellectual golden threads
of the craftsman's loom,
who copulated ecstatic and insatiate with a bottle of beer a sweetheart
a package of cigarettes a candle, and fell off the bed, and
~~(jissum)~~ continued along the floor and down the hall and ended fainting
gyzym on the wall with a vision of ultimate cunt and come eluding the
last ~~inbas~~ of consciousness,
who sweetened the snatch of a million girls trembling in the sunset,
flashing buttocks under barns, and were red-eyed in the morning
but prepared to sweeten the snatch of the sunrise, naked in the
lake,
who picked themselves up out of basements hungover with heartless
Tokay and 3rd Avenue horrors of dismantled iron and stumbled
to unemployment offices,
who ate the lamb stew of the imagination or digested the crab at the
muddy bottom of the rivers of Bowery ~~...~~ cooked rotten animals
lung heart feet tail borsht and tortillas dreaming of the pure
vegetable kingdom,
who —

8: scattered
45: jissum [canceled] gyzym

54: [Printer's paragraph mark]
Who [repeated below as insert]

place first strophe as indicated by [arrow] after "bad music"

their groans *bloody*

who sang out of their windows in dispair, or ~~threw up~~ ~~drunk~~ in the toilet,
    moans in their ears and the blast of colossal steamwhistles,
who plunged themselves under meat trucks looking for an egg,
who jumped off the Brooklyn Bridge this actually happened and walked away
    unknown and forgotten into the ghostly daze of Chinatown soup
    alleyways and firetrucks, not even one free beer,
who were expelled from the academies for crazy and publish*ing* obscene odes
    on the windows of the skull,
who wept at the romance of the streets with their pushcarts full of onions
    and bad music,
who walked all night on the snowbank docks with their shoes full of blood
    waiting for a door in the East River to open to a room full of
    steamheat and opium, who walked between the violet and the violet,
who created great suicidal dramas on the banks of the Hudson under
    the wartime floodlight of the moon,
who coughed on the sixth floor of Harlem under the tubercular sky surround-
    ed by orange crates of theology,
who burned on the highways of the past journying to each other's hot-rod
    Golgotha jail-solitude watch or Burmingham blues incarnation,
who drove crosscountry seventy~~eight~~ hours to find out if I had a vision
    or you had a vision or he had a vision, to find out the present,
who journeyed to Denver, who died in Denver, who came back and waited in
    Denver, watched and went away finally to find out the future,
who fell on their knees in hopeless cathedrals praying for each others'
    salvation and light and breasts, until the soul illuminated its
    hair for a second,
who threw their watches out of windows in the ballot of Eternity and
    alarm clocks fell on their heads everyday for the next decade,
who cut their wrists three times unsuccessfully and were forced to
    open antique stores where they thought they were growing old and cried
who were burned alive in their innocent flannel suits on Madison Avenue
    amid ~~explosions of popular novels and~~ blasts of leaden verse
    and the nitroglycerine shrieks of the faries of advertising and
    the mustard gas of sinister intelligent editors, or were run down by
    the drunken taxicabs of absolute reality,
who sat in boxes breathing in the darkness under the bridge and rose up
    to build harpsichords in their lofts,
who retired to Mexico to cultivate sex or Rocky Mount to Buddha or
    Tangiers to boys or Southern Pacific to the black locomotive or
    Harvard to narcissus to Woodlawn to the daisychain or grave,
who crashed through their minds in jail waiting for impossible
    criminals with golden heads and the charm of reality in their
    hearts who sang sweet blues to Alcatraz,
who demanded sanity trials accusing the radio of hypnotism and were
    left with their insanity and their hands and a hung jury,
who threw potato salad at CCNY lecturers on Dadaism and subsequently
    presented themselves on the granite steps of the madhouse with
    shaven heads and harlequin speech of suicide, demanding instantaneous
    lobotomy,
and who were given instead the concrete void of insulin metrasol elec-
    tricity hydrotherapy psychotherapy occupational therapy pingpong
    & amnesia,
and who in humorless protest overturned only one symbolic pingpong
    table, resting briefly in catatonia,
returning a few years later truly bald except for a wig of blood to
    the visible madman doom of the wards of the madtowns of the East,

Head of page: Place first strophe *as indicated*
    by [arrow sign] after "bad music"

1: their groans [in]to [the] bloody   17: the
7: [publish]ing   20: [seventy]two
13: walking

to bicker with ~~an~~ echo^s, rocking and rolling in the midnight solitude-
    bench dolmen-realms of love, Rockland's and Greystone's
    foetid halls, aching for the ancestors, dream of life a
    nightmare, laughing in eclipse, with body turned to stone
    as heavy as the moon, *at 4 A.M.*

with mother finally fucked, and the last book thrown out of the attic, *window*
    and the last door closed and the last telephone slammed at the
    wall in reply, and the last furnished room emptied down to the
    last piece of mental furniture, a yellow paper rose twisted
    on a wire hangar in the closet, and even that imaginary, nothing
    but a hopeful little bit of hallucination--

ah, Carl, while you're not safe ~~none of us are~~ safe, ~~for~~ now *I am not* *and*
    you're really in the total soup of Time,--

and who therefore ran through the icy streets obsessed with a sudden
    flash of the alchemy of the use of the ellipse, the catalogue,
    the meter and vibrating plane,

who dreamt and made incarnate gaps in time and space through images
    juxtaposed and trapped the archangel of the soul between 2
    visual images and joined the elemental verbs and set the noun
    and dash of consciousness together jumping with sensation of ~~the~~
    ~~of~~ Pater Onmipotens Aeterna Deus,

~~who~~ recreate~~d~~ the syntax and structure of poor human prose and ~~stood~~ *to stand*
    before you speechless and intelligent and shaking with shame,
    rejected, yet confessing out the soul to conform to the rhythm
    of thought in his naked and endless head, the madman bum and
    angel beat in time, unknown, yet putting down what might be left
    to say in Time come after death,

and rose reincarnate in the clothes of ghostly jazz in the goldhorn
    shadow of the band and blew the suffering of America's naked mind
    for love into ~~the~~ saxophone cry that shivered the cities down
    to the last radio

with the absolute heart of the poem of life butchered out of their
    own bodies good to eat a thousand years.

an eli eli lamma lamma sabacthani (saxophone cry)

1: an [canceled] [echo]s   7: at 4 A.M.
4: [bod]ies   12: I am not [safe,] and
6: window   22: [recreate]ing . . . to stand

30: eli eli lamma sabacthani [canceled] An eli lamma
    lamma sabacthani (saxophone cry) [as insert]

H O W L

for

Carl Solomon

by

Allen Ginsberg

Unscrew the locks from the doors!
Unscrew the doors themselves from their jambs!

N.B. Sequence of drafts was established in case-by-case examination of changes. Some three dozen alterations evidence progression from 4th to 5th draft, though another half dozen indicate ambiguous chronology. These may be caused by typist's lacunae, reversions to earlier phrasing, or uncertainty of phrasing solved in later drafts. —A.G.

HOWL

for

Carl Solomon

I

I saw the best minds of my generation destroyed by

     madness, starving, hysterical, mystical, naked,

dragging themselves through the negro streets at dawn

     looking for an angry fix,

angelheaded hipsters burning for the ancient heavenly

     connection to the starry dynamo in the machinery

     of night,

who poverty and tatters and hollow-eyed and high sat

     up smoking in the supernatural darkness of cold-

     water flats floating across the tops of cities

     contemplating jazz,

who bared their brains to heaven under the El and saw

     Mohammedan angels staggering on tenement roofs

     illuminated,

who ~~sat~~ cowered in unshaven rooms in underwear burning their

     money in wastebaskets amid the rubbish of mem-

     orable Barkeley manifestoes listening to the

     Terror through the wall,

who got busted in their ~~phallic~~ pubic beards returning

     through Laredo with a belt of marijuana for

     New York,

who passed through universities with radiant cool

     eyes hallucinating Arkansas and Blake-light

15: ["sat" canceled] cowered   19: pubic

who were expelled

> tragedy among the scholars of war,

who ate fire in paint hotels or ‸drank turpentined in Para-
        dise Alley, death, or purgatoried their torsos
        night after night,

with dreams, with drugs, with waking nightmares,
        alchohol and cock and endless balls;

incomparable blind streets of shuddering cloud and
        lightning in the mind leaping toward poles
        of Canada & Paterson, illuminating all the
        motionless world between,

Peyote solidities of halls, backyard green tree
                                              the
        cemetary dawns, wine drunkeness over/roof-
        tops, boroughs of teahead neon green and
        blinking traffic light, sun and moon and
        tree vibrations in the roaring winter dusks
        of Brooklyn, ashcan rantings and kind king
        light of mind,

who chained themselves to subways for the endless
        ride from Battery to holy Bronx on benzedrine
        until the noise of wheels and children
        brought them down shuddering mouth-wracked
        and battered bleak of brain all drained of
        brilliance in the drear light of Zoo,

who sank all night in submarine Bickfords and
        ~~rose up~~ *floated out* to sit all thru the stale ‸beer morning ‸afternoon
        in desolate Fugazzi's, listening to the crack
        of doom on the hydrogen jukebox,

Left margin: Who were expelled   2: drank   25: floated out . . . beer [morning] afternoon

who talked continuously seventy hours from park to
        pad to bar to Bellevue to museum to the Brook-
        lyn Bridge,
yackatayaking screaming vomiting whispering facts and
        memories and anecdotes and eyeball kicks and
        shocks of hospitals and jails and wars,
a lost batallion of platonic conversationalists
        jumping down the stoops off fire escapes off
        windowsills off Empire State out of the moon,
who vanished into nowhere Zen New Jersey leaving a
        trail of ambiguous picture postcards of At-
        lantic Cryptic Hall,
suffering eastern sweats and tangerian bonegrindings
        and migraines of china under junk-withdrawal
        in Newark's bleak furnished room,
who wandered midnight in the railroad yard wondering
        where to go, and went, leaving no broken hearts,
who lit cigarettes in boxcars boxcars boxcars racket-
        ing through snow toward lonesome farms in
        grandfather night,
who studied Plotinus and Fludd telepathy & bop
        kaballa because the cosmos instinctively
        vibrated at their feet in Kansas,
who loned it through the streets of Idaho seeking
        visionary indian angels who were visionary
        indian angels,

who jumped in cars with the Chinaman of Illinois on
        the impulse of winter midnight streetlight
        smalltown rain,
who lounged hungry and lonesome through Huston seek-
        ing jazz or sex or soup, and followed the
        brilliant Spaniard to converse about America
        and Eternity, a hopeless task, and so took
        ship to Africa,
who disappeared into the volcanos of Mexico leaving
        behind nothing but the shadow of dungarees
        and the lava and ash of poetry scattered in
        fireplace Chicago,
who reappeared on the West Coast investigating the
        FBI in beards and shorts with big pacifist
        eyes sexy in their dark skin passing out
        incomprehensible leaflets,
who limped penniless over city hills with half a
        mustache hanging on the sinister lip looking
        for an example of Baroque architecture, and
        spent hours thereafter in the bathroom wash-
        ing their few nickles with a Buffalo tooth-
        brush,
who broke down crying in white gymnaseums naked and
        trembling before the machinery of other skeletons,
who burned cigarette holes in their arms protesting
        the narcotic tobacco haze of capitalism,

who passed out super-communist leaflets in Union Sq.

        weeping and undressing, while the sirens of

        Los Alamos wailed them down, and wailed down

        Wall, and the Staten Island ferry also wailed,

who bit detectives in the neck and shrieked with

        delight in policecars for committing no crime

        but their own wild cooking pederasty & intox-

        ication,

who ~~screamed~~ *howled* on their knees in the subway, and were

        dragged off the roof waving genitals and man-

        uscripts,

who blew and were blown by those human seraphs, the

        sailors, caresses of Atlantic and Caribbean joy,

who let themselves be fucked in the ass by saintly

        motorcyclists, and screamed with joy,

who hiccupped endlessly trying to giggle but wound

        up with a sob behind a partition in a Turkish

        bath when the blond & naked angel came to

        pierce them with a sword,

who lost their loveboys to the three old shrews of fate

        the oneeyed shrew of the heterosexual dollar,

        the oneeyed shrew that winks out of the womb

        and the oneeyed shrew that does nothing but

        sit on her ass and snip the intellectual gold-

        en threads of the craftsman's loom,

who sweetened the snatches of a million girls tremb-

        ling in the sunset, flashing buttocks under

        barns, and were red-eyed in the morning but

        prepared to sweeten the snatch of the sunrise

        naked in the lake,

+ Bird was wailing the most at Birdland

4: & Bird was wailing the most at Birdland   9: howled

who went out whoring through the Midwest, ~~in~~ myriad

stolen night cars, N.C., (secret hero of these

poems, cocksman and Adonis of Denver, our long

old love, heart of ten thousand bodies on

either coast,) joy to the memory of his innum-

erable lays of girls in empty lots and diners, ~~or~~ *backyards*

moviehouses rickety rows ^*in caves* on mountaintops or with

gaunt waittresses in familiar roadside lonesome

petticoat upliftings & especially secret gas-

station solipsisms of johns, & hometown alleys

too,

who copulated ecstatic and insatiate with a bottle

of beer a sweetheart a package of cigarettes

~~and~~ a candle and fell off the bed, and con-

tinued along the floor and down the hall and

ended fainting on the wall with a vision of

ultimate cunt and come eluding the last gyzym

of consciousness,

who were ~~shifted in~~ *faded out* vast sordid movies ~~to~~ *& woke up in manhattan* sudden

Manhattans, ~~and~~ picked themselves up out of

basements hungover with heartless Tokay &

3rd Avenue horrors of dismantled iron and

stumbled to unemployment offices,

Who ~~or~~ ate the lamb stew of the imagination or digested

the crab at the muddy bottom of the rivers

of Bowery,

who wept at the romance of the streets with their

pushcarts full of onions and bad music,

6: backyards   7: in caves   19: faded out . . . & woke up in Manhattan   24: Who

who sat in boxes breathing in the darkness under the

Bridge and rose up to build harpsichords in

their lofts,

who coughed on the sixth floor of Harlem under the

tubercular sky surrounded by orange crates

of theology,

who cooked rotten animals lung heart feet tail borsht

& tortillas dreaming of the pure vegetable king-

dom,

who sang out of their windows in dispair or threw up

their groans into the bloody toilet, moans in

their ears and the blast of colossal steamwhistles,

who plunged themselves under meat trucks looking for

an egg,

who jumped off the Brooklyn Bridge this actually

happened and walked away unknown and forgotten

into the ghostly daze of Chinatown soup

alleyways and firetrucks, not even one free

beer,

who were expelled from the academies for crazy &

publishing obscene odes on the windows of

the skull,

who threw their watches off the roof and casting

their ballot for Eternity outside of Time,

and alarm clocks fell on their heads every day

for the next decade,

3/4: Who sat all nite rocking & rolling over lofty incantations which in the yellow morning were stanzas of gibberish

9, left margin: * Meat truck egg

10: lunged out of subway windows, jumped in the filthy Passaic, leaped on negroes, Cried al over the street, danced on broken wineglasses barefoot smashed their phonograph records of European 1930's German jazz finished the whiskey &

11: groaning

15: got hi [canceled]

20–2, left margin: See p 1 [proposed shift to page 1—A.G.]

23–6, left margin: After free Beer [proposed shift to follow verse 6 above—A.G.]

8

After Steamwhistles, p. 7

who created great national suicidal dramas on the

banks of the Hudson under the wartime *blue*

floodlight of the moon on apartment cliffs, *& their heads shall be crowned with laurel in oblivion*

who cut their wrists three times unsuccessfully

~~and~~ gave up and were forced to open antique

stores where they thought they were growing

old and cried,

who were burnt alive in their innocent flannel

suits on Madison Avenue amid blasts of

leaden verse ~~and~~ the clatter of ~~the~~ iron

regiments of fashion ~~and~~ the nitroglycerine

shrieks of the fairies of advertising ~~and~~

the mustard gas of sinister intelligent

editors, or were run down by the drunken

taxicabs of Absolute Reality,

who walked all night with shoes full of blood on

the snowbank docks, waiting for a door in

the East River to open to a room full of

steamheat and opium,

who ~~burned on~~ *barrelled down* the highways of the past journying to

each other's hotrod Golgotha jail-solitude watch

or Birmingham jazz incarnation,

who drove crosscountry seventy-two hours to find out

if I had a vision or you had a vision or he had

a vision to find out the present,

Left margin: After Steamwhistles, p. 7 [proposed shift to p. 7 of this draft as insert to verse 4a—A.G.]
2: [insert] the . . . blue

3: & their heads shall be crowned with laurel in oblivion.
20: barrelled down . . . [journ]e[ying]

who journeyed to Denver, who died in Denver, who came
      back to Denver & waited in vain, who watched
      and finally went away to find out the future,

who fell on their knees in hopeless cathedrals
      praying for each other's salvation and light
      and breasts, till the soul illuminated its
      hair for a second,

who crashed through their minds in jail waiting for
      impossible criminals with golden heads and
      the charm of reality in their hearts who sang
      sweet blues to Alcatraz,

who retired to Mexico to cultivate a habit or
      Rocky Mount to tender Buddha or Tangiers
      to boys or Southern Pacific to the black
      locomotive or Harvard to Narcissus to
      Woodlawn to the daisychain or grave,

who demanded sanity trials accusing the radio of
      hypnotism and were left with their insanity
      and their hands and a hung jury,

who threw potato salad at CCNY lecturers on Dadaism
      and subsequently presented themselves on the
      granite steps of the madhouse with shaven heads
      and harlequin speech of suicide, demanding
      instantaneous lobotomy,

and who were given instead the concrete void of

     insulin metrasol electricity hydrotherapy

     psychotherapy occupational therapy pingpong

     & amnesia,

and who in humorless protest overturned only one

     symbolic pingpong table, resting briefly

     in catatonia,

returning years later truly bald except for a wig of

     blood to the visible madman doom of the wards

     of the madtowns of the East,

Rockland's and Greystone's foetid halls, bickering

     with echoes, rocking and rolling in the mid-

     night solitude bench dolmen-realms of love,

     dream of life a nightmare, laughing in

     eclipse with bodies turned to stone as heavy

     as the moon,

with mother finally ***, and the last book thrown out

     of ~~the~~ Lexington attic window, and the last

     door closed at 4 AM, and the last telephone

     slammed at the wall in reply and the last under-

     wear stripped down to the floor and the last

     furnished room emptied down to the last piece

     of mental furniture, a yellow paper rose twisted

     on a wire hanger in the closet, and even that

     imaginary, nothing but a hopeful little bit of

     hallucination--

Ah, Carl, while you are not safe I am not safe, and

     now you're _really_ in the total trouble soup of Time--

28: really

and who therefore ran through the icy streets obsessed
        with a sudden flash of the alchemy of the use
        of the ellipse the catalogue the meter and the
        vibrating plane,
who dreamt and made incarnate heavenly gaps in time
        and space through images juxtaposed and
        trapped the archangel of the soul between
        2 visual images and joined the elemental verbs
        and set the breath and dash of consciousness
        together nouned and jumping with sensation of
        Pater Omnipotens Aeterna Deus
recreating the syntax and measure of poor human prose
        to stand before you speechless & intelligent
        & shaking with shame, rejected yet confessing
        out the soul to conform to the rhythm of thought
        in his naked and endless head,
the madman bum and angel, beat in Time, unknown yet
        putting down what must be left to say in Time
        come after death,
and rose reincarnate in the ghostly clothes of jazz
        in the goldhorn shadow of the the band and blew
        the suffering of America's naked mind for love
        into an eli eli lamma lamma sabacthani sax-
        ophone cry that shivered the cities down
        to the last radio
with the absolute heart of the poem of life butchered
        out of their own bodies good to eat a thous-
        and years.

21: of

HOWL

for

Carl Solomon

I saw the best minds of my generation destroyed by mad-
          ness, starving hysterical naked,
dragging themselves through the negro streets at dawn
          looking for an angry fix,
angelheaded hipsters burning for the ancient heavenly
          connection to the starry dynamo in the machinery
          of night,
who poverty and tatters and hollow-eyed and high sat up
          smoking in the supernatural darkness of cold-
          water flats floating across the tops of cities
          contemplating jazz,
who bared their brains to heaven under the El and saw
          Mohammedan angels staggering on tenement roofs
          illuminated,
who ~~crouched~~ *Cowered* in unshaven rooms in underwear burning
          their money in wastebaskets amid the rubbish
          of memorable Berkeley manifestoes listening to
          the Terror through the wall,
who got busted in their *pubic* beards returning through Laredo
          with a belt of marijuana for New York,

15: ["crouched" canceled] cowered   19: pubic

who passed through universities with radiant cool eyes
        hallucinating Arkansas and Blake-light tragedy
        among the scholars of war,
who were expelled from the academies for crazy & pub-
        lishing obscene odes on the windows of the skull,
who ate fire in paint hotels or drank turpentine in
        Paradise Alley, death, or purgatoried their torsos
        night after night
with dreams, with drugs, with waking nightmares, alchohol
        and cock and endless balls,
incomparable blind streets of shuddering cloud and
        lightning in the mind leaping toward poles of
        Canada & Paterson, illuminating all the motion-
        less world of time between,
Peyote solidities of halls, backyard green tree cemetary
        dawns, wine drunkenness over the rooftops, stoorfront
        boroughs of teahead joyride neon blinking
        traffic light, sun and moon and tree vibrations
        in the roaring winter dusks of Brooklyn, ashcan
        rantings and kind king light of mind,
who chained themselves to subways for ~~the~~ endless ~~rage~~ ride
        from Battery to holy Bronx on benzedrine until
        the noise of wheels and children brought them down
        shuddering mouth-wracked and battered bleak of
        brain all drained of brilliance in the drear
        light of Zoo,

21: the [endless] ["rage" canceled] ride

who sank all night in submarine Bickfords and ~~rose up~~ FLOATED OUT

     to sit all through the stale beer ~~morning~~

     afternoons in desolate Fugazzi's listening

     to the crack of doom on the hydrogen jukebox,

who talked continuously seventy hours from park to

     pad to bar to Bellevue to museum to the

     Brooklyn Bridge,

yacketayaking screaming vomiting whispering facts

     and memories and anecdotes and eyeball kicks

     and shocks of hospitals and jails and wars,

a lost batallion of platonic conversationalists

     jumping down the stoops off fire escapes

     off windowsills off Empire State out of

     the moon,

who vanished into nowhere Zen New Jersey leaving

     a trail of ambiguous picture postcards of

     Atlantic Cryptic Hall,

suffering Eastern sweats and Tangerian bonegrindings

     and migraines of China under junk-withdrawal

     in Newark's bleak furnished room,

who wandered at midnight in the railroad yard won-

     dering where to go, and went, leaving no

     broken hearts,

1: ["rose up" canceled] floated out   2: ["morning" canceled]   3: Fugazzi's

who lit cigarettes in boxcars boxcars boxcars racket-
ing through snow toward lonesome farms in
grandfather night,

who studied Plotinus and Fludd telepathy and bop
kaballa because the cosmos instinctively
vibrated at their feet in Kansas,

who loned it through the streets of Idaho seeking
visionary indian angels who were visionary
indian angels,

who lounged hungry and lonesome through Houston
seeking jazz or sex or soup, and followed
the brilliant Spaniard to converse about
America and Eternity, a hopeless task, and so
took ship to Africa,

who disappeared into the volcanoes of Mexico leaving
behind nothing but the shadow of dungarees
and the lava and ash of poetry scattered in
fireplace Chicago,

who reappeared on the West Coast investigating the
FBI in beards and shorts with big pacifist eyes
sexy in their dark skin passing out incompre-
hensible leaflets,

who limped penniless over city hills looking for an
example of Baroque architecture with half a
mustache hanging on the sinister lip, and spent
hours in the bathroom washing their poor
nickles with a buffalo toothbrush,

who jumped in limosines with the Chinaman of Oklahoma
        on the impulse of winter midnight smalltown
        streetlight rain,

who broke down crying in white gymnasiums naked and
        trembling before the machinery of other
        skeletons,

who burned cigarette holes in their arms protesting
        the narcotic tobacco haze of Capitalism,

who passed out Supercommunist leaflets in Union
        Square while the sirens of Los Alamos wailed
        them down, and wailed down Wall, and the
        Staten Island Ferry also wailed, and Bird
        was wailing the most at Birdland,

who bit detectives in the neck and shrieked with
        delight in policecars for committing no crime
        but their own wild cooking pederasty and
        intoxication,

who howled on their knees in the subway, and were
        dragged off the roof waving genitals and
        manuscripts,

who let themselves be fucked in the ass by saintly
        motorcyclists, and screamed with joy,

who blew and were blown by those human seraphim
        the sailors, caresses of Atlantic and
        Carribean love,

who hiccupped endlessly trying to giggle but wound up
        with a sob behind a partition in a Turkish Bath
        when the blond & naked angel came to pierce them
        with a sword,
who lost their loveboys to the three old shrews of fate
        the one eyed shrew of the heterosexual dollar
        the one eyed shrew that winks out of the womb
        and the one eyed shrew that does nothing but sit
        on her ass and snip the intellectual golden
        threads of the craftsman's loom,
who sweetened the snatches of a million girls trembling
        in the sunset, flashing buttocks under barns,
        and were red eyed in the morning but prepared
        to sweeten the snatch of the sunrise naked in
        the lake,
who went out whoring through midwest in myriad stolen
        night cars, joy to the memory of his innumerable
        lays of girls in empty lots & diners, backyards
        moviehouses' rickety rows in caves and mountain-
        tops, or with gaunt waittresses in familiar roadside
        lonely petticoat upliftings & especially secret
        gas-station solipsisms of johns, & hometown
        alleys too,
who copulated ecstatic and insatiate with a bottle of
        beer a sweetheart a package of cigarettes a
        candle and fell off the bed, and continued
        along the floor and down the hall and ended
        fainting on the wall with a vision of ultimate
        cunt and come eluding the last gyzym of
        consciousness,

who faded out in vast sordid movies and suddenly woke up
      in Manhattan, picked themselves up out of base-
      ments hung-over with heartless Tokay and horrors
      of dismantled Third Avenue iron dreams stumbled
      to unemployment offices,

who ate the lamb stew of the imagination or digested
      the crab at the muddy bottom of the rivers of
      Bowery,

who wept at the romance of the streets with their
      pushcarts full of onions and bad music,

who sat in boxes breathing in darkness under the
      Bridge, and rose up to build harpsichords
      in their lofts,

who sat all night rocking and rolling over LOFTY incantations
      which in the yellow morning were stanzas of
      gibberish,

who coughed on the sixth floor of Harlem under the
      tubercular sky surrounded by orange crates
      of theology,

who cooked rotten animals lung heart feet tail borsht
      & tortillas dreaming of the pure vegetable
      kingdom,

who plunged themselves under meat trucks looking for
      an egg,

who sang out of their windows in dispair, lunged out
      of subway windows, jumped in the filthy Passaic,
      leaped on negroes, cried all over the street,
      [finished the whiskey] danced on a broken wine glasses
      barefoot smashed their phonograph records of
      European 1930's German jazz & threw up groaning
      into the bloody toilet, moans in their ears and
      the blast of colossal steamwhistles,

who plunged themselves in to meat trucks looking for an egg,

who got high and jumped off the Brooklyn Bridge, this
actually happened and walked away unknown and
forgotten into the ghostly daze of Chinatown
soup alleyways and firetrucks, not even one
free beer,

who threw their watches off the roof to cast their
ballot for Eternity outside of Time, &
alarm clocks fell on their heads every day
for the next decade,

who created great suicidal dramas on the apartment
cliff-banks of the Hudson under the wartime
BLUE floodlight of the moon and their heads shall
be crowned with laurel in oblivion,

who cut their wrists three times successively un-
successfully, gave up, and were forced to
open antique stores where they throught they
were growing old and cried,

who were burned alive in their innocent flannel suits
on Madison Avenue amid blasts of leaden verse
& the tanked-up clatter of the iron regiments of
fashion & the nitroglycerine shrieks of the
fairies of advertising & the mustard gas of
sinister intelligent editors, or were run down
by the drunken taxicabs of Absolute Reality,

1: shifted around . . . up   14: blue
Left margin: East River
14: lofty

who walked all night with *their* shoes full of blood on the
      snowbank docks waiting for a door in the East
      River to open to a room full of steamheat and
      opium,

who barreled down the highways of the past journeying
      to eachother's hotrod-Golgotha jail-solitude
      watch or Birmingham jazz incarnation,

who drove crosscountry seventy-two hours to find out
      if I had a vision or you had a vision or he had
      a vision to find out the present,

who journeyed to Denver, who died in Denver, who
      came back to Denver & waited in vain, who
      watched and finally went away to find out
      the future,

who fell on their knees in hopeless cathedrals praying
      for each other's salvation and light and breasts,
      till the soul illuminated its hair for a second,

who crashed through their minds in jail waiting for
      impossible criminals with golden heads and
      the charm of reality in their hearts who sang
      sweet blues to Alcatraz,

who retired to Mexico to cultivate *a* habit, or Rocky
      Mount to tender Buddha or Tangiers to boys
      or Southern Pacific to the black locomotive
      or Harvard to Narcissus to Woodlawn to the
      daisychain or grave,

1: their

who demanded sanity trials accusing the radio of
        hypnotism and were left with their insanity
        and their hands and a hung jury,
who threw potato salad at CCNY lecturers on Dadaism
        and subsequently presented themselves on the
        granite steps of the madhouse with shaven
        heads and harlequin speech of suicide, de-
        manding instantaneous lobotomy,
and who were given instead the concrete void of
        insulin metrasol electricity hydrotherapy
        psychotherapy occupational therapy pingpong
        & amnesia,
who in humorless protest overturned only one symbolic
        pingpong table, rested briefly in catatonia,
returning years later truly bald except for a wig of
        blood ~~and helpless fingers~~ to the visible
        madman doom of the wards of the madtowns
        of the East,
Greystone's and Rockland's foetid halls, bickering
        with echoes, rocking and rolling in the mid-
        night solitude-bench dolmen-realms of Love,
        dream of life a nightmare, laughing in eclipse,
        with bod*ies* turned to stone as heavy as the moon,
with mother finally ***, and the last *magical* book ~~of magic~~
        thrown out of the attic window, and the last
        door closed at ~~four~~ 4 AM, and the last telephone
        slammed at the wall in reply and the last
        furnished room emptied down to the last piece

16: ["and helpless fingers" canceled]
23: [bod]ies

24: magical . . . ["of magic" canceled]
26: ["four" canceled] 4

of mental furniture, a yellow paper rose

twisted in a wire hanger in the closet, and

even that imaginary, nothing but a hopeful

little bit of hallucination--

ah, Carl, while you are not safe I am not safe, and

now you're ~~really~~ in the ~~total~~ animal soup

TOTAL

of Time--

and who therefore ran through the icy streets obsessed

with a sudden flash of the alchemy of the use

of the ellipse the meter the catalogue and

the vibrating plane,

who dreamt and made incarnate gaps in time and space

through images juxtaposed, and trapped the

archangel of the soul between 2 visual images

and joined the elemental verbs and set the noun

and dash of consciousness together ~~in a breath~~

~~and~~ jumping with sensation of Pater Omnipotens

Aeterna Deus,

to recreate the syntax and measure of poor human prose

and stand before you speechless and intelligent

and shaking with shame, rejected yet confessing

out the soul to conform to the rhythm of thought

in his naked and endless head, the madman bum and

angel, beat in time, unknown yet putting down

now what might be left to say in time come after

death,

6: ["total" canceled] total   16: ["in a breath" canceled]   17: ["and" canceled]

and rose reincarnate in the ghostly clothes of jazz
in the goldhorn shadow of the band and blew
the suffering of America's naked mind for love
into an eli eli lamma ~~lamma~~ sabacthani sax-
ophone cry that shivered the cities down to
the last radio
with the absolute heart of the poem of life butchered
out of their own bodies good to eat a thousand
years.

Guide to Original Manuscripts, Part II

Draft 1: This manuscript, handwrit on the last page of a scrapped late version of Part I, provided a form for the "Moloch" inspiration, a rhythmic logic.

Draft 2: First draft typed, cleaned up, cut, and tied together for clarity, with marginal note on antiphonal cadence implicit.

Draft 3: A worksheet, phrasings improved, verse divisions balanced neater, arrow re-orders last verse group to midsection.

Draft 4: Clear-typed to consolidate prior corrections, this draft provides a clean & strong skeleton on which to hang more appendages, meat and lungs.

Draft 5: Four pages of pleasure cadenzas on the anaphoric trochee "Moloch!" fill in the body of the monster vision. Since word combinations possible were inexhaustible, there was space for free mind play. Imagination was released to juxtapose disparate archetypes of electric modernity, condense naturalistic observation of the industrial landscape into hyperbolic images of metropolitan apocalypse. Any spontaneous majestic glimpse could be solidified merely by typing outrageous verbal associations on the page, free from any idea logic but phrase wit, auditory intuition of assonance and cadence, and beauty of picture.

These pages were written one afternoon late 1955 in the small backyard cottage I shared with Gary Snyder, 1624 Milvia Street, Berkeley. I sat at typewriter desk facing garden window bushes, he sat Japanese style cross-legged before a writing frame on the floor rug, translating Chinese, Han Shan. Must've heard me muttering, sometimes laughing aloud, and distracted by my trancelike self-absorption, he called out, "Moloch who reaches up at night thru the bottom of the toilet bowl and grabs my pecker everytime I try to take a crap!"

How cohere these inklings of extravaganza? The most glittering intense phrases were hand-underlined next, first pass at selecting pure gold nuggets—workable serious images—out of the mass of random associations.

Draft 6: Incorporates prior draft's experimental spontaneous rhapsody of "Moloch!"s. The task was, scan raw material of nonparagraphed improvisations, select best phrase elements, set them in "strophic" verses, experiment with balance and arrangement of the rhetorical flight. This typescript presumes the initial two-verse rhythmic statement up to "Old men weeping in parks!" and the entire closure following "Monstrous bombs!" Later this material is added into the midsection catalogue of Molochs fixed in Draft 4.

Draft 7: Adds the initial two verses, refines an extended list of Molochs, connects that directly to the Adonic apostrophe "Robot apartments!," suspending one verse ("broken backs lifting moloch to heaven") for use further on.

Draft 8: This fragment works out a problem of transition passage from panoramic to personal reference in Moloch midsection, changing "we sit lonely" to "I sit lonely."

Draft 9: Work here sets up whole structure, builds cadence & energy in middle section, extends all useful Moloch phrases, juggles and cuts them, summing up to reconnect with "breaking their backs" and the coda, "Visions, omens etc."

Draft 10: Surveys Moloch catalogue first page with cuts and transpositions, suspends "consciousness without body" for use later in section, adds key phrase, "whose name is the Mind."

Draft 11: Begins to untangle the bones of epithet for "congress and prison," and weigh proper placement for crucial Moloch name "Mind."

Draft 12: This fragment focused back on the problematic transition passage, somewhat clarifying the visual panorama, extending ecstatic personal confession—and here hit on more direct phrasing, the exclamatory "Wake up in Moloch!," to resolve thought rhythms and climax the imitation of vision.

Draft 13: The complete structure is consolidated, beginning to end. Some epithets within each strophic verse will be eliminated, and some phrases change, but the sequence of verses & the interior relations of phrases within these verses are in right rhythmic order.

Draft 14: Rehearses all but the coda, rearranging crucial images, progressively improving surface and sequence. "Consumer" & "slaughterer," etc., reincorporate unsuccessfully. "Consciousness without a body" has located a fitting place by hand, and "Moloch whose name is the Mind" still floats around looking for logical sonorous home among the verses.

Draft 15: This isolate worksheet is an attempt to account previous draft's corrections (elisions & transpositions) indicated for two verses, consolidating the good phrases lined up in order condensed into one fat strophe. With a few phrases eliminated, the original sequence will be restored, divided in two again.

Draft 16: "Cannibal dynamo" phrase moves ahead, Moloch's "poverty" finds right place, first seven verses run through near perfected, stumbling on the "bodiless God" transition. The two climactic verses follow almost completely in place. Moloch's "Mind" isn't settled.

Draft 17: The weak "star of Apocalypse" obstructs the spot where Moloch might be named "the Mind"; but "bodiless God" has been removed to the tail of the catalogue, temporarily out of the way. A rhythmic continuity moves between "a cloud of sexless hydrogen" and "Moloch in whom I sit lonely," only one phrase wants laying in place to couple the parts. Handmade brackets arrow "bodiless God" back in between them, halfway uncertain, well-wishing, rhythmic heart in the right place.

Draft 18: This is the last typescript stage surviving in author's possession. In this penultimate draft most everything's in place. The coda "They broke their backs . . . Into the streets!" from Draft 13 was to be added on, with minor variants. These further changes were, in order:

"Thousand blind windows," fifth verse, will come to follow not precede "machinery," sixth verse, for the sake of rhythmic buildup. "Moloch whose name is the Mind" follows in dactylic natural cadence after "a cloud of sexless hydrogen." The next three phrases, always excessive and metaphysically vague, will be dropped. "Frightened natural ecstasy" was still to be discovered in place of "a burned down world." Blake's satanic "mills" further down the line will turn into demonic "industries," following "blind capitals."

Other than first mimeo (Ditto process), final draft printer's copy in publisher City Lights Books archives is represented by published text.

returning to the magneta reality of the wards years later
        truly bald except for a wig of blood, with a
        handfull of Time, all fingers and tears, and the
        bleak scream of society blasting out of his ears,
with his visible madman doom, and his own mother finally
        fucked, and the last book burned on the windowsill,
        and the last anal prosepoem published as Apocalypse
        to the rats under the toilet, and the last door closed
        at 4 AM and the last helpless companion up in a plane,
        and the last telephone slammed against the wall in reply,
        and the last furnished room emptied down to the last
        piece of mental furniture, a yellow paper rose twisted
        on a wire hanger in the ghostly closet, and even that
        hallucination, --
Ah, Carl Solomon while you are not safe I am not safe,
        for now you're really in the total soup of Time, --
who sat years after bickering his echo in the madtowns of the
        east, rocking and rolling in the midnight solitude
        bench dolmen realms of love, Rockland and Greystone's
        foetid halls,
tangled in the hassels of imaginary shrouds and straightjackets,
        aching for ancestors, dream of life a nightmare,
        laughing in eclipse until the body turns to
        stone as heavy as the moon
and who therefore ran through the icy streets obsessed with
        a sudden flash of the alchemy of the use of the
        elipse, the catalogue, the meter and vibrating
        plane,
who dreamt and made incarnate gaps in time and space through
        images juxtaposed and blocks of color shoving back
        and forth in front of a flat dimension
who rose reincarnate in the clothes of music in the goldhorn
        shadow the the band and blew the suffering of
        America's naked mind for love into a saxaphone cry
        that shivered the cities down to the last radio,
who stood before you speechless and intelligent and shaking with
        shame, rejected, yet confessing out the soul, the
        madman bum and angel, beat in Time, unknown,
who recreated the synatx and structure of poor human prose
        to conform to the rhythm of thought in his naked
        and endless head, and set down here what might be left
        to say in Time come after death,
who trapped the archangel of soul between 2 visual
        images and joined the elemental verms and set the noun
        and dash of consciousness together jumping with sensation
        of Cezanne, Pater Omnipotens Aeterna Deus,
the absolute heart of the poem of life butchered out from
        their own bodies good to eat a thousand years.

Moloch! Moloch! whose head ripped out their brains ①
and scattered their minds the the wheels of subways!
Molloch! Filth! Ugliness! Ashcans and unobtainable dollars!
Beauties dying in lofts! Harpsichords unbuilt! Children
screaming under the stairways! old men weeping in the parks!

Children. Children! The very children breaking their
backs under the subway. Breaking their backs trying to lift the
Whole City on their backs — Pavements! Buildings! Trees
Rockefeller Center Tons — The whole damned lot of it — the
screaming radios — Hitler! Stalin! Christmas! Jesus!
The wires coming out of our ears — lifting the city on our
backs! To ~~heav~~ Heaven —

Heaven which exists and is everywhere about us

Dreams! Visions! Gone, Garbaged, in the morgue,
with the rest of them, the wholel boatload of sensitive bullshit,
raving insanity

Passed over the river, down on the rocks, Time gone,
10 years past, the flowers carried off by the stream, amid
screams and shrieking and laughter! real holy laughter in
the ~~strea strea~~ river. They saw it all, they heard it all,
each others desperate Cries, bade farewell as they jumped off
the roof to solitude, Carrying flowers, ~~the~~ down to the
river, down in the streat.

Moloch! Molock! Whose hand ripped out their brains
and scattered their minds on the wheels of subways?
Molloch! Filth! Ugliness! Ashcans and unobtainable dollars!
~~Beatit~~ Beauties dying in lofts! Harpsichords unbuilt! Children ~~never~~
screaming under the stairways! old men weeping in the parks!

Children! children! The very children breaking their
backs under the subways. Breaking their backs trying to lift the
Whole City on their backs—Pavements! Buildings! Trees
Rockefeller Center Tons—The whole damned lot of it—the
screaming radios—Hitler! Stalin! Christmas! Jesus!
The wires coming out of our ears—lifting the city on our
backs! To ~~heav~~ heaven—
Heaven which is exists and is everywhere about us
Dreams! Visions! Gone, Garbaged, in the morgue,
with the rest of them, the wholel boatload of sensitive bullshit,
raving insanity
Passed over the river, down on the rocks, Time gone,
10 years past, the flowers carried off by the stream, amid
screams and shriekings and laughter! real holy laughter in
the ~~strea strea~~ river. They saw it all, they heard it all,
each others desperate Cries, bade farewell as they jumped off
the roof to solitude, Carrying flowers, ~~the~~ down to the
river, down in the streat.

MOLOCH! MOLOCK! Whose hand bashed out their brains on the subway ~~wh~~
        wheels?
Moloch Filth Ugliness! Ashcans and unobta~~f~~able dollars! Unbuilt
        harpsichords! Beauties dying in lofts! Screaming under the
        stairways! Harpsichords unbuilt! Old men weeping in the parks!
Children! Children! breaking their backs lifting t~~h~~e city up into
        heaven. Pavements, trees, tons. The screaming radios. Xmas!
        Jesus! Wires coming out of the ears. Lifting the city on our
        backs
to Heaven which exists ~~and is~~ everywhere.

        Visions! Hallucinations! Omens! Dreams! Illuminations!
Garbage! Corpses!
        Gone down the river, the whole boatload of sensitive bullshit!
        Miracles! Ecstasies! Flips! Highs! Break-throughs! Telepathies!
        Over the river, gone down the flood, time gone, ten years,
animal screams, real holy laughter in the river!
        They saw it all, they heard the drowning yell!
        They bade farewell as they jumped off the roof to solitude,
carrying flowers, down to the street.

Moloch! Moloch! The ugly cities, the skullhead ~~buildings~~,
        monsterous warehouses, abbatoirs, treasuries, banks and
        robot hotels
        robot apartments, skullhead hotels, skeleton treasuries,
ghostly banks, bloody abbotoirs, monster ware~~h~~ouses, spectral
streets, ~~eyes in the~~ capitols, stone cock skyscrapers
                eyeless

antiphonal
river?
Breath!

10: ["and is" canceled]
Left margin: "*Antiphonal* river vs stacatto!" A struc-
    tural note, proposing that verse strung with ex-
    clamatory or "stacatto" single words ("Visions!")
alternate with verse made up of short phrasing
("Gone down the river!"). —A.G.
20: ["buildings" x-ed out]
25: ["eyes in the" x-ed out]

60   HOWL, PART II: DRAFT 2

Moloch! Moloch! What Sphinx of cement and alluminum bashed in their
        skulls and ate up imagination? up their brains & imagination
Moloch Moloch! Solitude! Ugliness! Ashcans and unobtainable dollars! Garbage
        heap of brains! Boys screaming under the stairways! Old men
        weeping in the parks! *Children*
    Moloch! Moloch! breaking their backs lifting Moloch to heaven!
        Pavements, trees, radios, tons! Lifting the city to heaven
        which exists everywhere!
                        and is
    Visions! Omens! Hallucinations! Miracles! Ecstasies! Gone down the
        American river!
    Dreams! Illuminations! Garbage! Corpses! The whole boatload of
        sensitive bullshit!
    Breakthroughs! Over the river! Flips! gone down the flood! Telepathies!
        Time gone! Highs! Animal screams! Ten Years! Epiphanies!
        Real holy laughter in the river!
    They saw it all! The wild eyes! The holy yells! They bade farewell!
        They jumped off the roof! to solitude! Carrying flowers!
        Down to the river! Into the street!

                                                    Dynasour
    Moloch! Moloch! Robot apartments! Eyeless capitols! Monsterous bombs!
        Skeleton treasuries! Ghostly banks! Granite phalluses!
                        crazy

1: ["Moloch! Moloch! canceled] . . . ["in" x-ed out]
2: ["up" x-ed out] . . . ["imagination?" canceled] up
   their brains & imagination
3: Moloch
4: ["Boys" canceled] children

8: and is
11: ["Garbage" canceled]
19: ["Monsterous" canceled] Dynasaur
20: ["Ghostly" canceled] craz[y]

II

What sphinx of cement and aluminum bashed in their skulls and
        ate up their brains and imagination?
Moloch! Solitude! Filth! Ugliness! Ashcans and unobtainable
        dollars! Garbage heap of eyebrows and brains! Children
        screaming under the stairways! Old men weeping in the parks!
Moloch! Moloch! Breaking their backs lifting Moloch to Heaven!
        Pavements, trees, radios, tons! lifting the city
to Heaven which exists and is everywhere!

Moloch! Moloch! Robot apartments! Invisible suburbs! Skeleton
        treasuries! Blind capitals! Ghostly bureaucracies!
        Invincible madhouses! Granite cocks! Monsterous bombs!

Visions! Omens! Hallucinations! Miracles! Ecstasies! Gone down
        the American river!
Dreams! Illuminations! Crosses! Religions! The whole boatload
        of sensitive bullshit!
Breakthroughs! Over the river! Corpses! Gone down the flood!
        Telepathies! Flips! Highs! Animal screams! Ten years!
        Mad generations! Epiphanies! Down on the rocks of time!
Real holy laughter in the river! They saw it all! The wild eyes!
        The holy yells! They bade farewell! They jumped off the
        roof! to solitude! Waving! Carrying flowers! Down to the
        river! Into the street!

Moloch! Moloch! Nightmare of Moloch! Moloch the buildings!

Moloch the battleship! Moloch the loveless!

Moloch the labor! Moloch Brokenleg Moloch!

Moloch the Money! Moloch the mental, moloch the

heavy moloch the ponderous moloch the inhuman

moloch the judger of men moloch the enfless

moloch the scientist moloch the President

moloch the priest moloch the prophet moloch the

Moloch the soulless moloch the, omen moloch the

avenger moloch the judger moloch the harbor

moloch the sity moloch the metropolis moloch the

capital moloch the labor loloch the vision molovh

theacademy moloch the lawful moloch the radio

moloch the soldier moloch the teacher moloch

the congress molochq the charity moloch the

dollar moloch/the ponderous moloch the powerful

moloch the s   sexless moloch   moloch the   *monarch*

marriage moloch thetelevision antennae moloch

the books amoloch the movies moloch the

New York Daily news, moloch the magazine of Time

moloch the heavy moloch of stone moloch the   *monolith*

heartless moloch the fearful moloch the

stone buildings moloch the vast stone of war

moloch the stunned intelligence moloch the   *kingdoms*

blind buildings moloch the buildings of

judgement moloch the incomprelensible prisons

moloch the electrical gallows ,moloch the lonely

streets moloch the empty/eyes moloch the mad

crowd of daytime moloch the

moloch the deathless government̶x moloch the mental jury
moloch the flags of the nations moloch the invisible
God moloch the slaughterer of sheep moloch the slaugh
terer of men moloch the slaughterer of mankind ,
moloch the slaughterer of a billion christs moloch
the b̶r̶i̶n̶g̶e̶r̶x̶o̶f̶ builder̶x̶x̶ of Hell moloch the bodiless
god moloch the god whose eyes are a thousand blind
windows moloch whose apartments stand in the
streets like lonely endless crazy geniusses and
spectral goliath l moloch whose names is America
Moloch whose name is Russia moloch whose name is
justice moloch whose name is religion moloch
whose name is poverty moloch whose name is plenty
moloch whose name is Congress moloch whose name is
Chicago and Moscow moloch whose name is democracy
moloch whose name is the Mind moloch whose name is
insanity moloch whose name is sanity moloch whose
h̶e̶a̶r̶t̶x̶i̶s̶z̶i̶z̶d̶x̶x̶ heart is Natural Resources Moloch
whose mind is machinery moloch whos legs are
pattleships moloch whose fingers are armies moloch
whose love is a stone moloch whose cock is the
washington monument moloch whose eyes are the atombombs
  moloch whose soul is physical fire moloch whose
conceptions are dreary

6: ["bringer of" x-ed out]   18: ["heart is indus[trial(?)] x-ed out]   22: the

moloch the man who interviewed me at the draftb
oard moloch for whom I sit lonely at the
typewriter moloch in whom I am homosexual moloch
in whom I am guilty moloch in whom I suffer mol
moloch in ~~whose xux~~ whom I am nightmare moloch
                              in whom
in whom I am mad moloch ~~inwhomxux~~ my mind has
abandoned itself moloch in whom we are mad mol
moloch in whom we are lovelorn moloch in whom
we live like dreams moloch for whome we are
fools moloch who entered our souls early
moloch from whom we waken in streaming
                      in
light from heaven moloch whom we hide moloch
whom we abandon with tears of pity & suffering
moloch that nurders the world moloch that stares
like a blind abysmal barren bleak beliefless
hellish god out of the win dows of the sirfrancis
dRake twoweyed god whose windows are lavatories
wwhose nose is a barroom and whose teeth are
the rooms of businessmen pulling million dollar
international deals and running the world.
Molich in whom I am a consciousness without
a body.

Moloch in whom I sit lonely! Moloch in whom I am gdäå
guilty! Moloch in whom I dream of angels! Moloch
in whom I am a hysterical fairy moloch in whom I
amd a nut moloch in whom I make insane prophecies
moloch in whom I am hopeless moloch of whivh I pseak
lightly moloch which is the lawyer moloch which is
my madness moloch in which I typewrite moloch in whom
I stare at the streets moloch in which I walk down
by the river moloch in whom I wander and stare at
rosebushes moloch wherein I fuck up moloch wherein I
cant get a hardom moloch what has me by the balls
moloch in whom I am manless moloch who gives me no
angel moloch who I give an angel moloch in whicj
I am my own angel moloch in whom I fall in the
battleship moloch whos e broken glasses I wear moloch
whose anesthesia and e ther I sip moloch where my love
is empty and eccentri c moloch where my love is a
void moloch in which I go to the hopspital to be anal
ysed moloch in whom I vomit moloch in whom I stare at
rosebushes moloch in which I eat garbage moloch in
which I ocook garbage moloch in which I hitchike.

Moloch whose name is America! Moloch whose poverty ~~is the~~ makes

spectre of genius! ~~Moloch whose insanity is justice!~~

Moloch whose name is Chicago! Moloch whose name is demo-

cracy! Moloch whose name is the Mind!

Moloch whose mind is pure machinery! Moloch whose fingers

are armies! ~~Moloch whose genitals are financial!~~

Moloch whose cock is the Washington Monument!

Moloch whose love is endless oil and stone! Moloch whose

soul is physical fire! Moloch whose ~~dream~~ amen is Apocalypse!

Moloch in whom I sit lonely! Moloch in whom I am guilty!

Moloch in whom ~~I suffer~~ I am mad! madness! Moloch in whom I suffer

~~we are~~ lovelorn in eternity!

Moloch who enters ~~our~~ my souls early! Moloch in whom ~~we~~ I hide!

Moloch whome ~~we~~ I abandon in tears of pity and fright!

Moloch who murders the world! Moloch from whom ~~we~~ I

waken in light streaming ~~down~~ from heaven!

Moloch! Moloch! ~~breaking~~ broken ~~my~~ backs lifting moloch to

heaven! Pavements, trees, radios, tons! Lifting

the cities to Heaven/which exists

and is everywhere!

Moloch! Moloch! Robot apartments! invisible suburbs!

skeleton treasuries! blind capitols! ghostly

bureaucracies! bloodie industries! invincible

madhouses! granite cocks! Monsterous bombs!

1: makes
9: ["dream" canceled] amen
11: I am mad! . . . I suffer
12: ["we are" canceled]

13: ["our" canceled] my . . . ["we" canceled] I
16: ["down" canceled]
17: broken ["my" canceled]

What spxinx of cement and aluminum bashed open their
        skulls and ate up their brains and imagination?

Moloch! Solitude! Filth! Ugliness! Ashcans and unob-
        tainable dollars! Garbage heap of eyebrows
        and brains! Children weeping under the stair-
        ways! Boys sobbing in armies! Old men weeping
        in the parks!

Moloch! Moloch! Nightmare of Moloch! Moloch the loveless!
        Moloch the mental! Moloch the heavy judger of
        men! Moloch the Avenger!

Moloch the economic monolith! Moloch the electrical
        prison! Moloch the incomprehensible Congress!

Moloch whose buildings are judgement! Moloch the vast
        stone of war! Moloch the stunned kingdoms!

Moloch in whom we are a consciousness without a body!
        Moloch the slaughterer of sheep! Moloch the
        slaughterer of men! Moloch the crucifier of a
        billion Christs! Moloch the bodiless God!

Moloch whose eyes are a thousand blind windows! Moloch
        whose apartments stand in the streets like
        endless dead Jehovahs!

Moloch whose name is America! Moloch whose poverty
        is the spectre of genius! Moloch whose name
        is Chicago! Moloch whose name is democracy!
        Moloch whose name is the Mind!

Moloch whose head is pure machinery! Moloch whose
        fingers are armies! Moloch whose cock is

5: Screaming
10: ["heartless" canceled]

11: of sorrow . . . avenger
14: governments!

17: slaughter

the Washington Monument!

Moloch whose love is endless stone and oil! Moloch
            Moloch whose eyes are the atom bombs!
    whose soul is physical fire!/Moloch whose

    omen is Apocalypse!

Moloch in whom we sit lonely! Moloch in whom we are

    guilty! Moloch in whom we suffer insanity!

    Moloch in whom we are lovelorn in eternity!

Moloch who enters our souls early! Moloch in whom

    we hide! Moloch whom we abandon in tears of

    pity and fright! Moloch from whom we waken

    in light streaming from heaven!

Moloch! Moloch! robot apartments! invisible suburbs!

    skeleton treasuries! blind capitols! ghostly

    bureaucracies! bloody industries! invincible

    madhouses! granite cocks! monsterous bombs!

Moloch whose mind is pure machinery! Moloch whose
         blood is green money! Moloch whose fingers
         are armies! Moloch whose ear is the tomb!
Moloch whose love is endless oil and stone! Moloch
         whose soul is physical fire! Moloch whose
         illuminations are atomic bombs! Moloch whose
         omen is øxøxzkx Apocalypse!
Moloch in whom I sit lonely! Moloch in whom I am
         guilty!

7: ["omen is" x-ed out]

What sphinx of cement and aluminum knocked open their
      skulls and ate up their brains and imagination?
Moloch! Solitude! Beatness! Filth! Ugliness! Ashcans
      and unobtainable dollars! Garbage heap of eyebrows
      and brains! Children screaming under the stair-
      ways! Boys sobbing in armies! Old men weeping
      in the parks!
Moloch! Moloch! Nightmare of Moloch! Moloch the loveless!
      Moloch the mental! Moloch the heavy judger of men!
      ~~Moloch the soulless!~~ Moloch the Avenger!
~~Moloch the vision of the radio! Moloch the lawful Congress!~~
      ~~Moloch the ponderous dollar!~~
~~Moloch the sexless monarch!~~ ~~Moloch the powerful marriage!~~
      Moloch the heartless monolithic ~~magazine of Time!~~
Moloch the incomprehensible prison! Moloch the electrical
      gallows! Moloch the _sorrowful_ ~~fearful~~ Congress!
Moloch _which_ the buildings ~~of~~ _are_ judgement! Moloch the vast stone
      of war! Moloch the stunned kingdoms!
Moloch in whom we are a consciousness without a body!
      ~~Moloch the deathless governments! Moloch the~~
      ~~flags of the nations! Moloch the builder of hell!~~
~~Moloch the invisible mental jury!~~ Moloch the slaughterer
      of mankind! Moloch the crucifier of a billion
      Christs! Moloch the bodiless God!
Moloch ~~whosex the god~~ whose eyes are a thousand blind
      windows! Moloch whose apartments stand in the
      streets like _endless_ ~~mad lonely~~ Jehovahs!

13: ["monarch" canceled]   17: whose [buildings] are   27: ["mad lonely" canceled] endless
16: sorrowful   25: ["whose" x-ed out] ["the god" canceled]

Moloch whose mind is pure machinery! Moloch whose
          blood is money! Moloch whose fingers are
          armies! Moloch whose ear is the tomb!
Moloch whose love is endless oil and stone! Moloch
          whose soul is physical fire! Moloch whose
          death is the atomic bomb! Moloch whose star
          is apocalypse!
Moloch in whom I sit lonely! Moloch in whom I am
          guilty!   Moloch in whom I am crazy! Moloch
          in whom I am lovelorn!
Moloch who entered my soul early! Moloch in whom I
          hide!   Moloch whom I abandon in tears of fright!
          Moloch who murders the world! Moloch from
          whom I waken in light streaming down from
          Heaven!
Moloch! Moloch! robot apartments! invisible suburbs!
          skeleton treasuries! blind capitals! ghostly
          bureaucracies! mournful industries! invincible
          madhouses! granite cocks! monsterous bombs!
Breaking their backs lifting Moloch to Heaven! pave-
          ments, trees, radios, tons! lifting the cities
          to Heaven
which exists and is everywhere!

--------Visions! omens! hallucinations! miracles! ecstasies!
          Gone down the American river.

What sphinx of cement and aluminum cracked open their
      skulls and ate up their brains and imagination?

Moloch! Solitude! Filth! Ugliness! Ashcans and
      unobtainable dollars! Garbage heap of eyebrows
      and brains! Children screaming under the
      stairways! Boys sobbing in armies! Old men
      weeping in the parks!

Moloch! Moloch! Nightmare of Moloch! Moloch the
      loveless! Mental Moloch! Moloch the heavy
      judger of men!

~~Moloch the heartless monolith in naked Time!~~ Moloch
      the incomprehensible prison! Moloch the
      ~~Congress of sorrows!~~

Moloch in whom ~~I am~~ we are a consciousness ~~without a body!~~
      Moloch whose buildings are judgement! Moloch
      the vast stone of war! Moloch the stunned
      governments!

Moloch the builder of hell! Moloch the slaughterer
      of sheep! Moloch the slaughterer of a
      billion Christs! Moloch the bodiless God!

~~Moloch whose name is America! Moloch whose name
      is Russia! Moloch whose name is Chicago!~~
      Moloch whose name is the Mind!

14: we are

What sphinx of cement and aluminum cracked open their
skulls and ate up their brains and imagination?
Moloch! Solitude! Filth! Ugliness! Ashcans and unob-
tainable dollars! Garbage heap of eyebrows
and brains! Children screaming under the
stairways! Boys sobbing in armies! Old men
weeping in the parks!
Moloch! Moloch! Nightmare of Moloch! Moloch the
loveless! Mental Moloch! Moloch the heavy
judger of men!
Moloch the granite skull monolith! Moloch the crossbone
congress and prison! Moloch whose buildings
are judgement! Moloch the vast stone of war!
Moloch the stunned govenments!
Moloch the slaughterer of men! Moloch the consumer
of a billion Christs! Moloch the builder
of Hell! Moloch the bodiless God!
Moloch whose name is the Mind! Moloch whose eyes are
a thousand blind windows! Moloch whose sky-
scrapers stand on the streets like endless
Jehovahs! Moloch whose smokestacks and antennae
crown the cities!

Moloch whose mind is greasy machinery! Moloch whose
       blood is running money! Moloch whose fingers
       are ten armies! Moloch whose ear is a smoking
       tomb!
Moloch whose love is endless oil and stone! Moloch whose
       soul is electricity and banks! Moloch whose fate
       is a cloud of sexless hydrogen! Moloch whose
       star is Apocalypse!
Moloch in whom I sit lonely! Moloch in whom I dream
       Angels! Crazy in Moloch! Cocksucker in Moloch!
       Lacklove and manless in Moloch!
Moloch who entered my soul early! Moloch whom I abandon!
       Moloch who murders the world! ~~Moloch I wake in!~~
       Light streaming out of the sky! *Wake up in Moloch!*

13: Wake up in Moloch!

II

What sphinx of cement and aluminum bashed open their
skulls and ate up their brains and imagination?

Moloch! Solitude! Filth! Ugliness! Ashcans and unob-
tainable dollars! Garbage heap of eyebrows and
brains! Children screaming under the stairways!
Boys sobbing in armies! Old men weeping in the
parks!

Moloch! Moloch! Nightmare of Moloch! Moloch the loveless!
Mental Moloch! Moloch the heavy judger of men!

Moloch the granite-skull ~~monolith~~ *monument*! Moloch the crossbone
Congress and prison! Moloch whose buildings
are judgement! Moloch the vast stone of war!
Moloch the stunned governments!

Moloch ~~the~~ consumer of mankind! Moloch the slaughterer
of a billion Christs! Moloch the builder of Hell!
Moloch the bodiless God!

~~Moloch whose name is the Mind!~~ Moloch whose eyes are
a thousand blind windows! Moloch whose sky-
scrapers stand in the streets like endless
Jehovahs! Moloch whose smokestacks and antennae
crown ~~the~~ cities!

10: ["[skull]ed" canceled] monument   17: ["Moloch whose name is the Mind!" canceled]
14: ["the" canceled]   21: ["the" canceled]

Moloch whose mind is pure machinery! Moloch whose

     blood is running money! Moloch whose fingers

     are ten armies! Moloch whose ear is a smoking

     tomb!

Moloch whose love is endless oil and stone! Moloch

     whose soul is electricity and banks! Moloch

     whose fate is a cloud of sexless hydrogen!

     Moloch whose star is Apocalypse!

Moloch in whom I sit lonely! Moloch in whom I dream

     Angels! Crazy in Moloch! Cocksucker in Moloch!

     Lacklove and manless in Moloch!

Moloch who entered my soul early! Moloch ~~which~~ who

     burned down my springtime! ~~Moloch in whom~~

     ~~I am a consciousness without a body!~~ Moloch

     who murders the world! Moloch whom I abandon!

     Wake up in Moloch! Light streaming out of

     the sky!

Moloch! Moloch! Robot apartments! invisible suburbs!

     skeleton treasuries! blind capitals! ghostly

     bureaucracies! ~~ghostly industries~~ *demonic mills* spectral

     nations! invincible madhouses! granite cocks!

     monsterous bombs!

12: ["which" canceled] who
20: demonic mills

Moloch! Moloch! breaking their backs lifting Moloch
      to Heaven! Pavements, trees, radios, tons!
      lifting the city to Heaven
Which exists and is everywhere!

Visions! omens! hallucinations! miracles! ecstasies!
      gone down the American river!
Dreams! adorations! illuminations! religions! the whole
      boatload of sensitive bullshit!
Break-throughs! over the river! Flips and crucifixions!
      gone down the flood! Highs! epiphanies! ten years!
      animal screams and suicides! Minds! new loves!
      Mad generations! down on the rocks of time!
Real holy laughter in the river! They saw it all!
      the wild eyes! the holy yells! They bade fare-
      well! they jumped off the roof! to solitude!
      waving! carrying flowers! Down to the river!
      into the street!

12: ["A" canceled] M[ad generation]s[!]

II

What sphinx of cement and aluminum bashed open their
skulls and ate up their brains and imagination?

Moloch! Solitude! Filth! Ugliness! Ashcans and unob-
tainable dollars! Garbageheap of eyebrows and
brains! Children screaming under the stairways!
Boys sobbing in armies! Old men weeping in the
parks!

Moloch! Moloch! Nightmare of Moloch! Moloch the love-
less! Mental Moloch! Moloch the heavy judger of
men!

Moloch the ~~granitestulled~~ incomprehensible prison!
Moloch the crossbone soulless jailhouse &
Congress of sorrows! Moloch the ~~Avenger~~
whose buildings are judgement! Moloch the
vast stone of war! Moloch the stunned govern-
ments!

Moloch whose eyes are a thousand blind windows! Moloch
whose ~~apartments~~ *skyscrapers* stand in the streets like endless
Jehovahs! ~~Moloch whose skyscrapers scream out~~
~~their rusty agony into the winter night!~~ Moloch
whose factories dream & creak in the fog!
Moloch whose smokestacks and antennae crown
~~the~~ cities!

18: skyscrapers   23: ["the" canceled]

Moloch whose mind is pure machinery! Moloch whose blood
    is running money! Moloch whose belly ~~is~~ a cannibal
    dynamo! ~~Moloch whose cock is the Washington
    Monument!~~ Moloch whose fingers are ten armies!
    Moloch whose ear is a smoking tomb!

Moloch whose love is endless oil and stone! ~~Moloch
    whose poverty is the spectre of genius!~~ Moloch
    whose soul is electricity and banks! Moloch
    whose fate is a cloud of sexless hydrogen! Moloch
    whose Star is Apocalypse!

Moloch whose name is the Mind! Moloch consumer of man-
    kind! Moloch the slaughterer of a billion ~~sheep
    of~~ Christ! Moloch the builder of Hell! Moloch
    the bodiless God!

Moloch in whom I sit lonely! ~~Moloch in whom I am a
    consciousness without a body!~~ Moloch in whom
    I dream Angels! Crazy in Moloch! Cocksucker
    in Moloch! Lacklove and manless in Moloch!

Moloch who entered my soul early! ~~Moloch who took away
    joy as the bringer of Justice! Moloch who
    burned down my Spring time!~~ Moloch our
    ~~merciless~~ Father! Moloch who murders the world!
    Wake up in Moloch! Light streaming out of the
    sky!

Moloch! Moloch! Robot apartments! invisible suburbs!
    skeleton treasuries! blind capitols! ghostly
    bureaucracies! spectral nations! demonic mills!
    invincible madhouses! granite cocks! monsterous
    bombs!

2: ["is" canceled] is   22: merciless
13: [Christ]s   26: [[gh]a[stly] canceled] [gh]o[stly]

Moloch who entered my soul early! Moloch in whom I am
a consciousness without a body! Moloch in whom
I sit lonely! Moloch in whom I dream Angels!
Moloch who murders the world! Crazy in Moloch!
Cocksucker in Moloch! Lacklove and manless in
Moloch! Wake up in Moloch! Light streaming out
of the sky!

N.B. This isolate draft attempts to condense corrections
& resolve problems indicated for two verses (Draft 14)
into one fat verse. Original sequence of exclamations
was later restored, a few phrases eliminated, then verse
divided in two again. —A.G.

II

What sphinx of cement and aluminum bashed open their

skulls and ate up their brains and imagination?

Moloch! Solitude! Filth! Ugliness! Ashcans and unob-

tainable dollars! Garbageheap of eyebrows and

brains! Children screaming under the stairways!

Boys sobbing in armies! Old men weeping in the

parks!

Moloch! Moloch! Nightmare of Moloch! Moloch the loveless!

Mental Moloch! Moloch the heavy judger of men!

Moloch the incomprehensible prison! Moloch the crossbone

soulless jailhouse and Congress of sorrows!

Moloch whose buildings are judgement! Moloch

the vast stone of war! Moloch the stunned gov-

ernments!

Moloch whose eyes are a thousand blind windows! Moloch

whose skyscrapers stand in the streets like

endless Jehovahs! Moloch whose factories ~~dream~~

~~&~~ croak in the fog! Moloch whose smokestacks and

antennae crown the cities!

Moloch whose mind is pure machinery! Moloch whose blood

is running money! ~~Moloch whose cock is the Wash-~~

~~ington Monument!~~ Moloch whose ~~belly's~~ belly's a cannibal

dynamo! Moloch whose fingers are ten armies!

Moloch whose ear is a smoking tomb!

17: ["dream" canceled]   18: ["&" canceled]   19: the   22: ["belly's" canceled] ["heart" canceled] belly's

Moloch whose love is endless oil and stone! Moloch whose
soul is electricity and banks! Moloch whose fate
is a cloud of sexless hydrogen! Moloch whose Star
is Apocalypse!

Moloch whose name is the Mind! Moloch consumer of man-
kind! Moloch the slaughterer of a billion Christs!
Moloch the builder of Hell! Moloch the bodiless
God!

Moloch in whom I sit lonely! Moloch in whom I dream
Angels! Crazy in Moloch! Cocksucker in Moloch!
Lacklove and manless in Moloch!

Moloch who entered my soul early! Moloch in whom I am
a consciousness without a body! Moloch who murders
the world! Wake up in Moloch! Light streaming
out of the sky!

Moloch! Moloch! Robot apartments! invisible suburbs!
skeleton treasuries! blind capitals! ghostly
bureaucracies! spectral nations! demonic mills!
invincible madhouses! granite cocks! monsterous
bombs!

2: poverty   14: Moloch whom I abandon!

II

What sphinx of cement and aluminum bashed open their
     skulls and ate up their brains and imagination?
Moloch! Solitude! Filth! Ugliness! Ashcans and unob-
     tainable dollars! Garbageheap of eyebrows and
     brains! Children screaming under the stairways!
     Old men weeping in the parks!
Moloch! Moloch! Nightmare of Moloch! Moloch the love-
     less! Mental Moloch! Moloch the heavy judger
     of men!
Moloch the incomprehensible prison! Moloch the cross-
     bone soulless jailhouse and Congress of sorrows!
     Moloch whose buildings are judgement! Moloch
     the vast stone of war! Moloch the stunned gov-
     ernments!
Moloch whose eyes are a thousand blind windows! Moloch
     whose skyscrapers stand in the/long streets like
     endless Jehovahs! Moloch whose factories dream
     and creak in the fog! Moloch whose smokestacks
     & antennae crown the cities!

19: the

Moloch whose mind is pure machinery! Moloch whose blood
      is running money! Moloch whose fingers are ten
      armies! Moloch whose belly is a cannibal dynamo!
      Moloch whose ear is a smoking tomb!
Moloch whose love is endless oil and stone! Moloch
      whose soul is electricity and banks! Moloch
      whose poverty is the spectre of genius! Moloch
      whose fate is a cloud of sexless hydrogen!
      Moloch whose Star is Apocalypse!
Moloch in whom I sit lonely! Moloch in whom I dream
      Angels! Crazy in Moloch! Cocksucker in Moloch!
      Lacklove and manless in Moloch!
Moloch who entered my soul early! Moloch in whom I am
      a consciousness without a body! Moloch who burned
             Moloch whom I abandon!
      down the world!/Wake up in Moloch! Light stream-
      ing out of the sky!
Moloch whose name is the mind! Moloch consumer of man-
      kind! Moloch the builder of hell! Moloch the
      bodiless god!

Moloch Moloch Robot apartments Invisible suburbs skel-
      eton treasuries demonic mills blind capitals
      silent bureaucracies spectral nations invincible
      madhouses granite cocks monsterous bombs

II

What sphinx of cement and aluminum bashed open their
skulls and ate up their brains and imagination?
Moloch! Solitude! Filth! Ugliness! Ashcans and unob-
tainable dollars! Garbageheap of eyebrows and
brains! Children screaming under the stairways!
Old men weeping in the parks!
Moloch! Moloch! Nightmare of Moloch! Moloch the love-
less! Mental Moloch! Moloch the heavy judger
of men!
Moloch the incomprehensible prison! Moloch the crossbone
soulless jailhouse and Congress of sorrows!
Moloch whose buildings are judgement! Moloch
the vast stone of war! Moloch the stunned
governments!
Moloch whose eyes are a thousand blind windows! Moloch
whose skyscrapers stand in the long streets like
endless Jehovahs! Moloch whose factories dream
and croak in the fog! Moloch whose smokestacks
and antennae crown the cities!

Moloch whose mind is pure machinery! Moloch whose
    blood is running money! Moloch whose fingers
    are ten armies! Moloch whose breast is a cannibal
    dynamo! Moloch whose ear is a smoking tomb!
Moloch whose love is endless oil and stone! Moloch
    whose soul is electricity and banks! Moloch
    whose poverty is the spectre of genius! Moloch
    whose fate is a cloud of sexless hydrogen!
Moloch whose name is the Mind! Moloch consumer of
    mankind! Moloch the builder of Hell! Moloch
    the bodiless God!
Moloch in whom I sit lonely! Moloch in whom I dream
    Angels! Crazy in Moloch! Cocksucker in Moloch!
    Lacklove and manless in Moloch!
Moloch who entered my soul early! Moloch in whom I am
    a consciousness without a body! Moloch who burned
    down the world! Moloch whom I abandon! Wake up
    in Moloch! Light streaming out of the sky!
Moloch! Moloch! Robot apartments! invisible suburbs!
    skeleton treasuries! demonic mills! blind
    capitals! cabalistic bureaucracies! spectral
    nations! invincible madhouses! granite cocks!
    monsterous bombs!

Guide to Original Manuscripts, Part III

Draft 1: This is the first stage of improvisation, retained mainly intact, rearranged. It was provisionally titled Part IV, for a time intended to follow "Footnote to Howl," now Part IV. Checks and crossouts were used to keep track of verses rearranged in third draft.

Draft 2: Fills out longish end of pyramid with thicker middle, & rearranges litany for progressively longer responses. Here it was opportune to expand this space to expound terms of spiritual revolution.

Draft 3: Consolidates phrasing & arranges the graduated litany in physical pyramid by eyeball order on one page, as in Schwitters' "Priimiitittiii" model (see p. 182).

Draft 4: Prior draft is revised & tightened, cleaned up, typed single space, and properly titled Part III.

Draft 5: Typed double space near final form.

Carl Solomon!
I am with you in Rockland
    where the faculties of the skull no longer admit the worms
    of the senses
I am with you in Rockland
    where you drink the tea of the breast of the spinsters
    of Utica
I am with you in Rockland
    where you pun on the bodies of your nurses the harpies
    of the Bronx
I am with you in Rockland
    where you imitate the shade of my mother
I am with you in Rockland
    where thirtyfive shocks will never return your soul to its
    body from its pilgrimage in the void
I am with you in Rockland
    where you're madder than I am
I am with you in Rockland
    where you write only letters which are invisible
I am with you in Rockland
    where you wanted to be
where you laugh at this invisible humor

I am with you in Rockland
    where you xxx stay for the rest of your life
I am with you in Rockland
    where your condition has become serious and is reported
    over the radio
I am with you in Rockland
    where you knock dripping from a sea journey at the door
    of my cottage in the Western night
I am with you in Rockland
    where you have murdered your secretaries
I am with you in Rockland
    where you play pingpong with Malcolm Ghazal and Christopher
    Smart
I am with you in Rockland
    where life is easy though you must feel very strange
I am with you in Rockland
    where there are twenty-five thousand mad comrades
    all singing the Internationale together
I am with you in Rockland
    where we are great writers together on the same
    dreadfuly typewriter
I am with you in Rockland
    where we hug and kiss the United States under our
    bedsheets, the United States that coughs all night,
    and won't let us sleep.

34: Appollinaire   42: ["together" canceled]

I am with you in Rocklaned   against
        where we plot a revolution in the United States
I am with you in Rockland
        where we plan a new republic based on free money
        and magnanimity
I am with you in Rockland
        where we committ that old blind whore Justice once and for
        all and help young Mercy escape
I am with you in Rockland
        where we make(icecream and mercy for the) merciful icecream
        for the multitudes

I am with you in Rockland
        where accuse America of insanity and plot a revolution
        against the doctors of your Golgotha
I am with you in Rockland
        where you call for a new god to split the heavens of Long Island
        and ressurect your living body from the tomb
I am with you in Rockland where you walk dripping from a sea-journey
        on the highway to my cottage in the Western night
I am with you in Rockland
        where there are thirtyfive thousand mad comrades all together
        singing the Internationale
I am with you in Rockland
        where we hug and kiss the United States under our bedsheets, the
        United States that coughs all night, and won't let us sleep.

Carl Solomon!
I am with you in Rockland
    where you're madder than I am
I am with you in Rockland
    where you'll stay for the rest of your life
I am with you in Rockland
    where you must feel very strange
I am with you in Rockland
    where you laugh at this invisible humor
I am with you in Rockland
    where you have murdered your secretaries
I am with you in Rockland
    where you imitate the shade of my mother
I am with you in Rockland
    where your condition has become serious and is reported on the
    radio
I am with you in Rockland
    where we are great writers on the same dreadful typewriter
I am with you in Rockland
    where fifty shocks will never again return your soul to its obody
    from a pilgrimage in the void
I am with you in Rockland
    where you play pingpong with the actual pingpong of the abyss William Appollinaire and Chris-
    topher Smart
I am with you in Rockland
    where the faculties of the skull no longer admit the worms
    of the senses
I am with you in Rockland
    where you drink the tea of the breasts of the spinsters of
    Utica
I am with you in Rockland where
    where you pun on the bodies of your nurses the harpies of the
    Bronx
I am with you in Rockland   existentialism atheism
    where you accuse your doctors of insanity and plot the final
    revolution against the national Golgotha
I am with you in Rockland
    where we hug and kiss the United States under our bedsheets,
    the United states that coughs all night, and won't let us sleep
I am with you in Rockland
    where there are thirtyfive thousand mad comrades all together
    singing the final stanzas of the Internationale
I am with you in Rockland/where you will split the heavens of Long
    Island and resurrect your living human Jesus from the tomb
I am with you in Rockland where you walk
    where you walk in my dreams, dripping from a sea-journey, on
    the highway across America in tears, to the door of my cottage
    in the Western night.

5: [you]'ll   35: existentialism atheism
23: with the [canceled] the actual pingpong of the abyss   44: living

III

Carl Solomon! I'm with you in Rockland
          where you're madder than I am
I'm with you in Rockland
          where you must feel very strange
I'm with you in Rockland
          where you laugh at this invisible humor
I'm with you in Rockland
          where you imitate the shade of my mother
I'm with you in Rockland
          where you've murdered your 12 secretaries
I'm with you in Rockland
          where your condition has become serious and is reported
          on the radio
I'm with you in Rockland
          where we are great writers on the same dreadful typewriter
I'm with you in Rockland
          where the faculties of the skull no longer admit the worms
          of the senses
I'm with you in Rockland
          where you drink the tea of the breasts of the spinsters of
          Utica
I'm with you in Rockland
          where you pun on the bodies of your nurses the harpy magdalines
          of the Bronx
I'm with you in Rockland
          where fifty more shocks will return your soul to its body again
          from its pilgrimage to a cross in the void
I'm with you in Rockland
          where you scream in a straightjacket that you're losing the game
          of the actual pingpong of the abyss
I'm with you in Rockland
          where you accuse your doctors of insanity and plot the Hebrew
          socialist rebellion against the facist national Golgotha
I'm with you in Rockland
          where you will split the heavens of Long Island and resurrect
          your living human Jesus from the superhuman tomb
I'm with you in Rockland
          where there are thirtyfive-thousand mad comrades all together
          singing the final stanzas of the Internationale
I'm with you in Rockland
          where we hug and kiss the United States under our bedsheets,
          the United States that coughs all night, and won't let us sleep
I'm with you in Rockland
          in my dreams you walk dripping from a sea-journey on the highway
          across America in tears to the door of my cottage in the Western
          night.

III

Carl Solomon! I'm with you in Rockland

     where you're madder than I am

I'm with you in Rockland

     where you must feel very strange

I'm with you in Rockland

     where you laugh at this invisible humor

I'm with you in Rockland

     where you imitate the shade of my mother

I'm with you in Rockland

     where you have murdered your 12 secretaries

I'm with you in Rockland

     where your condition has become serious and is

     reported on the radio

I'm with you in Rockland

     where we are great writers on the same dread-

     ful typewriter

I'm with you in Rockland

     where the faculties of the skull no longer

     admit the worms of the senses

I'm with you in Rockland

     where you drink the tea of the breasts of

     the spinsters of Utica

I'm with you in Rockland

     where you pun on the bodies of your nurses

     the harpies of the bronx

I'm with you in Rockland

>   where fifty more shocks will never return
>
>   your soul to its body again from its pil-
>
>   grimage to a cross in the void

I'm with you in Rockland

>   where you scream in a straightjacket that
>
>   you're losing the game of the actual ping-
>
>   pong of the abyss

I'm with you in Rockland

>   where you accuse your doctors of insanity
>
>   and plot the Hebrew socialist rebellion
>
>   against the ~~capitalist~~ Facist national Golgotha

I'm with you in Rockland

>   where you will split the Heavens of Long
>
>   Island and resurrect your living human
>
>   Jesus from the superhuman tomb

I'm with you in Rockland

>   where there are thirty-five-thousand mad
>
>   comrades all together singing the final
>
>   stanzas of the Internationale

I'm with you in Rockland

>   where we ~~scream~~ howl and dance on the piano
>
>   of spiritual knowledge the soul is inn-
>
>   ocent and immortal ~~and~~ it will never die
>
>   ungodly in an armed madhouse

12: Facist   22: howl   24: it

I'm with you in Rockland

      where we hug and kiss the United States under

      our bedsheets, the United States that coughs

      all night, and won't let us sleep

I'm with you in Rockland

      where we wake up electrified and hear our

      own souls' airplanes roaring over the roof

      they've come to drop angelic bombs the

      war is over forget your underwear we're

      free

I'm with you in Rockland

      in my dreams you walk dripping from a sea-

      journey on the highway across America in

      tears to the door of my cottage in the

      Western night.

Guide to Original Manuscripts, Part IV (Footnote)

Draft 1: This handscript is the original improvisation, date uncertain, probably written after public reading of Part I. The basic cadence, diction & phrasings are set, all extravagance driving toward redemption.

Draft 2: Begins with 14 "Holy"s, adds prefatory generic blessings, moving from World to bodily parts. Verse 13, adding "voice" and "audience," may refer to 6 Gallery reading. Then personal names and local underground imagery (junky cafeterias, etc.) are set in place, then international panoramic generalizations, "Skyscrapers & Antiquities." Some arrangement of form's begun.

Draft 3: The matter's condensed, beginning with 15 "Holy"s, for continuity of cadence, climaxed with three rolling locomotive comma-less exclamatory verses.

Draft 4: Phrasing boiled down to nonrepetitive usable concepts, the opening is cleaned up, but sequence gets stuck at the end. Bottom page, 15 vertical lines count the "Holy"s into one set of 3 and three sets of 4—upbeat 4/4 time with accented last syllable. If analyzed according to classical meters as suggested by scholar Ed Sanders, its primary reading is catalectic first paeonic tetrameter: a paean to Sacred World. Alternately, it can be read as five sets of 3 trochaic "Holy"s, with heavier stress varying from first to third trochee of each set; and heaviest stress of all on the last trochee of the fifth & last set of "Holy"s.

Draft 5: Lines have been arranged to strophic verse, sets of equivalent phrases grouped together more logically than before. Use of slightly longer verse than in original draft allows separation out of basic ideas, concepts, "angles," in this typescript.
Handscript completes the rhythmic run; this is the first notation of last verse. Kerouac's phrasings "Kind King Mind" (*Mexico City Blues*, 5th chorus) and "Adios, King" (last line of *Visions of Cody*, referring to Neal Cassady) are echoed.

Draft 6: Retyped double spaced & revised, with new key phrases invented: "hideous human angels," "mysterious rivers of tears under the streets," etc.

Draft 7: This final retype cleans up several single-word revisions and transpositions. A few phrases (of verse 11, oddly characterizing author's appearance, Beijing 1984) are omitted in published version.

Holy Peter Holy Allen Holy Kerouac Holy Huncke

Holy the numberless & the unknown beggars & bums

Holy the hipsters Holy the Thieves & Criminals

Holy the Damned Holy the Saved! Holy the Holy

Holy the Turks and the Cows Holy the Idiots

Holy the heavens & the pavements! Holy the Cafeterias

Holy the Jazzbands Holy the Marijuana Holy the Saxophones

Holy the Junkies Holy the Turd Holy the Needle

Holy the pants! Holy the babes! Holy the Reapers

Holy the lovers! Holy the fucking! Holy the Buggers Holy Cocksucking

Holy, Forgiveness! Mercy! Love! Charity! Faith! Magnanimity

Holy Rivers & the beggars

Holy the Juggernaut Holy the Murders Holy the Moloch

Holy the vast Middleclasses Holy the Bitters & Holy the rebellions

Holy Rebellions! Holy Skyscrapers & antiquities Holy the millions

Holy NY Holy SF Holy Paris Holy Tangiers Holy Istanbul

Holy the Bastards

Holy Rome

Holy the Visions Holy the hallucination Holy the Void Holy Holy the abyss

Holy Time in Eternity Holy Eternity in Time

Holy the clocks Holy Space Holy Infinity Holy the 4th dimension

Holy my mother in the insane asylum! Holy the cunt

Holy My father's cock Holy My cock & the cocks of my lovers!

Holy the cocks of the grandfather of Kansas!

Holy the aeroplanes! Holy the gardens! Holy the pavements! Holy the ——

Holy the Sea Holy the Desert Holy the Railroad Holy the locomotive

Holy the endless disciples of buddha Holy the Categories of beings Holy particulars

Holy the rumblings in my gut! Holy my shirt in the toilet!

Holy the come on the tip of my cock! Holy the cock in my mouth

Holy the cock in my asshole Holy the cock in between my legs.

Holy Peter Holy Allen Holy Kerouac Holy Huncke
Holy the numberless & the unknown beggars & bums
Holy the hipsters Holy the Junkies & Criminals
Holy the Damned Holy the Saved! Holy the Holy
Holy the Turks and the Cows Holy the Idiots
Holy the heavens & the pavements! Holy the cafeterias
Holy the Jazzbands Holy the Marijuana Holy the saxophones!
Holy the Junkies Holy the Junk Holy the Needle
Holy the Pants! Holy the babies! Holy the Diapers
Holy the lovers! Holy the fucking! Holy the Quers Holy Cocksucking.
Holy, Forgiveness! Mercy! Love! Charity! Faith! Magnanimity
    Holy Dimes to the beggars
Holy the Juggernaut Holy the Murders Holy the Moloch
Holy the vast Middleclasses Holy the Hitlers Holy the rebellios
Holy rebellions! Holy Skyscrapers & Antiquities Holy the millions
Holy NY Holy SF Holy Paris Holy Tangier Holy Istanbul
                                Holy Rome
                                Holy Lhasa
Holy the Bastards
Holy the Visions Holy the Hallucination Holy the Void Holy the abyss

Holy Time in Eternity Holy Eternity in Time
Holy the Clocks Holy Space Holy Infinity Holy the Cunt   4th Dimension
Holy my Mother in the insane asylum! Holy the Cunt
Holy My father's cock Holy My cock & The Cocks of my lovers!
Holy the Cocks of the grandfathers of Kansas!
Holy the aeroplanes! Holy the Heavens! Holy the Pavements! Holy the Concrete
Holy the Sea Holy the Desert Holy the Railroad Holy the locomotive
Holy the endless disciples of Bhudda Holy the Catagories of beings Holy
                               Particulars

Holy the rumblings in my gut! holy my shit in the toilet!
Holy the come on the tip of my cock! Holy the Cock in my mouth
Holy the Cock in my asshole Holy the Cock in between my legs

Holy! holy! holy! holy! holy! Holy! holy!
holy! holy! holy! holy! holy! holy! holy!
The World is holy! the soul is holy!
The skin is holy; the nose is holy!
the hand is holy! the eyeball holy!
The ~~nose~~ and cock and ears and asshole holy!

Everything is holy! everybody's holy everyone's an angel
Everywhere is heaven Everyplace is paradise
~~Every~~ every ~~is a seraph every everyness is God~~
        man

The pig is holy as the seraphim is holy
The bum is holy as you my soul are holy
The notebook is holy The poem is holy
the voice is holy the addience is holy the typewriter is holy

Holy ~~Peter~~ Holy Allen Holy Kerouac Holy Huncke
Holy the numberless unknown beggars and bums
Holy the hipsters Holy the Junkies and Criminals
~~(Holy the Damned Holy the Saved! Holy the Holy!)~~
~~(Holy the Turks and the Cows! Holy the Idiots)~~
Holy the heavens and the pavements! Holy the cafeterias
Holy the Jazzbands holy the Marijuana Holy the Saxophones!
Holy the Junkies Holy the Junk Holy the Needle
~~(Holy the pants! Holy the babies! Holy the diapers!)~~   the
Holy the lovers! Holy the fucking! ~~Holy the Queers!~~ Holy cocksucki
Holy, Forgiveness! Mercy! Love! Charity! Faith! Magnanimity!
~~Holy dimes to the beggars~~
Holy the Juggernauts Holy the Murders Holy the Moloch
Holy the vast Middleclass ~~Holy the Hitlers Holy the rebellious~~
Holy Rebellions! Holy Skyscrapers & Antiquities Holy the Millions
Holy NY Holy SF Holy Paris Holy Tangiers Holy Istanbul Holy Rome
~~Holy the Bastards~~
Holy the visions Holy the Hallucinations Holy the Void Holy the
                                             ~~Holy~~ vast abyss
Holy Time in Eternity Holy Eternity in Time
Holy the clocks Holy Space Holy Infinity Holy ~~the Cunt~~ 4th Dimens
                                                            ion
Holy my mother in the insane asylum! ~~Holy the Cunt~~
~~Holy my father's cock Holy my cock and the cocks of my lovers!~~
Holy the cocks of the grandfathers of Kansas!
Holy the aeroplanes! Holy the Heavens! Holy the pavements! Holy
                                         the concrete
Holy the sea Holy the desert Holy the railroad Holy the locomotive
~~Holy the endless disciples of Buddha Holy the Categories of Beings~~
                                     Holy particulars
~~Holy the rumblings in my gut! Holy the shit in my toilet!~~
Holy the come on the tip of my cock! ~~Holy the cock in my mouth!~~
~~Holy the cock in my asshole~~ Holy the cock in between my legs.

Holy!

9: man   14: Solomon [canceled] Carl   23: the   43: [insert] Holy

Holy! Holy! holy! holy! holy! holy! holy!
Holy! Holy! Holy! holy! holy! holy! holy! holy!
The World is Holy! the soul is holy!
The skin is holy! the nose is holy! *the madman is holy!*
~~The madman is holy! the sane man is holy!~~
The tongue and cock and ears and asshole holy!
Everything is holy! everybody's holy! everyone's an angel!
Everywhere is heaven! Everyday's eternity! everyman is god!
The pig is holy as the seraphim is holy!
The bum is holy as you my soul are holy!
The notebook is holy the typewriter is holy the poem is holy
the voice is holy the audience is holy the ecstasy is holy
Solomon is holy Allen is Holy Kerouac is Holy Huncke is holy
Holy the unknown numberless beggars and bums
Holy the hipsters holy the jazzbands holy the ~~Junkies~~ *Marijuana*
~~Holy the fuckers holy the marijuana holy~~ the saxophones
Holy my mother in the insane asylum holy the cocks of the
            grandfathers of Kansas
Holy the heavens and the pavements holy the cafeterias
Holy the Jauggernauts holy the vast middleclass holy the rebellions
Holy the millions holy the skyscrapers holy the moloch holy the
~~Holy the nations holy the seas holy the deserts holy the~~
                                    Nations
Holy ~~the~~ NY holy SF holy Paris HolyTangiers holy Jerusalem holy
                                    Istanbul
Holy the visions holy the hallucinations holythe Omens holy the
                                    abyss
Holy Time in Eternity Holy Eeternity in Time holy the clocks
        ~~holy space holy~~ in space holy the Fourth Dimension
Holyforgiveness holy mercy holy love holycharity faith magnanimity
        holy the soul!

Holy! Holy! holy! Holy! holy! holy! Holy!
Holy! holy! holy! holy! holy! holy! holy!
The world is holy! the soul is holy! the body holy!
The nose is holy! the hand is holy! the eyeball holy!
The cock and tongue and ears and dreams are holy!
Everything is holy! everybody's holy! everyone's an angel!
Everywhere is heaven ! everyplace is Paradise! everytime eterni
Everyman's a seraph! Everyday is Eden! Everynight eternity!
The sufferer is holy as the seraphim are holy!
The saint is holy the bum is holy as you my soul are holy!
The notebook is holy the typewriter is holy the poem is holy
the voice is holy the audience is holy the ecstasy is holy
Holy Solomon Holy Allen Holy Kerouac Holy Huncke
Holy the numberless unknown beggars and bums
Holy the hipsters holy the Junkies Holy the Junk & the Needle
Holy the jazzbands Holy their Marijuana Holy their Saxophones
Holy the lovers! Holy the fucking Holy the cocksucking
Holy my mother in the insane asylum! Holy the cocks of the
                              Grandfathers of Kansas!
Holy the juggernauts! Holy the vast middleclass! Holy the Molocl
Holy the Rebbellions! Holy the skyscrapers! Holy the Millions!
Holy NY Holy SF Holy Paris Holy Tangiers Holy Istanbul Holy Chi
Holy the visions! Holy the Hallucinations! Holy the void Abyss!
Holy the Heavens! Holy the Aeroplanes! Holy the Sea! Holy the
                              Concrete!
Holy the pavements! Holy the desert! Holy the RR! Holy the
                              locomotive!
Holy the endless disciples of Buddha! Holy the cafeterias!

' ((((((((((((

* (((= Holy's — trying to balance
the rychm as
1.234, 1234, 1234, 1
A4 85/12/27

Holy! holy! holy! holy! holy! holy! holy! holy! holy!
    holy! holy! holy! holy! holy! holy!
The world is holy! the skin is holy! the nose is holy!
    the hand is holy! the tongue and cock and ears
    and asshole holy!
Everything is holy! everybody's holy! everywhere is heaven!
    everyday is in eternity! everyman is angel!
The madman is holy as the seraphim is holy! The bum is holy
    as you my soul are holy!
The notebook is holy the tyepewriter is holy the poem is holy
    the voice is holy the ecstasy is holy the audience
    is holy!
Holy Solomon Holy Allen Holy Kerouac Holy Cassady Holy Lucien
    holy Burroughs holy Huncke holy the unknown numberless
    suffering beggars and angels!
Holy the hipsters holy the jazzbands holy themarijuana holy
    the junkies holy the saxophones!
Holy my mother in the insane asylum! Holy the cocks of the
    grandfathers of Kansas!
Holy the heavens and the pavements! holy the cafeterias and
    the millions!
Holy the juggernauts holy the vast middleclass holy the rebellious
    holy thskyscrapers holy the moloch!
Holy the nations holy NY holy SF Holy Paris holy Tangiers holy
    Jerusalem holy Istanbul!
Holy time in eternity holy eternity in time holy the clocks
    in space holy the fourth dimension!
Holy the visions holy the hallucinations holy the intelligence
    holy the omens holy the abyss!
Holy forgiveness holy mercy! holy love! holy charity! holy faith!
    holy magnanimity! holy the soul!

[Handwritten lines:]

Holy the supernatural extra brilliant kindness of the kindly brilliance of the Soul!

Holy the supernatural natural extra brilliant intelligent kindness of the Soul!

30–31: Holy the supernatural excess ["excess" canceled, replaced by:] natural brilliant kindness of the ["brilliant kindness of the" canceled, replaced by:] kindly brilliance of the soul! ["brilliant kindness of the" replaced by:] extra brilliant kindness intelligent [inserted between "brilliant" and "kindness" [Entire line canceled, replaced by:] Holy the supernatural natural extra brilliant intelligent kindness of the Soul! ["natural" canceled]

IV

Holy! Holy! Holy! Holy! Holy!Holy! Holy! Holy!

Holy! Holy! Holy! Holy!Holy! Holy! Holy!

The world is holy! the soul is holy! the skin is
holy! the nose is holy! the head is holy! the
tongue and cock and hand and asshole holy!

Everything is holy! everybody's holy! everywhere is holy
heaven! everyone is here! everyday is in
eternity! everyman is angel!

The pig is holy as the seraphim! the madman is holy
as you my soul are holy!

The notebook is holy the typewriter is holy the poem
is holy the voice is holy the ecstasy is holy
the hearer is holy!

Holy Peter holy Allen holy Solomon holy Lucien holy
Kerouac holy Cassady holy Huncke holy Burroughs
holy the unknown buggered and suffering bums!
Holy the hideous human angels!

Holy my mother in the insane asylum! Holy the cocks
of the grandfathers of Kansas!

Holy the groaning saxophones! Holy the bop apocal-
ypse! Holy the drunken jazzbands marijuana
hipsters peace & junk & drums!

Holy the solitude of skyscrapers and pavements!
Holy the cafeterias and the millions! Holy
the mysterious rivers of tears under the
streets!

6: holy   16: [b]u[gg]ered

Holy the lone juggernaut! Holy the vast lamb of
        the middle-class! Holy the crazy shepherds
        of rebellion! Denver is lonesome for her
        heroes!

Holy the glitter-eyed stranger digging the scene
        in Peking! he's in a sexual China! and who
        digs Los Angeles is Los Angeles!

Holy NY holy SF holy Paris holy ~~Jerusalem~~ holy
        Tangiers holy Moscow holy Istanbul!

Holy Time in Eternity holy Eternity in Time holy
        the clock in space holy the Fourth Dimension
        holy the Angel in Moloch!

Holy the sea holy the desert holy the railroad holy
        the locomotive holy the visions holy the omens
        holy the hallucinations holy the miracles holy
        the abyss!

Holy forgiveness! mercy! charity! faith! holy! ours!
        bodies! suffering! magnanimity!

Holy the supernatural extra brilliant intelligent
        kindness of the soul!

Holy! Holy! Holy! Holy! Holy! Holy! Holy! Holy!
        Holy! Holy! Holy! Holy! Holy! Holy! Holy!
The world is holy! The soul is holy! the skin is
        holy! the nose is holy! the heart is holy!
        the head is holy! the tongue and cock and
        hand and asshole holy!
Everything is holy! everybody's holy! everywhere
        is holy! everyman is here! everyday's eternity!
        everyone's an angel!
The bum is holy as the seraph! the madman is holy
        as you my soul are holy!
The notebook is holy the typewriter is holy the poem
        is holy the voice is holy the hearer is holy
        the ecstasy is holy!
Holy Peter holy Allen holy Kerouac holy Solomon holy
        Lucien holy Cassady holy Burroughs holy Huncke
        holy the unknown buggered and suffering beggars!
        Holy the hideous human angels!
Holy my mother in the insane asylum! Holy the cocks of
        the grandfathers of Kansas!
Holy the groaning saxophone! Holy the bop apocalypse!
        Holy the jazzbands marijuana hipsters peace &
        junk & drums!
Holy the solitude of skyscrapers & pavements! Holy
        the cafeterias and the millions! Holy the
        mysterious rivers of tears under the streets!

Holy the lone juggernaut! Holy the vast lamb of the
        middle class! Holy the crazy shepherds of
        rebellion! Denver is lonesome for her heroes!
Holy the glitter-eyed stranger digging the scene in
        Peking! he's in a sexual China! and who digs
        Los Angeles IS Los Angeles!
Holy NY holy SF holy Paris holy Hutchinson & Bellingham
        holy Tangiers holy Moscow holy Istanbul!
Holy time in eternity holy eternity in time holy
        the clocks in space holy the fourth dimension
        holy the fifth International holy the Angel
        in Moloch!
Holy the sea holy the desert holy the railroad holy
        the locomotive holy the visions holy the omens
        holy the hallucinations holy the miracles holy
        the eyeball holy the abyss!
Holy forgiveness! mercy! charity! faith! Holy! Ours!
        bodies! suffering! magnanimity! Holy the
        supernatural extra brilliant intelligent kindness
        of the soul!

CARL SOLOMON SPEAKS

Carl Solomon in his apartment, New York, circa 1953, several years after residence with author at N.Y. Psychiatric Institute, newly working at Ace Books editing W. S. Burroughs' *Junkie*. *Photo by A.G.*

Carl Solomon on his favorite Sunday outing, fishing under City Island bridge, N.Y., Summer 1983. *Photo by A.G.*

Reintroduction to Carl Solomon

Here the personage whose name was taken as the mythical dedicatee of "Howl: For Carl Solomon" steps forth. The poem was written in relative literary obscurity in a room on Montgomery Street, in North Beach, San Francisco; I dedicated it to Mr. Solomon by name and didn't have any clear idea that the poem would make its way around the world and proclaim a private reference to public attention. The first printing of 1,000 copies imported from England gave no promise of celebrity to the author or Carl Solomon outside a small circle of witty understanding readers in sophisticated poetry circles of the Bay Area mid 1950s.

Mr. Solomon had recently returned to a mental hospital 3,000 miles away on the East Coast, and I was heart-struck at what seemed his hopeless impasse.

As the poem accumulated public force, the private mythology bandied about between Mr. Solomon and myself solidified as an image notorious on a quasi-national scale. This had unexpected consequences: it put Mr. Solomon's actual person in the world with my stereotype—a poetic metaphor—as a large part of his social identity. (Similarly, *On the Road* readers confuse the heroic fictional Dean Moriarty with his equally heroic prototype, Neal Cassady.) I came to regret my naive use of his name; Mr. Solomon himself bore the burden uneasily, and later was sorely tried by the situation. I am thankful for his sanity and generosity in this strange karmic friendship.

I hadn't realized all the consequences of the Word. I'd thought the poem a gesture of wild solidarity, a message into the asylum, a sort of heart's trumpet call, but was mistaken in my diagnosis of his "case" ("You're madder than I am"). In hindsight, his lifelong virtues of endurance, familial fidelity and ultimate balance make my appeal seem hysterical, myself overwrought, as in 1963 dream printed below.

Beyond that I'd used Mr. Solomon's return to the asylum as occasion of a masque on my feelings toward my mother, in itself an ambiguous situation since I had signed the papers giving permission for her lobotomy a few years before. Thereby hangs another tale.

Hence follows a recent statement by Carl Solomon as background to our first encounter, also a brief selection of his essays relevant to "Howl" and its literary presumptions, as well as my own rueful dream dated 1963, "O Carl!"

His specific comments on my unlicensed poetic version of his adventures are integrated, with others' appropriately signed, and my own notes forethought and afterthought verse by verse, in the section Annotations.

May this writing sweep away Clouds of Ignorance
From sentient beings too much in pain to see dream humor
Metaphor & hyperbole as comedic personae of the Muse
& for those ill-affected by "Howl"'s text, redress the karmic balance.

February 1986

Allen Ginsberg

Statement by Carl Solomon

A kind of immature romantic at that time, full of flowery dreams of Paris—having just read to completion Romain Rolland's novel *Jean Christophe*—I deserted, very precipitously and foolishly, I later decided, the American Liberty ship *Alexander Ramsey*, in the port of La Pallice in Brittany (during May of 1947) and made my way to La Rochelle (the provincial capital). There my first move was to get a haircut.

Then, on to Paris, settled in Montparnasse, read *Tropic of Cancer*, and hired a French lady to teach me the language.

It was not long before I had developed a taste for nougat and haricots verts, attended a lecture on Kafka by Jean-Paul Sartre at the Salle Gaveau, seen the *Mona Lisa*, made friends at the Cité Universitaire who had turned me on to Prévert and Michaux, begun an amatory relationship with a lady in Montmartre, witnessed an Artaud reading on the rue Jacob, attended à CP rally at the Vel d'Hiv,* and discovered Isou and *lettrisme*.

Six weeks and it was all over (the Paris *séjour*) and I came back to the States. Letterism had already awakened an interest in me and I was especially interested in the new poets of my generation of whom Isou and his followers seemed to be very significant ones. The whole tendency toward the non-verbal as I witnessed its reflection even in such American phenomena as the scat singing of Jackie Cain and Ray Kraal.† I sat in the Forty-second Street library in those years reading the latest issues of *La Nouvelle Revue Française*. I remember a special issue devoted to "Young Men of Twenty" in the year 1948.

My protest against the verbal, the rational and the acceptable took the form of disruption of a critical discussion of Mallarmé and other neo-dada clowning, which resulted in my incarceration in a psychiatric hospital in Manhattan. Where I encountered Allen Ginsberg, a fellow patient who was intrigued by my collection of Paris-acquired books. Among the Artaud, Genêt, Michaux, Miller, and Lautréamont was Isou's *Nouvelle Poésie et une Nouvelle Musique*. We discussed all of these things by way of laying the groundwork for Allen's eventual publication of "Howl" in 1956.

After treatment at P.I., I was readmitted to Brooklyn College, dropped out after subsequent marriage and job offer in book publishing.

After release from Pilgrim State (post "Howl") I took a battery of aptitude tests administered by the N.Y. State Department of Vocational Rehabilitation which indicated an IQ slightly above average and aptitude in literature, sales and social service; deficiencies in mechanical, scientific and mathematical areas; I wasn't trying very hard.

I took courses in American literature at the New School. NYU has been trying to get me back into academic work offering credit for life experience. However I still prefer to work.

February 9, 1986

---

* Velodrome d'Hiver, Winter Garden, Paris assembly place for sports and political meets.

† Singers who performed at Birdland, New York bebop mecca.

Report from the Asylum
Afterthoughts of a Shock Patient
By Carl Goy

A book that is accepted, at the moment, as the definitive work on shock-therapy concludes with the astonishing admission that the curative agent in shock-treatment "remains a mystery shrouded within a mystery."[1] This confession of ignorance (and it is extended to both insulin and electric shock-therapies), by two of the men who actually place the electrodes on the heads of mental patients at one of our psychiatric hospitals, certainly opens this field of inquiry to the sensitive layman as well as to the technician. The testimony that follows is that of an eye-witness, one who has undergone insulin-shock treatment and has slept through fifty comas.

One may begin with amusement at the hashish-smokers and their conception of the sublime. They, who at the very most, have been "high," consider themselves (quite properly) to be persons of *eminence* and archimandrates of a *High* Church. A patient emerging from an insulin coma, however, cannot help being a confirmed democrat. There can be no hierarchization of different levels of transcendency when they are induced by an intravenously-injected animal secretion, the very purpose of which is to bombard insulin-space with neutrons of glucose-time until space vanishes like a frightened child and one awakens terrified to find oneself bound fast by a restraining-sheet (wholly supererogatory to the patient, since, in the waking state, spaceless, mobility seems inconceivable). The ingenuousness of the hashishins is stupendous.

It is as though the Insulin Man were to call his drug by a pet name and spend days thrashing out the differences between "gone pot" and "nowhere pot."

The difference between hashish and insulin is in many ways similar to a difference between surrealism and magic. The one is affective and is administered by the subject himself; the other is violently resisted by the subject (since this substance offers not even the most perverse form of satisfactions); it is forcibly administered in the dead of night by white-clad, impersonal creatures who tear the subject from his bed, carry him screaming into an elevator, strap him to another bed on another floor, and who, later, recall him from his "revery" (a purely polemical term employed in writing "down" to the hashishin). Thus, insulin comes as a succubus, is effective, suggests grace.

In this respect, the paranoid phantasies released by hashish lack substantiality and are of the nature of automatic writing or gratuitous acts. In the case of insulin-shock therapy, one finds onself presented with a complete symbolism of paranoia, beginning with the rude awakening and the enormous hypodermic-needle, continuing through the dietary restrictions imposed upon patients receiving shock, and ending with the lapses of memory and the temporary physical disfigurement.

Early in the treatment, which consists of fifty hypoglycemic comas, I reacted in a highly paranoid manner and mocked the doctors by accusing them of "amputating" my brain. Of course, my illness was such that I was perpetually joking (having presented myself to the hospital upon reaching my majority, I had requested immediate electrocution since I was now of age—how serious was this request, I have no way of knowing—and was discharged as cured exactly nine months later, the day before Christmas).

Nevertheless, I noted similar paranoid responses on the part of other patients in shock.

For those of us acquainted with Kafka, an identification with K. became inevitable. Slowly, however, the identification with K. and with similar characters came to imply far more than we Kafkians had ever dreamed. We knew it to be true that we had been abducted for the most absurd of reasons: for spending hours at a time in the family-shower, for plotting to kill a soldier, for hurling refuse at a lecturer. And, in this particular, the text had been followed quite literally. The need for a revision of the Kafkian perspective arose, however, when the bureaucracy suddenly revealed itself as benevolent. We had not been dragged to a vacant lot and murdered, but had been dragged to a Garden of Earthly Delights and had there been fed (there were exceptions and there is a certain small percentage of fatalities resulting from shock, making the parallel to grace even more obvious). This impression arose, somehow, from the very nature of the subjective coma.

Upon being strapped into my insulin-bed, I would at once break off my usual stream of puns and hysterical chatter. I would stare at the bulge I

First published in *Neurotica* 6 (Spring 1950). Reprinted in *Mishaps, Perhaps*.

1. Hoch and Kalinowski, "Shock Therapy."

made beneath the canvas restraining-sheet, and my body, insulin-packed, would become to me an enormous concrete pun with infinite levels of association, and thereby, a means of surmounting association with things, much as the verbal puns had surmounted the meaning of words. And beneath this wrathful anticipation of world-destruction lay a vague fear of the consequences.

The coma soon confirms all of the patient's fears. What began as a drugged sleep soon changes organically and becomes one of the millions of psychophysical universes through which he must pass, before being awakened by his dose of glucose. And he cannot become accustomed to these things. Each coma is utterly incomparable to that of the previous day. Lacking a time-sense and inhabiting all of these universes at one and the same time, my condition was one of omnipresence, of being everywhere at no time. Hence, of being nowhere. Hence, of inhabiting that Void of which Antonin Artaud had screamed (I had been conditioned in illness by classical surrealism).

Invariably, I emerged from the comas bawling like an infant and flapping my arms crazily (after they had been unfastened), screaming, "Eat!" or, "Help!"

The nurses and doctors would ignore me, letting me flap about until my whole aching body and my aching mind (which felt as if it had been sprained) pulled themselves by their bootstraps out of the void of terror and, suddenly, attained a perfectly disciplined silence. This, of course, won the admiration of the dispensers of grace, who then decided that I was eminently worth saving and promptly brought me my breakfast tray and a glucose aperitif. And in this manner, item by item, the bureaucracy of the hospital presents the insulin *maudit* with a world of delightful objects all made of sugar—and gradually wins his undying allegiance. If we are not deceived by appearances we will see clearly that it is the entire world of things which imposes itself upon the would-be *maudit* and eventually becomes the object of his idolatry.

All told, the atmosphere of the insulin-ward was one in which, to the sick, miracles appeared to be occurring constantly. And, most traumatic of all, they were concrete miracles. For example, I am reminded of the day I went into a coma free of crab-lice and emerged thoroughly infested (the sheets are sterilized daily). I had caught the lice in somebody else's coma, since these states of unconsciousness are concrete and are left lying about the universe even after they have been vacated by the original occupant. And this was so credited by one of my fellow patients that he refused to submit to the needle the next day out of fear of venturing into one of my old comas and infesting himself. He believed that I had lied and that I'd had crabs for some time, having caught them in some previous coma.

Meanwhile, on that following day, I was revived from my coma intravenously by an Egyptian resident psychiatrist, who then, very brusquely, ordered the nurses to wrap the sheets around me a bit tighter lest I should free myself prematurely; I shrieked, "Amenhotep!"

And there was the day a young patient who had given the impression of being virtually illiterate, received his intravenous glucose (one is revived from a deep coma in this manner), and then gave ample evidence that he had become thoroughly acquainted with the works of Jacob Boehme in the course of his coma. Simone de Beauvoir, in her book on her travels in America, expresses her consternation upon finding that a member of the editorial board of *Partisan Review* once openly admitted to being ignorant of the writings of Boehme.

Shortly after my mummification and defiance of Amenhotep, I encountered what appeared to be a new patient, to whom I mumbled amicably, "I'm Kirilov." He mumbled, in reply, "I'm Myshkin." The cadence of the superreal was never challenged; not one of us would dare assume responsibility for a breach of the unity which each hallucination required.

These collective phantasies in which we dreamed each others dreams contributed to the terror created by contact with the flat, unpredictable insulin void, which had not yet been rendered entirely felicitous (as it was to be later) by the persistent benevolence of man and glucose, and from which all sorts of incredible horrors might yet spring.

The concomitants of therapeutic purgation were, for me, a rather thoroughly atomized amnesia (produced by an insulin convulsion of a rare type and occurring in not more than 2% of cases) and a burgeoning obesity caused by the heavy consumption of glucose. Much later in my treatment, when intensive psychotherapy had replaced insulin, both of these phenomena came to assume places of great importance in the pattern of my reorientation. As my illness had often been verbalized, the first effect of the amnesia was to create a verbal and ideational aphasia, from which resulted an unspoken panic. I had quite simply forgotten the name of my universe, though it was also true that this name rested on the tip of my tongue throughout the amnesiac period. All ideas and all sense of the object had been lost temporarily, and what remained was a state of conscious ideational absence which can only be defined in clinical terms—as amnesia.[2] I had been handed, by skilled and provident men, the very concrete void I'd sought. During this period, I had gained sixty pounds, and upon consulting a mirror, I was confronted with the dual inability to recognize myself or to remember what I had looked like prior to treatment, prior to reaching my majority.

When I had recovered from my amnesia sufficiently to find my way about, I was permitted to leave the hospital on Sundays, in the company of a relative of whom I would take immediate leave. My relatives on these occasions seemed entirely oblivious to any change in my behavior or physique. Generally, still rather hazy, I would be escorted by an old neurotic friend to a homosexual bar where, I would be informed, I had formerly passed much time. However, the most appalling situations would arise at this point, since, in my corpulent forgetfulness, I no longer remotely resembled a "butch" fairy or "rough trade." I had lost all facility with "gay" argot and was incapable of producing any erotic response to the objects proffered me.

Almost imperceptibly, however, the process of object-selection began once more in all realms of activity, and gained momentum.

I amazed my friends in a restaurant one Sunday afternoon by insisting that the waiter remove an entree with which I had been dissatisfied and that he replace it with another. And even greater was their incredulity when they witnessed my abrupt handling of a beggar, this having been the first time that I had ever rejected a request for alms.

> "The yearning infinite recoils
> For terrible is earth."
> —Melville, "L'Envoi."

At about this time, I wrote a sort of manifesto, called "Manifest," which is a most pertinent artifact:

Corsica is an island situated off the coast of Sardinia. Its capital is Ajaccio and it was here that Napoleon Bonaparte was born. Though it is part of the French Empire, Corsica is not part of the mainland. It is an island. As Capri is an island, and Malta. It is not attached to the European mainland. I am in a position to insist upon this point. There is a body of water separating the two, and it is known as the Mediterranean Sea. This is borne out by the maps now in use. I brook no contradiction. If I am challenged on this point, the world will rush to my assistance in one way

or another. What I have just written is a standing challenge to all the forces of evil, of idiocy, of irrelevance, of death, of silence, of vacancy, of transcendency, etc. And I rest secure in the knowledge that my challenge will never be accepted by the *scum* to whom I've addressed it. I've spent considerable time in the clutches of the LOON and I've waited for this opportunity to avenge myself by humiliating the void. Thank you for your kind attention.

— A VEHEMENT ADULT

As the business of selection became increasingly complex, I appeared to develop an unprecedented (for me) suavity in operating within clearly defined limits. Madness had presented itself as an irrelevancy, and I was now busily engaged in assigning values of comparative relevance to all objects within my reach.

My total rejection of psychiatry, which had, after coma, become a fanatical adulation, now passed into a third phase—one of constructive criticism. I became aware of the peripheral obtuseness and the administrative dogmatism of the hospital bureaucracy. My first impulse was to condemn; later, I perfected means of maneuvering freely within the clumsy structure of ward politics. To illustrate, my reading matter had been kept under surveillance for quite some time, and I had at last perfected a means of keeping *au courant* without unnecessarily alarming the nurses and attendants. I had smuggled several issues of *Hound and Horn* into my ward on the pretext that it was a field-and-stream magazine. I had read Hoch and Kalinowski's *Shock Therapy* (a top secret manual of arms at the hospital) quite openly, after I had put it into the dust-jacket of Anna Balakian's *Literary Origins of Surrealism*. Oddly enough, I hadn't thought it necessary to take such pains with Trotsky's *Permanent Revolution* and had become rudely aware of the entire body politic I had so long neglected, when, one evening, I was sharply attacked by the Head Nurse of the ward for "communism." He had slipped behind me on little cat feet and had been reading the book over my shoulder.

The psychiatric ineptitude of the official lower echelons became incredible when, one week before Halloween, it was announced to the patients that a masquerade ball would be held on the appropriate date, that attendance was to be mandatory, and that a prize would be given to the patient wearing the "best" costume. Whereupon, the patients, among whom there was a high spirit of competition, threw themselves precipitously into the work of creating what, for each, promised to be the most striking disguise. The work of sewing, tearing, dyeing, etc., was done in Occupational Therapy, where, at the disposal of all, were an infinite variety of paints,

---

2. So great was the sense of tangible loss that I later insisted upon an electro-encephalographic examination, to reassure myself that no organic damage had resulted from the convulsion.

gadgets, and fabrics. Supervising all this furious activity was a pedagogic harpy, who had been assigned as Occupational Therapist to see that we didn't destroy any of the implements in the shop (she tried to persuade me to attend the masquerade made up as a dog). Furiously we labored, competing with one another even in regard to speed of accomplishment, fashioning disguised phalluses, swords, spears, scars for our faces, enormous cysts for our heads. When Halloween Night arrived, we were led, dazed and semi-amnesiac, into the small gymnasium that served as a dance floor. Insidious tensions intruded themselves as the time for the awarding of the prize approached. Finally, the Social Therapists seated themselves in the center of the polished floor and ordered us to parade past them in a great circle; one of the nurses sat at the piano and played a march; to the strains of the music, we stepped forward to present our respective embodied idealizations to the judges. There were several Hamlets, a Lear, a grotesque Mr. Hyde, a doctor; there were many cases of transvestism; a young man obsessed with the idea that he was an inanimate object had come as an electric-lamp, brightly-lit, complete with shade; a boy who had filled his head to the point of bursting with baseball lore had come as a "Brooklyn Bum," in derby and tatters. Suddenly, the music stopped; the judges had chosen a winner, rejecting the others; we never learned who the winner had been, so chaotic was the scene that followed. There was a groan of deep torment from the entire group (each feeling that his dream had been condemned). Phantasmal shapes flung themselves about in despair. The nurses and Social Therapists spent the next hour in consoling the losers.

Thus I progressed, after my series of fifty comas had ended, and finally reached my normal weight of 180 pounds and my true sexual orientation: adult heterosexuality (which became my true sexual orientation only after the basic androgynous death-wish had been redirected). It is probably true, however, that my case is atypical and that the great majority of such transformations are not quite as thorough-going, and in some cases, fail to materialize at all. There were those patients who were completely unmoved by the experience of the coma, and who found that it did nothing more than to stimulate their appetites. And there were those Kafkians who remained confirmed paranoiacs to the bitter end.

I should like to quote a passage from an article by the French poet, Antonin Artaud, published posthumously in the February, 1949, issue of *Les Temps Modernes*. Artaud had undergone both electric and insulin shock-therapies during his period of confinement which lasted nine years and terminated with his death in March, 1948.

I died at Rodez under electro-shock. I say dead. Legally and medically dead. The coma of electro-shock lasts a quarter of an hour. Another half-hour and the invalid is breathing. But, one hour after shock I hadn't awakened and had stopped breathing. Surprised by my abnormal rigidity, an attendant went to look for the chief-doctor, who after auscultation found in me no sign of life. I have my own memories of my death at that moment, but it is not upon them that I base my accusation.

I restrict myself to the particulars which were given to me by Dr. Jean Dequeker, young interne of the Rodez asylum, who got them from the mouth of Dr. Ferdiere himself.

And the latter had told him that day he believed me dead, and that he had summoned two asylum guards to instruct them to transport my body to the morgue since I had not returned to myself one hour and a half after shock.

And it appeared that at the very moment the attendants entered to remove my body it quivered slightly, after which I awakened all at once.

I have another recollection of it.

But this memory I had guarded in secret until that day when Dr. Jean Dequeker confirmed it for me from without.

And this recollection is that, confirming all Dr. Jean Dequeker had told me, I had seen not this side of the world but the other. . . .

What he describes above was the experience of us all, but with Artaud and so many others, it stopped short and became the permanent level of existence: the absence of myth represented by the brief "death" was accepted as the culminating, all-embracing myth. Artaud went on to write, in his essay on Van Gogh, that a lunatic "is a man who has preferred to become what is socially understood as mad rather than forfeit a certain superior idea of human honor"; and to write further that "a vicious society has invented psychiatry to defend itself from the investigations of certain superior lucid minds whose intuitive powers were disturbing to it"; and that "every psychiatrist is a low-down son-of-a-bitch." In Paris, quite outrageously, this heart-rendingly skewed essay written by a grievously ill man was honored with a Prix Sainte-Beuve and was underwritten by several of the most distinguished French critics.

I have a small mind and I mean to use it.

The sentence above epitomizes the real lesson of insulin, that of tragedy, and it was neither written nor would it have been understood by Artaud, who remains (he wrote that "the dead continue to revolve around their corpses") a sublime comic figure, one who averted his eyes from the spectre of reality, one who never admitted to having dimensions or sex, and who was incapable of recognizing his own mortality. (In the list of comic figures of our time we can include the homosexual.)

My release from the hospital was followed by a period of headlong and vindictive commitment to substance, a period which continues, which is full of tactical and syntactical retreats and rapid reversals of opinion. It is obvious by this time, though, that the changes of opinion are becoming less frequent, that the truculent drive toward compulsive readjustment, toward the "acting out" of one's adjustment, has been dissipated. My attitude toward the magic I've witnessed is similar to that of the African student I met a month ago, who told me that his uncle had been a witch-doctor. He had seen his uncle turn to a cat before his eyes. He had simply thrown the uncle-cat a scrap of meat, hadn't been particularly impressed by the magic (though conceding its validity), and had come to America to acquire the political and technological skills with which to modernize his country upon his return.

For the ailing intellect, there can be great danger in the poetizing of the coma-void. Only when it is hopelessly distorted and its concrete nature disguised can it serve as material for myth-making. To confront the coma full-face, one must adhere to factual detail and this procedure need not prove deadening. On the contrary, the real coma administers a fillip to one's debilitated thinking processes. Jarry's debraining-machine was not the surgeon's scalpel but was contained within his own cranium. It was to place the coma thus in context that I undertook this examination of its architectonics.

Artaud
by Carl Solomon

I witnessed an Artaud reading in 1947, the year before Artaud's death in Rodez* in 1948. Artaud was being described by a small circle of Paris admirers, some in very high places in the arts, as being a genius who had extended Rimbaud's vision of the poet seer. His name was even described by one admirer, known as "The Alchemist," as Arthur Rimbaud without the *hur* in Arthur and without the *Rimb* in Rimbaud. And this man later made a case for Artaud as being, literally, the reincarnation of Rimbaud and spiritually his descendant. Other admirers were André Gide and Jean Louis Barrault. Gide made a case for Artaud as an existentialist man of despair, and Barrault had been influenced by Artaud on the theater. Artaud's is a tenuous case, an ambiguous one in that he has been highly esteemed by almost everyone of note in the arts and yet widely banned and condemned by legal authorities. To me his case, his destiny has been the cause of considerable confusion since one knows that by accepting his theories one puts one's body in the social frying pan and by rejecting him you are going through life with blinders on. He is certainly the leading critic I have ever read of social hypocrisy and for this became known as a "Damned" poet. He was a junkie, a lunatic and had pursued his peculiar turn of thought so far that he had even rebelled against surrealism which itself is supposed to be rebellion against society deriving from a rebellion against the "rebel," Anatole France, who had been considered too lucid, too rational, by the early dadaists. And where does all this rebellion against rebellion lead but surely into one of many large nuthouses which are continually being constructed all over this country and others in the name of that mystical cause "Mental Health."

From *Mishaps, Perhaps*, pp. 13–15.

* "Je suis mort à Rodez sous l'électrochoc."

The book by Artaud which impressed me most was his *Van Gogh* written in 1948 in which he condemns all forms of psychiatry, and thereby all organized authority, since all countries practise psychiatry including the socialist wonderland. In it, he claims that every lunatic, everyone marked and branded, and believe me all lunatics are really marked and branded, is a person of superior lucidity whose insights society thinks disturbing to it. This book impressed me when I read it in 1948, the year of Truman's upset victory over Dewey. I was still in the school system at that time and the intellectual students, by these I mean the ones who weren't in favor of basketball and who read a book now and then which wasn't on the compulsory reading list, were mostly interested in either Marxism and folksongs or, in the advanced echelons, in Freud or Wilhelm Reich. Now I was interested in Artaud, who to me was a symbol of real rebellion truly meriting the name.

To illustrate the mood of the student body in college at that time, I should state that I walked into a classroom carrying a copy of Baudelaire and was immediately latched upon by a girl English major who seemed to think I was actually Baudelaire in person. Shortly after this I was deposited in a nut factory where I was shocked into a renunciation of all my reading, etc., etc. What books remained to me after I had been shocked then, were later stolen from me by various local hoodlums and I was soon thrown into another more savage nuthouse.

The case of the so-called lunatic opened up by Artaud and no other writer is really the case of Socrates, who was condemned to death for being what, in his day, was considered "bright," that is to say not stupid. I say that we live in a generation of charlatanry, propaganda and corruption, and that there is no room for an honest man on either side of the Iron Curtain.

"O Carl!" A Dream: 1963
By Allen Ginsberg

I go up to room in a big apartment. Mental hospital—family quarters—I have changed— How is Carl Solomon?— He comes in from Elevator, in a blue business suit and tie his face at first looks the same but, as he sits down in Easychair I see he has great swollen spongy belly and huge lumps of football size fat on his arms and white basketball ass—I drift—must be from metrosol, what the doctors did to him with shock, deformed and added to his flesh, however— I explain, walking up and down—"Carl I did do wrong to you, I made you an object, a thing, an image—I didn't mean that, I loved you— I did discover finally what it is I—we—were seeking then in Psychiatric Institute, what it is we felt we thought we wanted all along— I made a mistake Carl. Forgive me, I have the answer now—"

"What is it? What is it?" he cries in his chair, his head is big and his face is red.

While talking I'd said "felt" we were seeking and I thought maybe I'd tipped it off too early without building it up right, formulating it so he'd feel what it was I was screaming about— He cried "What is it?"—

I say, "It's this image, the Mind, the reporters, the interviews, the fame, the image—it was our identity we were seeking wasn't it, our own identity?"

"Yes, yes," he says, but I see the anguish in his eyes—the reporters are waiting downstairs for me, to interview me again, now I see our chance to break thru our Names and Forms in public— I was all wrong to conspire with *Time* to create this Beatnik myself and to throw out into world a howl of Carl Solomon which fixed him in my idea of him a name

a madness a hospital a mass public image surrounding him confusing him furthermore—

I am striding up and down in front of him taking control of the situation, "Look, there are reporters outside waiting to come up and cast the image again, let's do it *now*, let's together make a break, escape the Names, escape our minds, escape their minds, escape the words, break through ourselves, Cut *out*! Cut out!"

"But how?" he says looking at me unhappily from couch—

"Don't you see?" I said—"it's our feelings, our feelings who we are—that's our identity not all these thoughts and ideas and angrys"—

He falls back in chair, his face turns even redder —I am afraid he'll strike me, "But I was depending on you, you let me down, you still don't realize my—"

He begins slapping his palm to his red square Frankenstein forehead—hard, hard slaps—as if hitting a solid bone red object— I get frightened—have I misunderstood?—have all things been mixed so now I am lost and he's damaged:

He: "My feelings always been the trouble, I am split in that organically by the shock"—he points to his freak grotesque sponge swollen doctored body— "How can this . . . ?"

I am desperate, I break down, I think how can I now love this body with my body, how can I touch him and isn't that what he wants and I wanted that we touch with love at last in the end and I cry.

"O Carl!" weeping to him not to desert me, "O Carl! I need you! O Carl! O Carl! O Carl!" broken down as he gazes at me at last, but I am hopeless like a baby with him wanting him to hold me, "O Carl! O Carl! O Carl!" and wake.

Allen Ginsberg, *Journals* (Vancouver), August 10, 1963.

Carl Solomon Bibliography

Mishaps, Perhaps. San Francisco: Beach Books, Texts and Documents/City Lights Books, 1966.

More Mishaps. San Francisco: Beach Books, Texts and Documents/City Lights Books, 1968.

AUTHOR'S ANNOTATIONS

Correspondence Chart: Final and First Drafts, HOWL, *Part 1*

Only objectified emotion endures.   —*Louis Zukofsky*

Author, Berkeley hills in background, U.C. graduate student, engaged with *Howl* Part II late drafts, 1956. *Photo by Peter Orlovsky?*

Correspondence Chart: Final and First Drafts, HOWL, Part I*

Verse-by-verse annotation following original draft of "Howl," Part I (and final drafts, Parts II, III and IV) includes analysis of revisions, root reference of vivid phrases, & images traced to personal anecdote; letters, commentary, testimony & clarifications by persons obliquely modeled in the poem, including Philip Lamantia, Carl Solomon, Louis Simpson & Tuli Kupferberg; with currency of author's private image bank declared and deconstruction of his projections; minute particulars and supplementary details background to starry dynamos & hydrogen jukeboxes displayed; rhythmic measures & verse tactics noted, mini-histories behind metaphors unburdened, bibliographic hints for inquisitive readers, and relevant journal jottings emplaced, with literary origins quoted, & visible referents reproduced.

Final Draft	First Draft	Final Draft	First Draft	Final Draft	First Draft	Final Draft	First Draft
1	1	21	18	41	22	61	36
2	2	22	69	42	76	62	23
3	(2)	23	66–67	43	(22)	63	78
4	3	24	19	44	27	64	61
5	4	25	(25)	45	56	65	43
6	9	26	26	46	52	66	46
7	50	27	66–67	47	65	67	46
8	5–6	28	51	48	54	68	46
9	7	29	41	49	63	69	47
10	11	30	73	50	55	70	42
11	11	31	34	51	(55)	71	48
12	12	32	31	52	53	72	49
13	12	33	40	53	52	73	44
14	13	34	28–30, 37	54	60	74	81
15	14	35	28–30, 37	55	59	75	80, 82, 84
16	15–16	36	20	56	50	76	79, 84
17	15–16	37	21	57	32	77	64
18	15–16	38	—	58	23–24	78	83
19	15–16	39	62	60	35		
20	17	40	45				

* Final-draft verses not derived from original draft are annotated in context of original verses, which are enclosed in parentheses.

First and Final Drafts, HOWL, Part I

1 [1]*

Crucial revision: "Mystical" is replaced by "hysterical," a key to the tone of the poem. Tho the initial idealistic impulse of the line went one way, afterthought noticed bathos, and common sense dictated "hysteria." One mind can entertain both notions without "any irritable reaching after fact and reason," as Keats proposed with his definition of "Negative Capability." The word "hysterical" is judicious, but the verse is overtly sympathetic. "Do I contradict myself?/Very well then I contradict myself,/(I am large, I contain multitudes.)" (Whitman, "Song of Myself," 51.) The poem's tone is in this mixture of empathy and shrewdness, the comic realism of Chaplin's *City Lights*, a humorous hyperbole derived in part from Blake's style in *The French Revolution*. "If you have a choice of two things and can't decide, take both," says Gregory Corso. Negative Capability = One Taste.

2 [2]

Herbert Huncke cruised Harlem and Times Square areas at irregular hours, late forties, scoring junk. See Herbert Huncke, *The Evening Sun Turned Crimson* (Cherry Valley, N.Y.: Cherry Valley Editions, 1980).

— [3]

"Starry dynamo" and "machinery of night" are derived from Dylan Thomas's mixture of Nature and Machinery in "The force that through the green fuse drives the flower / Drives my green age . . ."

3 [4]

Ref.: Bill Keck, Anton Rosenberg and other contemporaries who gathered often at the San Remo bar, living in Lower East Side, N.Y., early 1950s—their circle was prototype for Kerouac's fictional description in *The Subterraneans*, written 1953. The jazz was late bop Charlie Parker played in Bowery loft jam sessions in those few years.

4 [5]

Jack Kerouac had given anecdote of Philip Lamantia's celestial adventure to author in early

* Annotations of Part I are set in order according to verses of first draft (pp. 13–25) to provide background and references for final draft (pp. 3–8). Verse numbers at left refer to first draft. Bracketed numbers refer to corresponding verses of final draft. Final-draft verses not derived from the first draft (indicated by a dash) are annotated in context of first draft. To trace annotations directly from final back to first draft, see Correspondence Chart, on preceding page.

1950s. Poet Lamantia in note written for author May 25, 1986, New Orleans, provides this accurate account:

> 1953, Spring, aged 25, reading the Koran on a couch, one night, I was suddenly physically laid out by a powerful force beyond my volition, which rendered me almost comatose: suddenly, consciousness was contracted to a single point at the top of my head through which I was "siphoned" beyond the room, space and time into *another* state of awareness that seemed utterly beyond any other state before or since experienced. I floated toward an endless-looking universe of misty, lighted color forms: green, red, blue and silver, which circulated before me accompanied by such bliss that the one dominant thought was: This is it; I never want to return to anywhere but this *place*—i.e., I wanted to remain in this Ineffable Blissful Realm and explore it forever—since I felt a radiance beyond even further within it and so, suddenly the outline of a benign bearded Face appeared to whom I addressed my desire to remain in this marvel—and who calmly replied: "You can return, after you complete your work."

Part of Manhattan's subway system, the Third Avenue elevated railway, one of those familiarly called the "El," was demolished in the mid-'50s. See Kerouac's "sketches" in *Visions of Cody* (New York: McGraw-Hill, 1972), p. 6; as well as pictures in *Berenice Abbott: American Photographer*, ed. Hank O'Neal (New York: McGraw-Hill, 1982), pp. 90, 97, 119, 123, 140.

5 [8]

Ref. Carl Solomon, an anecdote.

6 [8]

Carl Solomon writes: "I burned money while upset about the evils of materialism in 1956, prior to commitment to Pilgrim." Date may have been earlier; "Howl" written in 1955.

7 [9]

Anonymous anecdote, possibly re John Hoffman (see note 41 [29]). Final draft of the poem reads: "Who got busted in their pubic beards . . ." The phrase comes by a simple mechanical method of intensifying a line by unusual juxtaposition of things or concepts, "doctoring" the verse.

9 [6]

Refers to author's adventures at Columbia College.

"Anarchy" changes to "Arkansas," in order to substitute a more concrete thing-name for an abstract word.

"Post-war cynical scholars" refers to some of Lionel Trilling's students, perhaps an inkling of literary "cold-warrior" Norman Podhoretz—see *Making It* (New York: Random House, 1967), pp. 39–40, 215–16. *Time* magazine in the fifties portrayed American intellectuals as comfortable, complacent. *Time*'s negative review of Rachel Carson's *Silent Spring* showed early (& anti-feminist) antagonism toward the inchoate ecology movement.

In final text, "scholars of war": During author's residence, 1944–48, Columbia scientists helped split atoms for military power in secrecy. Subsequent military-industrial funding increasingly dominated university research, thus two decades later rebellious student strikes had as primary grievance that the trusteeships of the university interlocked with Vietnam War–related corporations. That cold war influence darkened the complexion of scientific studies and humanistic attitudes. Columbia President D. D. Eisenhower himself had warned against such military-industrial complexity in his farewell address as U.S. Chief Executive. However, two decades after 1968 student activism, secret military-industrial research reached cosmic proportions, and "Star Wars" era university contracts swelled academic coffers with little hint of an historical scandal. Common private complaint against this "monstrous exotic" rarely flashed on TV.

10–11 [10]

This verse evolves into "Paradise Alley," a cold-water-flat courtyard at 501 East 11th Street, NE corner of Avenue A, Lower East Side New York, bricked up in the '70s and demolished after fire in 1985. As sketched by Kerouac in *The Subterraneans*, the prototype of his heroine Mardou Fox lived there in 1953 in friendly contact with the author, Corso and Kerouac, and typed the original ms. of Burroughs' *Yage Letters* and *Queer*.

Various artists lived in cheap hotels in the area, St. Mark's Place, their small rooms suffused with the smell of turpentine.

Supplemental ref. "apartments": 419 West 115th Street, #51, frequented 1945–46 by the author, William Burroughs, Joan Vollmer (later Joan Burroughs) and Jack Kerouac, among others. Use of Benzedrine inhalers was common, introduced by friends of Herbert Huncke visiting regularly.

"Bodies" changes to "torsos," final draft, for sound and sex.

"Cock & endless balls" ref. vernacular "have a ball."

12 [13]

The "backyard green tree cemetery dawns," ref. Bill Keck's apartment on East 2nd Street off Second Avenue, in New York City, overlooking cemetery; see author's April 17, 1952, entry, *Journals Early Fifties, Early Sixties*, ed. Gordon Ball (New York: Grove Press, 1977). Keck's early poem ended: "Life is the green lime tree." The author tried peyote (sold from East 10th Street storefront) two days later.

The "teahead joyride" likely refers to drive Neal Cassady and Jack Kerouac took thru Brooklyn to hear some early-morning jazz late 1940s. Final draft "kind king light of mind" paraphrases Kerouac's epithet "Kind King Mind" in *Mexico City Blues* and his last phrase in *Visions of Cody*, "Adios, King."

"Tree vibrations" ref. author's first peyote experience—see *Journals*, pp. 7–13.

13 [14]

From an anecdote, trying to score for morphine from an old doctor in the Bronx, 1945, told by Herbert Huncke in the 115th Street apartment.

This verse, the longest so far in its original composition, was a conscious attempt to go all the way from A to Z (Zoo) in associative flash and extension of breath.

14 [15]

Author's casual college job was mopping floors at various Manhattan cafeterias including Bickford's 42nd Street.

Fugazzi's Sixth Avenue Greenwich Village bar was early 1950s alternative to the noisier San Remo nearby. "Fugazzi" phrasing was added to accommodate "jukebox"; cafeterias had no jukeboxes.

Some end-of-the-world or apocalyptic vibration was noticed by the "subterraneans" in the roaring of the jukebox, thus "hydrogen [bomb] jukebox."

15–16 [16]

Ruth G——, an intelligent dreamy young Jewish woman ("meat for the synagogue" [19]), who wore Salvation Army granny dresses in times of Eisenhower prosperity, and associated with author, Carl Solomon and others in early 1950s Greenwich Village, one day began a flight of talk in Washington Square that continued through the day and night for 72 hours until she was finally committed to Bellevue.

Ref. also Neal Cassady's nonstop monologues; see Kerouac's *Visions of Cody*, pp. 268–74, for comic paraphrase of same.

"Eyeball kicks": See note re Cézanne, 44 [73] below.

17 [20]

"Nowhere Zen New Jersies of amnesia": Composite image of a few post-college "career failures" characteristic of 1950s, including author's own two-year sojourn in Paterson 1950–51 on leaving Columbia Psychiatric Institute. Author's family spent many 1930s summers at the shore in Belmar—"Atlantic City," final draft. "Sharks" ref. recurrent seaside newspaper reports and souvenir postcards.

18 [21]

"Tangerian bone-grindings": Details of W. S. Burroughs' withdrawals from heroin are found in his letters to the author, *Letters to Allen Ginsberg 1953–1957* (Geneva: Editions Claude Givaudin/Am Here Books, 1978; New York: Full Court Press, 1982).

Author saw "Newark's bleak furnished room" with Eugene Brooks, his brother, who lived in one such studying law, late forties.

19 [24]

Author had read in Wilhelm Reich's *Function of the Orgasm* and *Mass Psychology of Fascism*, Vico's *Scienza Nuova*, a smattering of Gurdjieff (at Burroughs' suggestion, 1945), little on kabbalah, and knew Robert Fludd's name only thru reference in W. B. Yeats and random illustrations of cosmographic human form. Change to final draft "Plotinus Poe St. John of the Cross telepathy and bop kabbalah" focused on matter closer to author's reading, juxtaposing hermetic sublime with Americanist esoterica for sake of sound and provincial sense. Plotinus and St. John of the Cross (and Plato's *Phaedrus*) were arranged in bookcase "orange crates of theology" in Russell Durgin's 121st Street Spanish Harlem 6th-floor apartment, where author experienced Wm. Blake illumination described otherwise. Journal entry April 1953: "to read recommended by [Meyer] Schapiro. Robt. Fludd—Cosmographia . . ." A brief paper on Vico was written as special study of cyclical history for Prof. Jacques Barzun's Columbia College class 1946.

Overt intention of this mystical name-dropping was to connect younger readers, Whitman's children already familiar with Poe and Bop, to older Gnostic tradition. Whitman dropped such hints to his fancied readers.

20 [36]

"Saintly motorcyclists" ref. Marlon Brando's film *The Wild One*, 1954.

"And screamed with joy": Popular superstition had it that one screamed with pain in such a circumstance. "Howl" 's enthusiastic version is more realistic. For its time the iconoclastic "shocker" of the poem, this verse reversed vulgar stereotype with a statement of fact. Tho "screamed" is hyperbole—"moaned" more common.

This crucial verse militated against author's thinking of the writing draft as "poetry" or "publishable" in any way that would reach the eyes of his family, thus author was left free to write thenceforth what he actually thought, from his own experience.

21 [37]

The poet Hart Crane picked up sailors to love on Sand Street, Brooklyn, etc. Suffering alcoholic exhaustion and rejected by the crew on his last voyage, from Veracruz, Crane disappeared off the fantail of the Caribbean ship *Orizaba*.

22 [41]

Hyperbolic ref. to one of Neal Cassady's accounts of sexual enthusiasm (see next entry). "Gyzym" ref. author's recollections of learned New Critical article *Hudson Review* late 1940s perhaps entitled "W. B. Yeats and the Gyzym of Eternity."

— [43]

Ref. Neal Cassady, 1926–1968, author *The First Third & Other Writings* (San Francisco: City Lights Books, 1971). His account of adolescent adventures stealing cars, seducing waitresses and haunting Denver alleyways written in long "Joan Anderson Letter" inspired Kerouac to forms of spontaneous personal narrative that involved continuous scanning of writer's consciousness during time of original composition for simultaneous multilevel references sufficiently swiftly to include them in extended prose sentences.

It was Cassady's profusion of physical energy and abundance of self-recollection that brought him to Kerouac's attention as prototype of Dean Moriarty in *On the Road* (1950) and Cody Pomeroy in its grander sequel, *Visions of Cody* (1952), among other books.

For twelve years with wife, house and children an exemplary senior brakeman on S. P. Railroad till entrapment by marijuana tax agents, Cassady served thereafter as central figure and model driver of Ken Kesey's "Merry Prankster" psychedelic Trips Festival crosscountry and Bay Area celebrations, inspiring songs and attitudes of The Grateful Dead.

Solitary during withdrawal from the exhaustions of amphetamine in San Miguel Allende, Mexico, Feb. 3, 1968, he passed by the door of a wedding party, was invited in, drank alcoholic pulque, later was found collapsed and suffocating on railroad tracks outside town and died in hospital. His ashes reside with his widow, Carolyn.

"Secret hero of these poems": The plural ref.

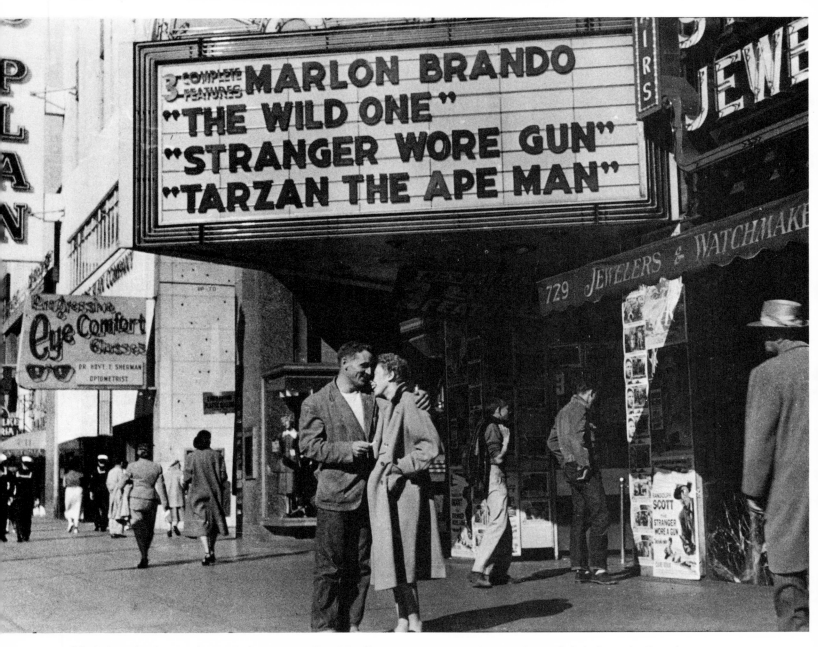

Neal Cassady, "secret hero of these poems," & Natalie Jackson (d. 1955) Conscious of their loves in Eternity on Market Street, San Francisco, Spring 1955.   *Photo by A.G.*

various other works by author, Kerouac and others (later Ken Kesey) accounting his heroic energy. For contemporary chronicle of author's early intense erotic liaison and extended friendship with this figure, see *As Ever: The Collected Correspondence of Allen Ginsberg and Neal Cassady*, ed. Barry Gifford (Berkeley, Cal.: Creative Arts, 1977).

23–24 [62, 59]
Author worked as night copyboy Associated Press office, Rockefeller Center, 1948–49, and stopped in across Fifth Avenue at St. Patrick's Cathedral on his way home, praying for Neal Cassady and friends returning to West Coast after visiting him in an apartment on York Avenue. The season is described in N.Y. chapters of *On the Road*.

"Send me a letter, send it by mail / Send it in care of the Birmingham Jail."—Huddie (Leadbelly) Ledbetter

25 [—]
See "The Trembling of the Veil," in Allen Ginsberg, *Collected Poems 1947–1980* (New York: Harper & Row, 1984), p. 14: "Today out of the window / the trees seemed like live / organisms on the moon."

— [25]

American Indian old ways included "vision quest" as mark of maturation, or resolution of life crisis. Some among the postwar generation of white Americans initiated themselves into this tradition. See Gary Snyder, *The Old Ways* (San Francisco: City Lights Books, 1977).

26 [26]

First and final versions ref. author's Blake illumination E. Harlem 1948. See *Paris Review* interview collected in *Writers at Work, Series 3* (New York: Viking Press, 1967), pp. 301–11. Author also dimly remembered an anecdote from conversation about surrealist poet Philip Lamantia, mostly apocryphal. For "Baltimore," Poe association, his brick house and grave are there.

27 [44]

"Heartless Tokay" ref. Kerouac's letters, an account of occasional drinking on weekends in New York.

28 [58]

"Fell out of windows . . . vomit in the toilet" ref. William Cannastra, legendary late 1940s New York bohemian figure, life cut short by alcoholic accident, body balanced out of subway window, knocked against a pillar, fell at Astor Place, Manhattan. Final draft: "Leaped . . . cried . . . danced . . . smashed . . . records" ref. same saga.

"Nostalgic . . . German jazz": *Rise and Fall of the City of Mahagonny* Brecht-Weill opera arias "O Show Me the Way to the Next Whiskey Bar" and "Benares Song," which echoed loud late nights repeatedly in Cannastra's West 21st Street Manhattan loft 1949.

"The filthy Passaic": In W. C. Williams "The Wanderer: A Baroque Fantasy," 1915, the youthful poet plunges his hands in her waters requesting sacrament of Goddess of Passaic River for his Muse: "and the filthy Passaic consented."

29 [35]

"on all fours": see 28 [58] above re Cannastra.

30 [34]

See 28 [58] re Cannastra.

See oblique references to Cannastra as prototype of Alan Harrington's novel figure Genovese in *The Secret Swinger* (New York: Knopf, 1966). Kerouac's portrait of "Finistra" is found in *Visions of Cody*. "Howl" text's brief summons of this shade is fleshed out two years later as Bill King in "The Names," *Collected Poems*, p. 178.

31 [32]

Living Theater director Judith Malina writes:

June 15, 1955, Julian [Beck] and I and about 27 others refused to take shelter when "the sirens . . . wailed." It was City Hall Park and not in Union Square, and I was sent to Bellevue for sassing the judge. The trial (with lawyers from the Ford Foundation's 20th Century Fund) was prolonged.

"We were an *all star* set of *defendants*; [including] Hugh Corbin, Dorothy Day, Ralph diGia, Ammon Hennacy, Richard Kern, Jackson MacLow, A. J. Muste, James Peck and Bayard Rustin. . . . I tell the story in my Grove Press diary [*The Diaries of Judith Malina 1947–1957* (New York, 1984)] on pps. 367–374.

"There's another telling of the story of the trial, etc. in a booklet called *What Happened On June 15th?* put out by the War Resisters' League. I don't think that anyone took their clothes off for that demo (with Day and Muste!), though surely at many others."

Account in Malina's *Diaries* is invaluable for those who wish to be acquainted with the genesis of postwar peace protest movement, for its humor and simplicity.

32 [57]

"Meat trucks": This apocryphal burlesque conforms with Chaplinesque tone of "hysterical" verse 1. Tuli Kupferberg writes:

In the Spring of 1945 at the age of 21, full of youthful angst, depression over the war and other insanities and at the end of a disastrous love affair, I went over the side of the Manhattan Bridge.

I was picked up tenderly by the crew of a passing tug and taken to Gouveneur Hospital.

My injuries were relatively slight (fracture of a transverse spinal process) but enuf to put me in a body cast.

In the hospital wards I met other suicide attempters less fortunate than me: one who wd walk on crutches and one who wd never walk again.

Thruout the years I have been annoyed many times by "O did you really jump off the Brooklyn Bridge?" as if that was a great accomplishment.

Remember I was a *failure* at the attempt.

Had I succeeded there wd have been 3 less wonderful beings (my children) in the world, no Fugs, and a few missing good poems & songs, & some people (including some lovely women, *hey!*) who might have missed my company.

In the US today, over 5000 young people between the ages of 15 & 24 do succeed *every year* in destroying themselves.

Fools!

There's nothing glamorous about it. (I know first hand of someone who regretted the act the day after & died a lingering death of throat burns 2 weeks later.)

There's time, there's time.

You'll be dead a long long while, & sooner than you imagine.

Patience patience, my young, wild, beautiful, damned friends!

See Tuli Kupferberg's *1001 Ways to Live Without Working* (New York: Birth Press, 1961), illustrated edition (New York: Grove Press, 1967); *Kill for Peace* (being *Yeah* 10), (New York: Birth Press, 1965); *1001 Ways to Beat the Draft* (with Robert Bashlow), (New York: Layton, 1966), illustrated edition (New York: Grove Press, 1967); *1001 Ways to Make Love* (New York: Grove Press, 1969). Also *Birth* magazine and all the recordings of The Fugs, significant intellectual breakthrough rock band of the 1960s returned to play their old and new lyric satires even more brilliantly in the mid 1980s.

33 [—]

Ref. Iris Brody, Lower East Side artist, whose work author collected. Unstable materials used to compose her pictures deteriorated within two decades. Her painting of poet-musician Jackson Mac Low with recorder can be seen in background of author's photographs of William Burroughs 1953.

34 [31]

A specialized Columbia College jape or fad.

"Narcotic . . . haze of capitalism": "WASHINGTON—The tobacco industry spent $1.24 billion advertising cigarettes in 1980 and got the average American smoker to buy 11,633 cigarettes that year, the Federal Trade Commission said. . . ."—*Washington Post*, November 22, 1982

35 [60]

"Crosscountry in 72 hours": To author's recollection, Neal Cassady literally did so in one late-'40s coast-to-coast auto trip on the road to see Kerouac and compare recent illuminations and despairs.

36 [61]

Lyric lines by Kerouac: "Down in Denver,/ Down in Denver,/ All I did was die."

Final-text verse ends "& now Denver is lonesome for her heroes," a line taken intact from December 1951 journal entry, drafts for the poem "Shroudy Stranger of the Night." See also note, verse 66 [23].

37 [34]

"Bit detectives" ref. William Cannastra, not literal.

38–39 [—]

Description of an unfortunate car crash 1948 on Utopia Blvd, Queens, New York, which resulted in

Neal Cassady with dealer looking over used cars, S.F., 1955.   *Photo by A.G.*

arrest of author, Herbert Huncke and friends. Stolen car was filled with stolen loot from second-story jobs, as well as several years' journals, address books, letters from William Burroughs, etc., being transported for safekeeping with author's brother prior departure from N.Y.C. See Jane Kramer, *Allen Ginsberg in America* (New York: Random House, 1969), pp. 123–30.

41 [29]

Ref. Malcolm Lowry, *Under the Volcano*. More specifically the myth of John Hoffman, N.Y. acquaintance of author and Carl Solomon. Solomon writes: "John Hoffman, 1930?–1950 or 1951. Hometown: Menlo Park, California. Friend of Gerd Stern, poet, born circa 1930. Also friend of Philip Lamantia, Chris Maclaine, both California poets. Blond, handsome, bespectacled, long hair. Spaced out quality that amused many people. Girl friend blonde girl named

Karen. Went to Mexico in 1950. Experimented with peyote. Died of mononucleosis while in Mexico. Poems highly regarded by avant-garde connoisseurs." Philip Lamantia read Hoffman's work at the seminal Six Gallery poetry reading where author first read Part I of "Howl."

Chicago as fireplace ref. Mrs. O'Leary's cow, which kicked over kerosene lantern, starting the celebrated fire of 1871 which consumed that city.

42 [69–70]

Ref. somewhat to Carl Solomon & those we left behind at Psychiatric Institute, 1949. Dolmens mark a vanished civilization, as Stonehenge or Greystone and Rockland monoliths. At time of writing, author's mother dwelled in her last months at Pilgrim State Hospital, Brentwood, N.Y., housing over 25,000, the largest such mental hospital in the world. Description of the wards and halls is drawn from Greystone State Hospital, near Morristown, N.J., which author frequented in adolescence to visit Naomi Ginsberg. New York's Rockland State Hospital's name was substituted for rhythmic euphony. Poem was occasioned by unexpected news of Carl Solomon's recent removal to Pilgrim State.

At this point, with an unusually extended line, the triadic form of William Carlos Williams definitely broke down and author realized it couldn't be restored as measure for the verse. The only option was to expand the verse line beyond that of Christopher Smart, as on occasion Whitman did, and the modernist Kenneth Fearing, more loosely. Paragraphic prose poetry by Rimbaud and St.-John Perse provided more electric model.

43 [65]

"Accusing the radio of hypnotism": Naomi Ginsberg was convinced circa 1943 that doctors had planted "three big sticks" down her back during insulin and electric shock treatments as antennae to receive radio broadcasts from the ceiling—voices sent by President Roosevelt that alternately praised her as a "great woman" or mocked her as a "radical" and "bad girl."

After shock treatments at Rodez asylum, circa 1943, Artaud, in his "Van Gogh" text, accused his doctors (and modern society itself) of materialist hypnotism. His idea was that electroshock drives the spirit down, from its flight to liberty from God, back into the mortal body, which he calls a pile of shit. See also the brilliant vehemence of accusation in his text "To Be Done with the Judgement of God," and Carl Solomon's mordant refutation of this concept, derived from greater experience with the issue: "Afterthoughts of a Shock Patient," p. 113 above.

Idiomatic metaphor "insanity on their hands" is the subvocal "phrasing." Variant options would have been: "left with *their* insanity on *their* hands & a hung jury" or "left *with* insanity on their hands *with* a hung jury." Neither option was graceful, so the idiomatic phrase was x-ed out on the spot. "And" sounded better, repeated.

44 [73]

This stanza concerns itself with aesthetic technique: the mechanisms of surrealist or ideogrammatic method, the juxtaposition of disparate images to create a gap of understanding which the mind fills in with a flash of recognition of the unstated relationship (as "hydrogen jukebox"); viz. Aristotle's "apt relation of dissimilars," his analysis of traditional metaphor.

L.-F. Céline punctuates the jump cuts in his prose with three dots of *ellipsis*. ("Ellipse" is a solecism in original mss. and printings; "ellipsis" is correct.) One theory of haiku is that it presents two opposite images that connect only in mind of reader. In Buddhist psychology, ordinary mind includes the space between thoughts, awareness of *sunyata*. Or, as in Cézanne: the space gap between hot and cold colors. According to George Wald's Nobel Prize theory of optics, the muscles of the retina can focus on only one plane of color at a time, narrowing or widening the lens in relation to varying intensities of light presented by "hot" and "cold" colors.

Whitman's *catalogues* present such grand spaciousness in "list poems" moving thru varying geographies, trades, sounds, stages, multiple precise but discrete observations. Cézanne re-composed his *"petite sensation"* of space on the flat canvas by interlocking squares, cubes and triangles of "hot" colors advancing and "cold" colors retreating in the optical field. His innovative paintings create the appearance of gaps in space without recourse to conventional perspective lines. Early cubist praxis entered this new space after his breakthrough. Paul Klee's "magic squares" may be viewed in this light. Apollinaire appreciated this mode in poetics, thus his pre-surrealist image montage. Eisenstein applied this insight to film, thus the terms "montage" and "jump cut."

Ezra Pound constructed an epic out of vivid ideograms, and extended the *meters* of English-language poetry to include classic quantity among other neglected measures of verse length. W. C. Williams moved forward into the "variable foot" or "relative measure" to include his own breath's spoken cadences.

A further extension of this model of sense consciousness into open space may be seen in "nonlinear" or "aleatoric" art: work by Gertrude Stein, Jackson Mac Low, John Cage and William S. Burroughs.

Contemporary mass swift-shifting-image music television (MTV) falls into place with the same mind. "Spontaneous prosody" in Kerouac's novels and poetry and in "Howl" text composition rely on the same notion of sense consciousness.

N.B. Phrasing in this verse has been clarified for present edition, from: "use of the ellipse the catalog the meter & the vibrating plane" in *Collected Poems*, to: "use of the ellipsis catalog a variable measure and the vibrating plane," to conform more precisely to above referents.

45 [40, 74]

"Blocks of pigments": A summary reference to Cézanne's theory as author understood it. "Aeterna" (*Collected Poems*) corrected to "Aeterne."

[Regarding the second half of the stanza (40), Ginsberg has tended to leave this out in recent years' public readings. —B.M.]

This line continues the invention of paragraph-long verse formation (see the note to verse 42).

46 [66–67–68]

Carl Solomon writes about the incident in a letter to the author, September 29, 1985:

This section of the poem garbles history completely and makes light of what to me was an extremely serious matter. I was attending Brooklyn College; the lecturer was Wallace Markfield (later a friend); it was an off-campus affair; Markfield's subject was Mallarmé and Alienation; The potato salad throwing was supposed to be Dadaism and also an illustration of alienation; it was done in jest and also as a gift-gesture to a campus girl-friend whose birthday it was and who thought the idea very funny. Contradiction: "in jest" and "quite a serious matter," this was typical of the black humor of dada.

The harlequin speech of suicide and request for lobotomy was meant to be the absurd humor a lot of people were into then which stemmed from the ill-conceived hard-boiled manners of American students—especially New York students in the 1940s. The perfect existential gesture in those days was supposed to be putting an apple in your mouth and jumping into a fire.

Of the second part of the line, Carl Solomon writes: "No Metrazol or electricity for me. Electricity followed six years later at Pilgrim. But I think Dr. Benway (*Naked Lunch*) treatment seems typical of modern psychiatry."

Of the third part, "who in humorless protest," he writes:

This sounds good but the catatonia I doubt as P.I. (where it occurred) diagnosed me as neurotic. Can you make sense of this legalistic diagnostic shit? (More, even further compounding the confusion, has been

offered since, like "as normal as apple pie"—so long as your politics are OK, and anxiety neurosis thrown in.) In short, whatever [diagnosis] has suited the occasion or the needs of the examiner. Also anybody who yelps is called paranoid even by book-thieves who are trying to ward off a conscientious clerk. *They* call you paranoid too. Pardon the use of the word bullshit, but it should be lavishly applied to most aspects of our culture.

The incident of the Ping-Pong table is described by Solomon as a "big burst anti-authoritarian rage on arrival at P.I. by me."

Author received hydrotherapy, psychotherapy, occupational therapy (oil painting) and played Ping-Pong with Carl Solomon at N.Y. State Psychiatric Institute, July 1948–March 1949.

Carl Solomon writes: "Further addendum, perhaps of some pertinence. I first learned of dadaism in an English class at Townsend Harris H.S. (a school for the academically gifted and a prep school for C.C.N.Y.) conducted by Mr. Melvin Bernstein. He described dada, jocularly, as a pro-Dad protest against Mama. This apparently had no relationship to Philip Wylie's protest against 'Momism.' "

47 [69]

"Uncle-lawyer scream": Author had in mind Ilo Orleans, member of Poetry Society of America, and friend of his father Louis, hired as counsel on author's stolen-car crash bust that led to retirement to P.I. as alternative to law court judgment.

48 [71]

In a passage in his book *More Mishaps*, called "Background to *Howl*: Memoirs of the Waugh Years," Solomon writes:

History moves in strange ways, I met for the first time my fellow Beatnik to be, Allen Ginsberg. I gave Allen an apocryphal history of my adventures and pseudo-intellectual deeds of daring. He meticulously took note of everything I said (I thought at the time that he suffered from "the writer's disease," imagined that he was a great writer). Later, when I decided to give up the flesh and become a professional lunatic-saint, he published all of this data, compounded partly of truth, but for the most raving self-justification, crypto-bohemian boasting a la Rimbaud, effeminate prancing, and esoteric aphorisms plagiarized from Kierkegaard and others—in the form of *Howl*. Thus he enshrined falsehood as truth and raving as common sense for future generations to ponder over and be misled. [P. 51.]

Author replaced letters with asterisks in final draft of poem to introduce appropriate element of uncertainty. In a letter regarding this project received

September 29, 1985, Carl Solomon wrote: "Mother finally ***. Crap. Sorry Allen. Also 'heterosexual dollar' is crap; much of our literature is crap. And so on ad infinitum. Howl is a good poem but poetry isn't life."

"Last hopeless companion flown West" ref. the author's 1954 move to West Coast, thinking that also meant "abandoning Carl to Doom and Fate."

Final draft alters to "last fantastic book flung out of the tenement window." Carl Solomon comments: "That's what the best people read in Manhattan. Chic and expensive; not aberrated. Ginsberg was just having a verbal orgy at this point. He likes words. No hallucinations were involved in the 'breakdown'; just overexposure to the metaphysical imagination of Manhattan's crackpot intelligentsia vintage 1956."

The end of the stanza includes author's own associations to Naomi Ginsberg's clothes closet, the "Rosebud" flashback in last scene of *Citizen Kane*; also a paraphrase of L.-F. Céline's "vomiting up the last raspberry" description of shipboard mass seasickness, in *Journey to the End of the Night*.

49: [72]

On the line "Ah, Carl, while you are not safe . . ." Carl Solomon writes: "It's safer in hospital than outside. Vide Neal Cassady's fate. Allen and I are probably both physical cowards anyway which is why he addresses me in such terms.

"I do acknowledge Allen's great skill in describing the maze of thoughts of upset people and conveying this to the reader. A kind of Malcolm Lowry, Virginia Woolf, William Styron expertise. I don't deny he's a great writer."

50 [7, 56]

Verse opens with author's adventures at Columbia College, 1945. Author traced the words "Fuck The Jews," "[N. M.] Butler has no balls," and images of male genitalia and skull and crossbones on the dirty glass of his window to draw the attention of an Irish cleaning lady who consistently overlooked it. The action was seen by Dean Nicholas D. MacKnight as offensive and author was suspended from classes for a year. Final draft: "obscene odes on the windows of the skull."

Ref. Vance Packard's novel *The Man in the Grey Flannel Suit* and Mary McCarthy's story "The Man in the Brooks Brothers Suit," mild aspects of 1950s conformism that clothed the more savage animosity of McCarthyism.

"Blasts . . . of leaden verse": Refers to academic poetry of '40s–'50s, Eliotic tone with J. C. Ransom and Alan Tate text models, rejection of Whitman and W. C. Williams tone and form as naive, crude, raw, provincial. See the modish anthology *New Poets of England and America*, ed. D. Hall, R. Pack and L. Simpson (Cleveland: World Publishing Company, 1957).

"Nitroglycerine shrieks of fairies": See Lorca's "Ode to Walt Whitman" ("shrieks of pansies").

"Sinister intelligent editors" ref. Robert Giroux and other editors' early 1950s rejections of Kerouac's *On the Road* manuscript.

"Subconscious bloops of the hand grenades": Très Beatnik! Phrasing in this verse coincides with Kenneth Koch's "Fresh Air," a contemporaneous comment on the same theme: "Farewell, stale pale skunky pentameters (the only honest English meter, gloop gloop!)!"

— [51]

Ref. Benzedrine exhaustion all night writing experiments 1945; author's crosshatched dawn revisions terminally indecipherable.

51 [28]

In September 1947, author waited a week in Houston-Galveston area for a job on ship to Dakar, W. Africa, after summer with Neal Cassady in Denver and at William Burroughs' marijuana farm, New Waverly, Texas.

"Brilliant Spaniard": *Journals Early Fifties Early Sixties*, entry for June 17, 1952:

In Houston, 1947—I was broke, stealing Pepsi Cola bottles to cash in and buy candy bars for hunger, waiting for a ship. Outside the old Union Hall, walking down the street, a latin animal, Cuban, Spanish, I don't know. Electricity seemed to flow from his powerful body—black hair, curled wildly, looked impossible for him to live in society, to me—powerful malignant features—he was perhaps 22 or less—springing down the street in a tense potent walk, dungarees, powerful legs, not too tall, blue shirt opened several buttons on the chest, black hair curling sparsely on chest—he seemed made of iron, no sweat—or brown polished rock. I never saw in my life a more perfect being—expression of vigor and potency and natural rage on face—I couldn't conceive of him speaking English. I wonder what loves he had. Who could resist him? He must have taken any weak body he needed or wanted. Love from such a face I could not imagine, not gentleness—but love and gentleness are not needed where there was so much life. He just passed me by and I stood there amazed staring at him as he disappeared up the block & around the corner scattering the air in spiritual waves behind him. I couldn't believe he was human. He had thick features, black eyebrows, almost square face, powerful chest, perfect freedom of walk.

Herbert E. Huncke, Fall 1953, Manhattan hotel room N.E. corner 8th Ave & 47th Street. *Photo by A.G.*

52 [46]

Ref. a story told in Jack Kerouac's fiction, *Vanity of Duluoz*, Book 12, Chap. VIII.

53 [52]

Author's mother cooked lungen (lung stew) and Russian borscht (beet soup) when not eating nature-community vegetarian.

54 [48]

Ref. Naomi Ginsberg's Chaplinesque recollections of Orchard and Rivington streets, Manhattan 1905, after debarking ship from Russia. See "Kaddish," Part IV, the "with your eyes" section, for similar images: ". . . with your fingers of rotten mandolins . . . arms of fat Paterson porches . . . belly of strikes and smokestacks . . ."

55 [50]

Russell Durgin (d. August 28, 1985), Columbia theology student in whose sublet apartment, 321 East 121st Street, East Harlem 1948, author read

William Blake, left Manhattan that summer for medical treatment, tubercular lungs. Treatment may have involved filling chest space with celluloid balls to prevent collapse.

"Orange crates of theology": Durgin's books were displayed in wooden orange crates, then commonly used as bookcases, as plastic milk crates serve four decades later.

56 [45]

After homeless weeks on New York's winter streets upon release from Rikers Island prison on an addict sentence, 86'd from Times Square by police who called him "a creep," friend Herbert Huncke knocked at author's door in this condition one winter's day, 1948.

"Scabs": Huncke's skin disturbances 1945–48, related to junk needles and amphetamine.

57 [—]

See William M. Garver in Jack Kerouac's *Mexico City Blues* (Choruses 57–61, 80–84) and other books; in *Junky*, by William S. Burroughs, the character Bill Gains. Garver purloined overcoats from semi-elegant restaurants, pawned them, used the money to score and pay rent—a good Russian overcoat was worth a week's rent. He'd sit at a table nursing coffee and apple pie till he spotted expensive unprotected apparel on a wall hanger.

Author sent Kerouac this original ms. of "Howl" (first six pages of Part I) in Mexico City. Kerouac showed it to Garver, who commented, "No coathangers in Longchamps [restaurants]." See Kerouac's annotation bottom p. 5 thus. Entire verse is dropped in final draft.

"Coat hanger apparition" alludes to W. B. Yeats' "The Apparitions": "Fifteen apparitions have I seen;/ The worst a coat upon a coat hanger."—*The Poems of W. B. Yeats* (New York: Macmillan, 1983), p. 334.

58 [—]

An image of Herbert Huncke hustling Bryant Park, N.Y., which author associates with opening pages of Jean Genêt's *Our Lady of the Flowers* (New York: Grove Press, 1963): ". . . the Negro Angel Sun . . . eyes are clear and sky-blue . . . vacant like the windows of buildings under construction, through which you see the sky . . ."

59 [55]

Ref. some of author's Columbia College gay contemporaries' later careers.

60 [54]

As author remembers anecdote, friend Walter Adams visited poet Louis Simpson's high-floored apartment near Columbia in 1946:

L.S.: Do you have a watch?

W.A.: Yes.

L.S.: Can I have it?

W.A.: Here.

L.S. (throwing watch out window): We don't need time, we're already in eternity.

In letter November 21, 1985, kindly responding to query from author, Louis Simpson writes:

It seems this does apply to me. I say "seems" because I don't remember doing this, but a man whose word I could trust once wrote me a letter in which he said that I thought "that technology had destroyed time so that all lives ever lived were being lived simultaneously, which was why you could ask Walter Adams for his watch, throw it out the window and remark that we didn't need such instruments any more."

This must have happened shortly before I had a "nervous breakdown"—the result of my experience during the war. There may have been other causes, but I think this was the main. I have no recollections of the months preceding the breakdown, and if people say I threw watches out of windows, OK.

61 [64]

William Burroughs, among others, "retired to Mexico [and Tanger] to cultivate sex," Garver to Mexico for his "habit," Jack Kerouac to his sister's North Carolina house in "Rocky Mount to Buddha," Neal Cassady worked for S.P. Railroad, John Hollander among others went on to Harvard. Naomi Ginsberg's window 1953 overlooked Woodlawn Cemetery in the Bronx; see "Kaddish."

Poe wrote "Annabel Lee," "The Bells," "Ulalume" and "Eureka" 1846–48 in his Fordham cottage, now moved to Grand Concourse, Bronx.

62 [39]

One night 1945, author and William Burroughs visited Everard Baths, rumored to be owned by Police Athletic League, at 28 West 28th Street, N.Y., accompanied by Jack Kerouac, who consorted with several French sailors who blew him. Phallic reference is mostly imaginary.

63 [49]

Bill Keck built a harpsichord in his 2nd Street loft. Other artists had cold-water flats under Brooklyn Bridge, some furnished with Wilhelm Reich's wardrobe-sized Orgone Accumulator boxes to which they repaired sitting in daily sessions to replenish their cosmic-energy monad "orgones." See Reich's *The Function of the Orgasm* (New York: Touchstone, 1974).

Large packing crates were adapted for use as furniture, closets, beds, etc., in this milieu.

64 [77]

"Goldhorn shadow" in this verse paraphrases some sentence by Kerouac.

Lester Young, Coleman Hawkins, Charlie Parker, Illinois Jacquet saxophones were heard on "Symphony Sid" all-night bebop radio program mid-'40s Manhattan.

First draft's concluding phrase, "last blue sad jelly of Time," ref. Jelly Roll Morton's "Jelly, Jelly, Jelly, Jelly stays on my mind," Ma Rainey's "Jellybean Blues," etc., as black metaphor for erotic squish.

"Lamma lamma sabacthani"—"My God, my God, why have you forsaken me?" Christ's last words from the cross ("Eli, Eli, lama sabachthani": Matthew 27: 46)—of final draft was lifted from Tristan Corbière's version in "Cris d'Aveugle" ("Cries of the Blindman") in *Poems*, trans. Walter McElroy (Pawlet, Vt.: Banyan Press, 1947), p. 30:

Les oiseaux croques-morts	The birds those under-takers
Ont donc peur a mon corps	Facing my body show fear
Mon Golgotha n'est pas fini	This Golgotha lasts on for me
Lamma lamma sabacthani	*Lamma lamma sabacthani*
Colombes de la Mort	You doves of Death
	· hover
Soiffez apres mon corps	In thirst for my body here

The poem ends:

J'entends le vent du nord	I hear the north wind roar
Qui bugle comme un cor	It bellows like a horn
C'est l'hallali des trepasses	That halloos for those who are gone
J'aboie apres mon tour assez	I have howled for my turn too long
J'entends le vent du nord	I hear the north wind roar
J'entends le glas du cor	I hear the knell of the horn

65 [47]

Basically it's just Bowery bums.

66–67 [23, 27]

See Hart Crane's "The Bridge":

Behind
My father's cannery works I used to see
Rail-squatters ranged in nomad raillery,
The ancient men—wifeless or runaway
Hobo-trekkers that forever search
An empire wilderness of freight and rails.
Each seemed a child, like me, on a loose perch,
Holding to childhood like some termless play.
John, Jake or Charley, hopping the slow freight
—Memphis to Tallahassee—riding the rods,
Blind fists of nothing, humpty-dumpty clods.

Yet they touch something like a key perhaps.
From pole to pole across the hills, the states
—They know a body under the wide rain;
Youngsters with eyes like fjords, old reprobates
With racetrack jargon, —dotting immensity
They lurk across her, knowing her yonder breast
Snow-silvered, sumac-stained or smoky blue—
is past the valley-sleepers, south or west.
—As I have trod the rumorous midnights, too.

See also the Circus of Oklahoma in Kafka's *Amerika*, trans. Edwin Muir (New York: New Directions, 1946).

70–71 [—]

Peter Du Peru, San Francisco friend of author 1954 and at time of "Howl"'s writing. See photograph.

72 [—]

The late Guy Wernham, early translator Comte de Lautréamont's *The Chants of Maldoror* (New York: New Directions, 1947), served as bartender at Gino and Carlo's, poet Jack Spicer's favored bar on Green St., North Beach, San Francisco, late 1950s–early 60s.

73 [30]

Joffre Stewart, Chicago vegetarian pacifist war-tax resister, signal member of 1948 "Peacemakers" meeting with Dave Dellinger, Dwight Macdonald, A. J. Muste and Bayard Rustin at Yellow Springs, Ohio, called to plan resistance to reinstatement of draft in peacetime. A strong anarchist, visiting Kenneth Rexroth S.F. 1955 he remarked to author that he was investigating the FBI. Familiarly active around folk clubs and on Chicago's streets thru 1968 police riots to the 1980s, he carried a large white cloth bag filled with peace leaflets and his own provocative anarchist broadsides.

Peter Du Peru, North Beach remittance man wanderer, Broadway corner a few doors below 1010 Montgomery Street. Author had worked as market researcher in financial district several blocks downhill thru Spring 1955. *Photo by A.G.*

75 [—]

Next drafts eliminate this ponderous lineage. "Howl" was originally co-dedicated to Burroughs, Kerouac, Cassady and Lucien Carr; the last preferred his name be dropped lest it cause his life to cast a shadow beyond its actuality.

76 [42]

My own version of Neal Cassady's Western myth, here exaggerated as erotic comedy.

77 [—]

Ref. verse beginning "Nous n'avions pas fini de nous parler d'amour," from "Le Condamné à Mort" by Jean Genêt. Quoted earlier, author's letter to Neal Cassady and Jack Kerouac, February 15, 1952: *As Ever: The Collected Correspondence of Allen Ginsberg & Neal Cassady* (Berkeley, Cal.: Creative Arts, 1977), p. 120.

> We didn't get time to finish talking about love.
> We didn't get time to smoke our cigarettes, Gitanes.
> You ask yourself why the courts passed death sentence
> On a man so beautiful he made the dawn pale.
>
> Nous n'avions pas fini de nous parler d'amour.
> Nous n'avions pas fini de fumer nos gitanes.
> On peut se demander pourquoi les Cours condamné
> Un assassin si beau qu'il fait pâlir le jour.

78 [63]

Ref. Genêt, above. Four years after this draft, Neal Cassady was incarcerated in San Quentin for over two years on conviction of having passed two grass cigarettes to agents in exchange of a lift to work at the S.P.R.R. station. After 1957 publication of *On the Road*, Cassady's association with Jack Kerouac's Dean Moriarty on his picaresque road was well known around San Francisco Bay Area. By 1959 the energetic Cassady gained further underground fame as "Johnny Appleseed" of the local marijuana movement, and was under surveillance for his literary and countercultural celebrity.

In San Quentin he enrolled in religion classes taught by astrologer Gavin Arthur (grandson of Pres. Chester A. Arthur), who in later years housed and befriended Cassady at various times of crisis. Author visited Cassady in San Quentin 1959 invited by Gavin Arthur and read text of "Howl" to his class.

79 [76]

Ref. author's idiomatic adaptation of Catullus XXXVIII, "Malest Cornifici Tuo Catullo" (*Collected Poems*, p. 123) to his domestic situation on meeting Peter Orlovsky.

Catullus returned home to Sirmio after visit to Asia Minor (XXXI); visiting his brother's grave in Asia Minor, he wrote "Ave Atque Vale," his eternal Hail and Farewell (CI): "What might be left to say anew in time after death . . ."

Original ms. ref. also L. Zukofsky's translations of Catullus, and the lyric title of his collection of short poems: *Anew.*

Also: "I'm writing this book because we're all going to die— In the loneliness of my life, my father dead, my brother dead, my mother faraway, my sister and wife far away, nothing here but my own tragic hands that once were guarded by a world, a sweet attention, that now are left to guide and disappear their own way into the common dark of all our death, sleeping in me raw bed, alone and stupid: with just this one pride and consolation: my heart broke in the general despair and opened up inwards to the Lord, I made a supplication in this dream." —Jack Kerouac, *Visions of Cody* (1952; New York: McGraw-Hill, 1972), p. 368.

80 [75]

Ref. Jack Kerouac as creative breakthru artist, especially for *Visions of Cody*'s long-breathed prose-poem "sketches" and "Imitation of the Tape" section; for *Mexico City Blues* (circa 1954–55, same time as "Howl") a seminal volume of poetry; earlier-invented rhapsodic paragraphs in *Book of Dreams*, and *Doctor Sax*; the naked spontaneous-minded pages of "Brakeman on the R.R." prose so much appreciated by Robert Creeley circa 1955 Bay Area, thus first published in his *Black Mountain Review* two autumns later; and supreme improvisations in *Old Angel Midnight* of endless vocal sounds entering the window of the ear. These examples catalyzed the scantier improvisations of "Howl."

Kerouac's superior formal genius as poet, much misnoted by academic criticism, was much appreciated in ms. at the time by his peers Robert Duncan and Robert Creeley, and had strong encouraging influence on the writing of his friends William S. Burroughs, Gary Snyder, Philip Whalen, Lew Welch, Michael McClure, Philip Lamantia and the author of "Howl" among many others, including Bob Dylan a half-decade later.

Kerouac's slogans for composition are outlined in "Belief and Technique of Modern Prose,"* excellent instruction, when well understood, for "First thought, best thought" clarity and sincerity:

---

* In *Heaven and Other Poems* (San Francisco: Grey Fox Press, 1977), pp. 46–7.

List of Essentials

1. Scribbled secret notebooks, and wild typewritten pages, for yr own joy
2. Submissive to everything, open, listening
3. Try never get drunk outside yr own house
4. Be in love with yr life
5. Something that you feel will find its own form
6. Be crazy dumbsaint of the mind
7. Blow as deep as you want to blow
8. Write what you want bottomless from bottom of the mind
9. The unspeakable visions of the individual
10. No time for poetry but exactly what is
11. Visionary tics shivering in the chest
12. In tranced fixation dreaming upon object before you
13. Remove literary, grammatical and syntactical inhibition
14. Like Proust be an old teahead of time
15. Telling the true story of the world in interior monolog
16. The jewel center of interest is the eye within the eye
17. Write in recollection and amazement for yourself
18. Work from pithy middle eye out, swimming in language sea
19. Accept loss forever
20. Believe in the holy contour of life
21. Struggle to sketch the flow that already exists intact in mind
22. Dont think of words when you stop but to see the picture better
23. Keep track of every day the date emblazoned in yr morning
24. No fear or shame in the dignity of yr experience, language & knowledge
25. Write for the world to read and see yr exact pictures of it
26. Bookmovie is the movie in words, the visual American form
27. In praise of Character in the Bleak inhuman Loneliness
28. Composing wild, undisciplined, pure, coming in from under, crazier the better
29. You're a Genius all the time
30. Writer-Director of Earthly movies Sponsored & Angeled in Heaven

This list was tacked on wall above author's bedstead in North Beach hotel a year before "Howl" was written. See Robert Duncan's comments apropos in *Allen Verbatim*, ed. Gordon Ball (New York: McGraw-Hill, 1974), pp. 143–47.

81 [74]

Regarding haiku and prose syntax, reworking and expanding the aesthetic program of verses 44–45

Jack Kerouac with R.R. Brakeman's Rule Book in pocket, visiting Burroughs & author at 206 East 7th Street, N.Y.C., around the time of spontaneous prose mode composition of *Dr. Sax, The Subterraneans* & *MacDougal St. Blues*, Fall 1953.   *Photo by A.G.*

(see note above), reference here is to Cézanne's method of composition. Letters and conversations of Cézanne from which author derived this aesthetic, applied somewhat to "Howl" poetics including paraphrase of key words ("sensation") and phrases, were first encountered in Erle Loran's *Cézanne's Composition* (Berkeley, Cal.: University of California Press, 1943). At the time, author was writing term paper on Cézanne for Prof. Meyer Schapiro at Columbia University. Correct Latin line should read: "Pater Omnipotens Aeterne Deus." Relevant passages from Loran follow:

"The study of arts is very long and badly conducted. Today a painter must discover everything for himself, for there are no longer any but very bad schools, where one becomes warped, where one learns nothing. One must first of all study geometric forms: the cone, the cube, the cylinder, the sphere. When one knows how to render these things in their form and their planes, one ought to know how to paint." —Emile Bernard, *Souvenirs sur Paul Cézanne* (Paris: Chez Michel, 1912).

"The form and contour of objects is given to us by the oppositions and contrasts which result from their individual coloration." —John Rewald, *Cézanne: Sa Vie, son oeuvre, son amitie pour Zola* (Paris: Albin Michel, 1939).

"This is absolutely indisputable—I am very positive: an optical sensation is produced in our visual organ which causes us to classify the planes represented by color modulations into light, half-tone, or quarter-tone." —Bernard, *Souvenirs.*

On Gauguin: "Well, he hasn't understood me; I have never wanted and I shall never accept the absence of modeling or of gradations; it's nonsense. Gauguin isn't a painter, he has only made Chinese images . . . [he has] stolen [my] little sensation and paraded it before the public." —Ibid.

"In an orange, an apple, a ball, a head, there is a culminating point; and this point is always—in spite of the terrible effect: light, shade, sensations of color —the nearest to our eye. The edges of objects recede toward a center placed at our horizon." —Ibid.

"Lines parallel to the horizon give extension, whether it be a section of nature or, if you prefer, of the spectacle that the *Pater Omnipotens aeterne Deus* spreads before our eyes. The lines perpendicular to this horizon give depth. Now for us, nature is more in depth than in surface." —Paul Cézanne to Emile Bernard, April 15, 1904. Ibid.

Cézanne: I have my motif [he joins his hands]. A motif, you see, is this. . . .

Gasquet: How's that?

Cézanne: Eh? Yes—[he repeats his gesture, draws his hands apart, fingers spread out, and brings them together again, slowly, slowly; then joins them, presses them together and contracts them, making them interlace] there you have it; that's what one must attain. If I pass too high or too low, all is ruined. There mustn't be a single link too loose, not a crevice through which may escape the emotion, the light, the truth. I advance, you understand, all of my canvas at one time—together. I bring together in the same spirit, the same faith, all that is scattered. All that we see disperses, vanishes; is it not so? Nature is always the same, but nothing remains of it, nothing of what comes to our sight. Our art ought to give the shimmer of its duration with the elements, the appearance of all its changes. It ought to make us taste it eternally. What is underneath? Nothing, perhaps. Perhaps everything. You understand? Thus I join these straying hands. I take from left, from right, here, there, everywhere, tones, colors, shades. I fix them, I bring them together. They make lines. They become objects, rocks, trees, without my thinking about it. They take on volume. They acquire value. If these volumes, these values, correspond on my canvas, in my feeling, to the planes and patches of color which are there before our eyes, very good! my canvas joins hands. It does not vacillate. It does not pass too high or too low. It is true; it is full. But if I feel the least distraction, the least weakness, above all if I interpret too much one day, if today I am carried away by a theory which is contrary to that of the day before, if I think while painting, if I intervene, why then everything is gone.

—Joachim Gasquet, *Paul Cézanne* (Paris: Editions Bernheim-Jeune, 1926).

For earlier articulation of ideas from Cézanne applied to "Howl," see author's 1965 *Paris Review* interview in *Writers at Work: Third Series* (New York: Viking, 1967), pp. 291–97.

82 [75]

On improvised sound track of the Al Leslie– Robert Frank film *Pull My Daisy*, 1959, Kerouac explains: "Well, they turn over their little purple moonlight pages in which their secret naked doodlings do show. Secret scatological thought, and that's why everybody wants to see it." —*Pull My Daisy* (New York: Grove Press, 1961), p. 23.

83 [78]

Ref. Lionel Trilling, *The Liberal Imagination* (New York: Viking, 1950). Author sat in Prof. Trilling's Romantic Literature class at Columbia College, studying Wordsworth, Keats, Shelley, Byron, little Blake, and did paper comparing Rimbaud to Keats. See Trilling's response to "Howl" on p. 156.

Latter half of verse unused in final draft. "Accept no substitute": 1950 slogan for commercial advertisement of a name-brand product forgotten by author.

84 [76]

Attempt to clarify the role of poetry as revealing naked mind, identical itself with the experience (and suffering) of love. See Whitman's poetics "of perfect personal candor," in 1855 preface, *Leaves of Grass.*

"Madman bum & angel [beat in Time]": See note to verse 79 above, re Kerouac's *Visions of Cody*, as quoted.

Final Draft, HOWL, Part II

80*

"Moloch": or Molech, the Canaanite fire god, whose worship was marked by parents' burning their children as propitiatory sacrifice. "And thou shalt not let any of thy seed pass through the fire to Molech" (Leviticus 18:21).

"Boys sobbing in armies": Postwar U.S.A. reinstitution of peacetime draft, 1948; see note to verse 31.

81

Law apparatus is too crude to cover human body of manslaughter, per author's experience; ref. Burroughs et al. See *Queer*, W. S. Burroughs (New York: Viking Press, 1985) pp. xvii–xxii.

"Heavy judger of men": Ref. also world-shock 1953 N.Y. electric chair executions Julius & Ethel Rosenberg spy convicts. (Later, Caryl Chessman gas execution 1960, California.)

82

"Buildings are judgment": See William Blake's spectre of the Jehovic hyper-rationalistic judgmental

* Line numbers from here on refer only to final published text (pp. 3–8).

lawgiver Urizen, creator of spiritual disorder and political chaos. His abstract calipers limit the infinite universe to his egoic horizon, a projection of unmindful selfhood, the result of aggressively naive mental measurements which substitute hypocrite or modish generalizations for experience of event, and oppress physical body, feelings and imagination.

83

"Whose mind is pure machinery": N.B. Marshall McLuhan's apposite axiom, "The medium is the message."

82–84

"Crossbone . . . jailhouse," etc.: Ref. Lynd Ward block-print novel *God's Man* (New York: Jonathan Cape and Harrison Smith, 1929), ex libris author's family 1930s, reprinted in Ward's *Storyteller Without Words* (New York: Harry W. Abrams, 1974), wherein Ward noted that *God's Man* was "published . . . in the same week that saw the crash of the New York stock market." Lynd Ward illustrated "Howl"'s "Moloch" in 1980, his block print thus completing the circle of imagination.

Lynd Ward blockprints: The artist enters the City of a Thousand Blind Windows. The artist sees Buildings of Judgment from the Soulless Jailhouse (likely New York Tombs prison). The artist flees the City whose skyscrapers stand in the long streets like endless Jehovahs.

Illustration for Howl II, *Moloch. Lynd Ward, 1980.*

Cannibal dynamo in Metropolis Centrum. Fritz Lang, Berlin 1932. *Courtesy Museum of Modern Art, Film Stills Archives.*

"Skyscrapers . . . endless Jehovahs," etc.: Ref. cinema images for robot megalopolis centrum, Fritz Lang's *Metropolis*, Berlin, 1932.

83

"Cannibal dynamo": Ref. the opening industrial-heartbeat sound track of Fritz Lang's terrific film *M* (1931); also his *Last Will of Dr. Mabuse* (1933).

84

"Thousand blind windows": Appearance of upper stories Sir Francis Drake Hotel, corner Powell & Pine streets, San Francisco, which image directly inspired this section of the poem. Entry 1954 journal reads:

On peyote, San Francisco, October 17–18, Sat nite. 1:15— Apartment window wide open looking across down downtown the aspect of ferocious building reared in the center looming up in the clouds wisp fog sliding across the flat blue sky.

Uprising in the timeless city gloom, dark tower over ruddy building suddenly a vision the Death Head —the building an evil monster—a tower in Hell—

("Those poor lost souls making it up in the tower") two eyes blast light far apart brick glass illuminated from within—too corny for a painter to make the surrealistic reality—no—deep gong religious

Impassive robot (antennalike structures) of Sir Francis Drake Hotel.

And quite vegetable that monster too—it may be coming to eat me someday—

That was what was familiar all along.

It's got a crown—

Smoke curling up from it—working rooted in the basements

Snub nosed monster—the hideous gorgonian aspect— . . .

Description of the Tower of Baal or Azriel? of Lucifer "The Tower of Lucifer." The star goes out at one A.M.—the monster appears most grim staring into the sky, small noselite—with snout near darkened —someone up late in the tower . . .

With fog rolling by down from Twin Peaks & South San Fran to the bridge and Embarcadero edge of the cock peninsula in the bottom of the vale of the town arranged skyline peyotl buildings:

I came to the window and glanced out into the night space at the unreal city below in which I inhabit a building—

as walking street today I noticed the battlement uprearing facade appearance of the ranges of blocks of houses with fantastic Graeco-mediaeval ornamentation juttings and false stone wood pillars and arches porches & crossbow tower'd bedrooms—

Came to the window to stare at the thousand eyed buildings in the smoke filled stone vale crowded with monstrous edifices shouldering each other rocking stolid on the streets, red lights below and haze purple sky light above as in Rembrandt it was brown—

and fixed eye & noticed the vegetable horror of the Sir Francis Drake Hotel—had waited long for this perception having spent four hours total over a week looking out the window at the wrong building waiting for something to happen—nothing had but that I'd noticed how modern and large and isolate the Sutter St. Med. building stood in my way, too large for the more homely old Drake and downtown other S P and Insurance edifices making a New York Gotham midtown Murray Hill unreal Wall Street miniature

Allen Ginsberg and Peter Orlovsky visiting Moloch with theatric gaze, Nob Hill's Pine Street corner, facing Powell Street downtown, Sir Francis Drake Hotel tower background night-lit, San Francisco, 1959.
Photo by Harry Redl.

Moloch. Athanasius Kircher, Oedipus Aegyptiacus, Rom, 1652.

panorama [sweep] toward [Bay] Bridge—another coast's apple for the eye—

Found suddenly the Gothic eyes of the skull tower glaring out bleak blind blank smoking above in stillness in the atmosphere of the real primeval city world, down-grown out of earth—with horrible cross check dollar sign skull protrusion of lipless jailbarred inhuman longtooth spectral deathhead brick columns making abstract teeth. This phantom building robot was smoking in inaction as it had been stuck there in eternity a golem waiting for the Rabbi of electricity to pull the switch for it to topple forward into the city destroying— Meanwhile serving as an evil tower of thought, glaring profound and open above the streets (into my window)—for every eye to see that could wake from the daily dream to register its central presence in the atmosphere of night.

On top a star of David in great blue silly neon that goes off at 1 A.M. leaving the impression of the continually Death-in-Life robot zombie presence of the Drake (mad cranes tear down the bldgs.) fixed for the night to wait sleepless and unseeing while physicists tinker in its bowels toward the day of resurrection.

85
"Whose soul is electricity and banks": See Ezra Pound's theory of usury as canker of state, *Cantos,* XLV.

"Specter of genius": William Blake's use of "spectre" as disordered shadow states of mind, body, heart or imagination, when mutually unbalanced dominated by or dominating one the others. See S. Foster

Damon, *A Blake Dictionary* (Boulder, Colo.: Shambala Books, 1980), "The Four Zoas," as well as Blake's prophetic book, same name.

"Whose name is the Mind": This verse seems to objectify a recognition uncovered in the act of composition, a crux of the poem.

86
"Cocksucker in Moloch": Ref. also Jean Genêt, another literary cocksucker.

87
Ref. Blake illumination; see note to verse 26.

"Whom I abandon": This verse seems to objectify a decision uncovered in the act of composition and is the crux of the poem.

88
Topographical associations: "Robot apartments," giant downtown money buildings; "invisible suburbs," perhaps Levittown, N.Y.; "skeleton treasuries," early cold war budget debts; "demonic industries," Southern California's night-lit war plants viewed from highway on author's first West Coast trip; "spectral nations," mainland China "unrecognized" by U.S.A., Soviet gulags' ghostly bureaucracies, Western imperium covering Guatemala, Vietnam, Algeria with war; "invincible madhouses," Naomi Ginsberg, Carl Solomon then immured in Pilgrim State Mental Hospital; "monstrous bombs," contemporaneous atomic and hydrogen nuclear weapons.

89
"Heaven which exists and is everywhere": See Arthur Rimbaud, "Morning": "When shall we go beyond the mountains and the shores, to greet the birth of new toil, of new wisdom, the flight of tyrants, of demons, the end of superstition, to adore —the first to adore!—Christmas on the earth." —*Season in Hell,* trans. Louise Varese (New York: New Directions, 1945).

91
"Sensitive bullshit": See note to verse 1 re "starving hysterical naked" for key to contradiction.

92
"Ten years . . . Mad generation": Poem's specific reference was to decade 1945–55.

Final Draft, HOWL, Part III

94*

Carl Solomon writes: "I was never in Rockland . . . Neither of us has ever been in Rockland. Ginsberg never even on a tour." (Not at the time, though I visited a friend of Leary's there later '60s.—A.G.)

96

Naomi Ginsberg then at Pilgrim State Hospital.

97

In early 1950s, Carl Solomon worked as editor for his uncle A. A. Wynn's Ace Books, publishing Burroughs' *Junky* and contracting Ur-text of Kerouac's *On the Road.*

99

Typescript drafts of letters unsent to T. S. Eliot and Malcolm de Chazal from N.Y. Psychiatric Institute fall–winter 1948 co-written by Carl Solomon and Allen Ginsberg.

October 13, 1949

My dear Chevalier de Chazal:

Graciously aware of the poverty of the correspondence, and above all of its tendentious nature, between the mainland and your forlorn Indian domicile, a mere man among monsoons as you undoubtedly hold yourself to be, we have taken advantage of the favorable winds, perhaps over-abruptly, but as a last recourse, to ask for money.

We are determined upon this course only upon considering the favorable rate of exchange. If however, you have nothing but goldfish out there we will accept these, as there is a shortage of exotic goldfish in this hospital. Perhaps we are too exacting. Therefore perhaps we could justify our very inconsiderate demands on your person by inquiring if you are bald.

Uncle Malcolm, we have come upon a stupendous discovery which promises to be the work of a theology student. It would be thoughtful of you to send us a short note of encouragement a mere morsel as we are dying of hunger. We have dyed our hair purple to attract the attention of other theology students but we have met with no encouragement in the eyes of those false hearted ambassadors from Moscow, who will not stop their endless accusations of Chinoiserie.

Since our natal light comes not from China but from Mauritius we feel that you are our last resort.

Can you tell us how much you charge for a season? We can live in goldfish bowls and thereby bring in much revenue from admiring Japanese tourists.

We have poignant types of children to the number of seven.

No more need be said. Beyond a certain point

there can be no spoken communication and all speech is useless.

Shirley Temple and Dagwood Bumpstead
(who affixes his name under protest)*

December 19, 1949

[To T. S. Eliot]
Most distinguished Number 1 poet of 1949:

The year is fast running out. We wish to affirm, if we may use so banal a word, that the year is running out. Does this not frighten you?

"Uneasy wears the crown that wears the head." etc.

Now we know all about cold spots on the moon and other items that probably preoccupy you at this, shall we say turbulent?, moment, so close to Christmas as it is. We understand very well that your conversion was fraudulent. You carried it off very well. Now to get on to business.

We have here crowded into this very room, 45 potential applicants, young legislators to be from various walks of society, together packed tight, and we constitute as you must be aware, a very formidable bloc. What we want to say, though its very difficult to explain pointedly, [is] that we want to represent ourselves as your Maginot line, though it is getting late in the year. We'll make riots for you. We'll make bonfires. There you have it, 45 young legislators (incidentally, to illustrate the prosletysing vigor of our legislators, one of those has just come in and announced to us that he has just converted one John Puccio, tinker, to our cause) scurrying through the night starting—there you have it—bonfires, all over, in order to advance your candidacy under the theory (we know you will sympathize) that every vote counts.

To illustrate the quality of self criticism in our ranks, one of our younger members has just criticised your body. You have a big nose. But we tend to regard this this way—for you to have a big nose is for us to have a big nose. (The ace of spades, the tarot cards, the dying king, the rituals and everything, we all know that.) So now to get on to business as we are legislators.

To illustrate some more of the self criticism, another young legislator of our ranks (the same one as before, it so happens—but he is very vociferous, and is promised to a grey dramatic critic, on Broadway, America) has interjected

" 'Uneasy wears the crown that wears the head' etc. kills the whole program."

The fact is, that some 85% of our young legislators are schemers, and you cannot count on them to be real firebrands (you know our position on that, personally, and you need not worry about us, I am sure you will be gratified by us). We know exactly where you stand

* Line numbers refer to final published text only (pp. 3–8).

* *Sens Plastique* (Paris: Gallimard, 1948); trans. Irving Weiss (New York: Sun Books, 1979).

on the question of the existence of your great mind. We are prepared to publicly back up our charges, defying libel, lawsuits, the stupid comments of newspaper would be litterateur editorialists manque.

Certain literary dirigibles (we use the term figuratively) claim that you are a dictator. But these people have nothing to do with the main body of traditional literature, but these people are stinkers. Has a stinker ever occupied a famous place in literature, English or French? I am not speaking of Russians, as they have always been bolsheviks, even before you became a dictator.

We send our regards and highest genuflections to Mrs. literary Dictator and all the little literary dictators. This was decided on at the last meeting, after much debate. Schwamp, who is earnest, but a fool at heart, says that you want to keep them in the background, but we know that your family is really mongoloid. But as an illustration of our total participation in your decades we voted to mention them too. This shows how completely we are of your camp.

We are waiting for marching orders. Some of our younger and less responsible young legislators to be want us to embark en masse, to China, thinking to join you there, on the theory that you'll soon contract a non-aggression pact with the reds in order to play for time. They feel our arrival there would give you an extra card up your sleeve to bargain with. The time will come when you won't have anybody to depend on but us, and young as we are, we still are legislators who know our minds and have taken a blood oath to respect you, no matter what happens. Anybody that reneges on the agreement, we will kill them. We do this with your tacit approval, in order that you need not be implicated if we get caught by the American police who are very brutal. But we vow not to involve you, because we know all about abysses already. In war there is no umpire, but nevertheless do not attempt to use your powers of divination: as regards the powers of divination, il s'agit de guerre moderne, (Clausewitz, Rommel, etc.) but you know all that.

Now to get back to speaking of you, personally, if we may make so bold. There are no atheists in foxholes. This definitely settles the religious question. Some of our younger legislators are Jews (you don't know their names), but we have decided to treat them as if they were dopey daffodils, a special category of legislator which we have invented for your approval. They think they are all budding young Clemenceaus. Perhaps there is a place for them in France.

The meeting is fast becoming a farce, indistinguishable from a pepper steak party, the like of which was given last week, or two weeks ago at the very most, by the young Chevaliers of Malcolm De Chazal, where they did nothing but eat. Therefore, much as we would like to go on chatting with you, exchanging literary gossip, news that would be of mutual interest, we will simply conclude by rephrasing a question that was made from the floor, by one of your young devotees who will not get up, whether you have epilepsy like Dostoievsky. If so (and Dostoievsky we consider from the very first to have been a dead issue, as far as this meeting is concerned—next month being set aside for our Dostoievsky memorial—) we want to know if you have not neglected it. We care for you and would be reassured that you have taken all available steps to curtail this dreadful disease which would turn you into a feebleminded mongolian idiot, too, which would make our position rather embarrassing.

Before saying farewell, we want to assure you that we know a good literary dictator when we see one: A smart young fellow like you, a real hustler.

In case you are wondering who is responsible for this transcription of the meeting, I may be permitted to speak of myself as a young poet who though passing through a position of temporary and purely transitional sterility, as far as productivity presently counts, will soon be bigger than you.

We take our leave by asking us to kiss you goodbye.

Signed,
Your 44 favorite legislators,
(one dissenting vote)
who are your brightest acolytes,
Yisraeli Soccer Team.

101

See note to verse 43 [65] re Artaud's "Judgement of God."

102

Likely association with Apollinaire's *Mamelles de Tirésias*; New York's Utica was named for classical Mediterranean city.

103

"Harpies of the Bronx": Solomon's and author's mother and aunts had lived in the Bronx.

104

Carl Solomon was not straightjacketed at N.Y. State Psychiatric Institute while in company with author. Solomon writes: "Not at P.I.; later at Pilgrim rather often." Ping-Pong was actual.

105

Not Solomon but author was rebuked for percussive experiments on piano once in P.I. common room.

"Armed madhouse": "Howl" marks 10th anniversary of Winston Churchill's Fulton, Missouri, "Iron Curtain" speech acknowledging cold war.

106

"Shocks": "Received 50 insulin comas at P.I. and 21 electroshocks at Pilgrim." —Carl Solomon, letter to author, September 29, 1985.

"A cross in the void": See note to verse 43 [65] re Artaud, etc.

107

Of this line, Carl Solomon writes: "At this time I was an admirer of Adlai Stevenson and had all the feelings toward America of a disappointed Democrat." —Letter to author, September 29, 1985

"Accuse your doctors of insanity": See note 43 [65], Artaud, etc.

108

"The heavens of Long Island": Ref. Pilgrim State Hospital, Brentwood, Long Island.

109

"Twenty-five thousand mad comrades": Pilgrim State population; see note to verse 42 [69–70].

> 'Tis the final conflict
> Let each stand in his place
> The International Soviet
> Shall be the human race.

Eugène Pottier, "The Internationale," June 1871, trans. C. H. Kerr, in *I.W.W. Songs* ("Little Red Songbook") 34th ed. (Chicago: International Workers of the World, 1973), pp. 6–7.

110

Democratic Vistas, 1871, limns Walt Whitman's amative affection for these United States. W.W. feared an America "on the road to a destiny, a status, equivalent in its real world, to that of the fabled damned," for want of spiritual adhesiveness.

Carl Solomon writes: "Gay sex reference with late 1940's gay typology involved [sailors in U.S. uniforms]—this typology changed later—different gestalt."

Certain patients on 6th-floor wards of P.I. remained agitated, talking to themselves, coughing all night.

111

"Starry spangled shock of mercy": Old Glory. Perhaps an echo of "star-yspangled," Elizabethan archaism.

112

"Cottage in the Western night": One-room cottage backyard 1624 Milvia Street, Berkeley, California, visited often by Peter Orlovsky and Jack Kerouac. Cottage was shared with Philip Whalen and Gary Snyder early fall 1955, during composition of Parts II and III of "Howl." See "A Strange New Cottage in Berkeley," "Supermarket in California," "Transcription of Organ-Music," in Allen Ginsberg, *Collected Poems*.

1624 Milvia Street Berkeley Cottage back garden 1955. Gesture imitating that painted by Bellini (*St. Francis in Ecstasy*, Frick Collection, N.Y.). Part II *Howl* completed here; Kerouac, Gary Snyder, Philip Whalen, Orlovsky, & others shared author's cottage that year. *Photo by Jack Kerouac?*

Final Draft, HOWL, Part IV (Footnote)

115*

"Everyday is in eternity": "Hold Infinity in the palm of your hand / And Eternity in an hour." —Blake, "Auguries of Innocence." "Only through time time is conquered." —T. S. Eliot, "Burnt Norton"

117

"The typewriter is holy": Part I "Howl" original draft was typewritten; "Footnote" was in holograph.
"Voice" and "hearers": Ref. original reading Part I at Six Gallery.

119

"Grandfathers of Kansas": General ref. mid-America; associated ref. Michael McClure, Wichita participant in "Six Poets at Six Gallery" reading. See *Scratching the Beat Surface* (San Francisco: North Point Press, 1982), pp. 11–33, for his complete account of the occasion and hindsights on the poets' texts.

120

"Bop apocalypse": "When the mode of the music changes the walls of the city shake." —Pythagoras
"Peace and junk and drums," City Lights edition, 1956, changes to "Peace peyote pipes & drums" in certain later editions: *Howl* (San Francisco: Grabhorn-Hoyem, 1971), and *Collected Poems 1947–1980* (New York: Harper & Row, 1984).

121

"Solitudes . . . cafeterias": Ref. also Lynd Ward block prints, Edward Hopper's silent night street corner café paintings.

122

"Lone juggernaut": A burgeoning military-industrial complex.
"Vast lamb of the middleclass": Ref. Dharma slogan "Regard each sentient being as a future Buddha."

* Line numbers refer to final published text (pp. 3–8).

"Who digs Los Angeles": i.e., the Angels; see William Blake's "They became what they beheld."

123

"Holy Tangiers": W. S. Burroughs' letters from Tanger to author in Bay Area 1954–56 contained major portions of *Naked Lunch*. Author had no connection to Peoria or Istanbul other than the sound of their names.

124

"Clocks in space": See note to verse 54.
"Fifth International": First International Workingman's Association, London 1864, under the leadership of Marx and Engels. Second Socialist and Labor International, Paris 1889. Third Communist International (Komintern), Zimmerwald, Switzerland, 1919. Trotskyite Fourth International, Paris, 1938. Fifth International of workers, entrepreneurs, peasants and indigenous communities of world has not yet assembled to propose survival norms in era of imperial private and state monopoly capital's near-absolute and potentially suicidal power.

126

"Charity": Rimbaud: "Charity is that key.— This inspiration proves that I have dreamed." —*A Season in Hell*.
"Ours! bodies! suffering! magnanimity!": Buddhadharma's Four Noble Truths including Eightfold Bodhisattva path, beginning with First Noble Truth of suffering, expounds the latent implication of this verse.

127

"Supernatural" here may be considered hyperbole.
Dharma equivalent of "extra brilliant intelligent kindness" is found in notion of Bodhicitta, "seed of enlightenment" or "essence of awakeness" in ordinary mind.

"*The road of excess leads to the palace of wisdom.*"
—William Blake

APPENDIXES

Bob Donlon (see Rob Donnelly, Kerouac's *Desolation Angels*), Neal Cassady, Peter Orlovsky, painter Robert La Vigne, poet-proprietor Lawrence Ferlinghetti at City Lights Bookshop, San Francisco, 1955. We were just hanging around, *Howl* book wasn't printed yet, Neal looks good, Peter 21.   *Photo by A.G.*

Appendix I
Contemporaneous Correspondence & Poetic Reactions

Response by poets and peers, author's cover letters and explanations, critical reaction, family advice and publisher's plans. (*Footnotes by Barry Miles*)

**Jack Kerouac, in Mexico City,
to Allen Ginsberg, in San Francisco***

August 19, 1955

(Summarized by A.G. in courtesy to Kerouac's family)

Kerouac wrote that my HOWL FOR CARL SOLOMON† was very powerful, but he didn't want it arbitrarily negated by secondary emendations made in time's reconsidering backstep—He wanted my LINGUAL SPONTANEITY or nothing, that went for me & Gregory Corso, he wouldn't read hackled handicapped poetry manuscripts. . . .

Said I should send some spontaneous pure poetry, ORIGINAL Ms. of "Howl" . . . and fuck Carl Solomon. He was a voyeur in the madhouse. HE WAS ALRIGHT. . . .

Said he wrote a poem dedicated to Peter Orlovsky (whoever he was) containing the following parenthesis: "(this madhouse shot of yours is not exactly the immemorial meil)" which he thought of changing to *meow*, thinking of me. . . .

And—he liked, in "Howl," "with a vision of ultimate cunt and come"—and—"waving genitals and manuscripts" (which was like my prose about Peter hitchhiking Texas with "Illuminations" under arm)—and especially he liked "died in Denver again" (I should leave his Dying Denvers) and "self delivered Truth's final lobotomy." . . .

* Abstracted from a ten-page letter.
† The ms. that A.G. sent to Kerouac consisted of the first six pages of "Howl," Part I, which A.G. had titled, in pink pencil, "Howl For Carl Solomon," presumably at the same time that he reorganized the running order of the stanzas, since the same pencil is used for both annotations. When Kerouac received the ms. he naturally referred to it in his letter using Ginsberg's title. A.G., however, had forgotten that he gave the poem a title and thought that Kerouac was suggesting the title to him, thus the reference on the dedication page: "Several phrases and the title of *Howl* are taken from him [Kerouac]." (The title could not have been added by Ginsberg at a later date because the ms., sent by Kerouac to John Clellon Holmes, did not return to Ginsberg's hands until the summer of 1980.)

**Allen Ginsberg, in San Francisco, to Jack
Kerouac, in Mexico City**

August 25, 1955

Dear Jack,
. . . The pages I sent you of Howl (right title) are the first pages put down, as is. I recopied them and sent you the 100% original draft.* There is no preexistant version. I typed it up as I went along, that's why it's so messy.

I realize how right you are, that was the first time I sat down to blow, it came out in your method, sounding like you, an imitation practically. How advanced you are on this. I don't know what I'm doing with poetry. I need years of isolation and constant everyday writing to attain your volume of freedom and knowledge of the form.

Love,
Allen

* See Kerouac's letter of September 6, 1955. Kerouac seemed to be aware that it was the original draft he had; his objection was to the fact that A.G. x-ed out words and phrases, revising during the process of composition.

**Allen Ginsberg, in San Francisco, to Jack
Kerouac, in Mexico City**

August 30, 1955

Dear Almond Crackerjack:
. . . City Lights bookstore here putting out pamphlets—50 short pages—of local poets & one of W.C. Williams reprint & one of Cummings & will put out Howl (under that title) next year, one booklet for that poem, nothing else. It will fill a booklet. . . .

Love,
Allen

**Jack Kerouac, in Mexico City,
to Allen Ginsberg, in San Francisco**

September 1-6, 1955

(Summarized by A.G. in courtesy to Kerouac's family)

J.K. wrote at beginning of September that he'd lit incense to my image and wandered into Tibetas with his incense stick and scroll. He said that I might tell Neal he'd been very high in Mexico, but he didn't come "to Mexico to cultivate sex," came to Mexico to study Madam Green and dance with Mustaphah Fustaphah Fearcrow— Result: Mexico City Blues & long short story. . . .

He said my battleship deodorants* were rather strange, like beautiful masonic rings, and that Garver noticed that line. . . .

He said that Anything is good because it is everything. And things are said in time, and time is of the essence, and when you change yr mind even for an instant and muss up with x-marks (as in "original" ms. of "Howl") you lie. He wrote that *the truth is already there*. He was not interested in what I had to hide, i.e., my "craft," he was interested in what I had to show, i.e., blow. . . .

Kerouac continued same letter September 6, reporting that Garver said I put too much homosexual material in my poems, "See what his reaction is," Garver winked.

Said my Moloch Solitude was great wild poetry—but granite phalluses & eyeless capitols with the "o" spontaneously blurt-blouted? "The whole boatload of sensitive bullshit" had that right sound of genuine eloquent raging appeal, like Jewish prophets of old.

J.K. added that his prophetic reminders were more delicate and gentle and Buddhist now. . . .

* Ref. "My Alba," *Collected Poems*, p. 89.

Allen Ginsberg, in Berkeley, California, to William Carlos Williams, in Rutherford, New Jersey

December 9, 1955

Dear Dr. Williams:

I enclose finally some of my recent work.*

Am reading Whitman through, note enclosed poem on same,† saw your essay a few days ago, you do not go far enough, look what I have done with the long line. In some of these poems it seems to answer your demand for a relatively absolute line with a fixed base, whatever it is (I am writing this in a hurry finally to get it off, have delayed far too long)—all held within the elastic of the breath, though of varying lengths. The key is in Jazz choruses to some extent; also to reliance on spontaneity & expressiveness which long line encourages; also to attention to interior unchecked logical mental stream. With a long line comes a return [to], (caused by) expressive human feeling, it's generally lacking in poetry now, which is inhuman. The release of emotion is one with rhythmical buildup of long line. The most interesting experiment here is perhaps the sort of bachlike fugue built up in part III of the poem called Howl.

This is not all I have done recently, there is one other piece which is nakeder than the rest and passed into prose,‡ I'll send that on if you're interested—also I have a whole book building up since 1951 when you last saw my work. I wish you would look at it but have not sent it on with these, is there enough time?

Enclosed poems are all from the last few months.

* Enclosed were "Howl," Part I, as of Draft 3, and early draft of Parts II and III (Ditto'd version—see note to Carr to Ginsberg letter below. Part I still had its verses in their original order and Parts II and III were much shorter than the final version. Also enclosed were "A Supermarket in California," "In the Baggage Room at Greyhound," and probably "Sunflower Sutra" and "Transcription of Organ Music."
† "A Supermarket in California."
‡ "Transcription of Organ Music."

I hope these answer somewhat what you were looking for.

As ever,
Allen

No time to write a weirder letter

[Holograph note follows as a P.S.]
The poems are arranged in chronological order to show development & uses of the line. They are best & clearest read aloud.

Lucien Carr, in New York City, to Allen Ginsberg, in Berkeley, California

February 13, 1956

Dear Allen,

. . . Thought your *Howl** very good indeed. Must be quite a spectacle to see you perform it. A considerable departure and improvement over earlier stuff. Keep it up, as we of the petit Bourgeoise say.

Lucien

* Probably the version typed by Robert Creeley, Ditto-mimeographed in 50 copies by Martha Rexroth circa May 1956 at San Francisco State College and sent to various friends.

Louis Ginsberg, in Paterson, New Jersey, to Allen Ginsberg, in Berkeley, California

February 29, 1956

Dear Allen,

. . . I am gratified about your new ms. It's a wild, rhapsodic, explosive outpouring with good figures of speech flashing by in its volcanic rushing. It's a hot geyser of emotion suddenly released in wild abandon from subterranean depths of your being. I'd like to see it in its entirety; and, moving back a bit, I'd like to discern its main outlines. I still insist, however, there is no need for dirty, ugly, words, as they will entangle you unnecessarily in trouble. Try to cut them out. . . .

Love,
Louis

William Carlos Williams, in Rutherford, New Jersey, to Allen Ginsberg, in San Francisco

March 14, 1956

Dear Allen,

I remember having spoken to Ferlinghetti telling him I would be glad to do an introduction for your book of poems and now that you have given me a chance to look at them I'll do just that. In a week or so, or just as soon as I can, I'll get to work. But if I don't like 'em I'll say so frankly—in general long poems do not appeal to me, I have a hell of a job reading them.

Best
Bill

[As a postscript]
The first look is favorable, sounds good to me, in my ears. W.

William Carlos Williams, in Rutherford, New Jersey, to Allen Ginsberg, in Berkeley, California

March 17, 1956

Dear Allen,

Flossie read it to me yesterday during the storm. It has a we[a]k spot toward the end of the first part, then it picks up again and goes on powerfully toward the end. It wouldn't be harmed by a little pruning at that point.

In general though it is the most suc[c]essful poems of yours that I have seen. You have something to say and say it supremely well. Congratulations.

Best luck
Sincerely
Bill

Allen Ginsberg, in Berkeley, California, to Louis Ginsberg, in Paterson, New Jersey

[March 1956]

Dear Louis:

. . . W.C.Williams read Howl and liked it and wrote an introduction for the book; and meanwhile there is the possibility of expanding and making a whole book of poems. . . .

English publishers wont handle Howl, that is English printers (Villiers) and so there is now difficulty in getting it through unexpurgated. I revised it and it is now worse* than it ever was, too. We're now investigating Mexico, if necessary will spend extra cost and have it done here tho. Civil Liberties Union here was consulted and said they'd defend it if it got into trouble, which I almost hope it does. I am almost ready to tackle the U.S. Govt out of sheer self delight. There is really a great stupid conspiracy of unconscious negative inertia to keep people from "expressing" themselves. I was reading Henry Miller's banned book Tropic Of Cancer, which actually is a great classic—I never heard of it at Columbia with anything but deprecatory dismissal comments—he and Genet are such frank hip writers that the open expression of their perceptions and real beliefs are a threat to society. The wonder is that literature does have so much power.

Love
Allen

* I.e., more unprintable words.

Allen Ginsberg, in San Francisco, to Jack Kerouac, in Mexico City

[May 1956]

Dear Jack,

. . . I sent copies* of Howl to T.S.Eliot, Pound, Faulkner, Van Doren, Meyer Schapiro, Eberhart, Trilling, till they were exhausted. I wonder what T.S.Eliot

will do. I wrote them each about you too. Funny letters to each. Imagine to T.S.Eliot! . . .

Allen
Love

* This refers to the mimeographed version of "Howl," not the final printed one.

Allen Ginsberg, in Berkeley, California, to Eugene Brooks, in New York City

May 18, 1956

Dear Gene:

. . . My book is being printed in England. There was a long delay while I held on to the MSS for revisions, & also I added 3 other poems. It will be quite a volume. I sent Louis a complete MSS this week. I don't know how he'll react to the wilder parts but I am very pleased with the whole deal. I have a feeling he'll be too scandalized to want the family to see it but it really is quite a high spirited & funny & serious collection of statements. I sort of feel unchallengeable on the solidity of the contents & expressions. W.C.Williams has written another introduction* and 1000 copies will be made. I'll even make a little money on it says my publisher who's so pleased he decided to give me royalties in addition to publishing it. . . .

Allen

* Williams' first introduction was to Ginsberg's 1952 collection, *Empty Mirror*, unpublished until 1961.

Allen Ginsberg, in Berkeley, California, to Richard Eberhart, in New York City

May 18, 1956

Dear Mr. Eberhart:

Kenneth Rexroth tells me you are writing an article on S.F. Poetry and asked for a copy of my MSS. I'll send it.

It occurred to me with alarm how really horrible generalizations might be if they are off-the-point as in newspapers.

I sat listening sans objection in the car while you told me what you'd said in Berkeley. I was flattered and egotistically hypnotized by the idea of recognition but really didn't agree with your evaluation of my own poetry. Before you say anything in the *Times* let me have my say.

1) The general "problem" is positive and negative "values." "You don't tell me how to live," "you deal with the negative or horrible well but have no positive program" etc.

This is absurd as it sounds.

It would be impossible to write a powerful emotional poem without a firm grasp on "value" not as an intellectual ideal but as an emotional reality.

Reprinted by permission from longer text in *To Eberhart from Ginsberg*, ed. Michael McCurdy (Great Barrington, Mass.: Penmaen Press, 1976).

You heard or saw *Howl* as a negative howl of protest.

The title notwithstanding, the poem itself is an act of sympathy, not rejection. In it I am leaping *out* of a preconceived notion of social "values," following my own heart's instincts—*allowing* myself to follow my own heart's instincts, overturning any notion of propriety, moral "value," superficial "maturity," Trilling-esque sense of "civilization," and exposing my true feelings—of sympathy and identification with the rejected, mystical, individual even "mad."

I am saying that what seems "mad" in America is our expression of natural ecstasy (as in Crane, Whitman) which suppressed, finds no social form organization background frame of reference or rapport or validation from the outside and so the "patient" gets confused thinks he is mad and really goes off rocker. I am paying homage to mystical mysteries in the forms in which they actually occur here in the U.S. in our environment.

I have taken a leap of detachment from the Artificial preoccupations and preconceptions of what is acceptable and normal and given my yea to the specific type of madness listed in the Who section.

The leap in the imagination—it is safe to do in a poem.

A leap to actual living sanctity is not impossible, but requires more time for me.

I used to think I was mad to want to be a saint, but now what have I got to fear? People's opinions? Loss of a teaching job? I am living outside this context. I make my own sanctity. How else? Suffering and humility are forced on my otherwise wild ego by lugging baggage in Greyhound.

I started as a fair-haired boy in academic Columbia.

I have discovered a great deal of my own true nature and that individuality which is a value, the only social value that there can be in the Blake-worlds. I see it as a "social value."

I have told you how to live if I have wakened any emotion of compassion and realization of the beauty of souls in America, thru the poem.

What other value could a poem have—now, historically maybe?

I have released and confessed and communicated clearly my true feelings tho it might involve at first a painful leap of exhibition and fear that I would be rejected.

This is a value, an actual fact, not a mental formulation of some second-rate sociological-moral ideal which is meaningless and academic in the poetry of H——, etc.

Howl is the first discovery as far as *communication* of feeling and truth, that I made. It begins with a catalogue sympathetically and *humanely* describing excesses of feeling and idealization.

Moloch is the vision of the mechanical feelingless inhuman world we live in and accept—and the key line finally is "Moloch whom I abandon."

It ends with a litany of active acceptance of the suffering of soul of C. Solomon, saying in effect I am *still* your amigo tho you are in trouble and think yourself in a void, and the final strophe states the terms of the communication.

"oh starry spangled shock of MERCY"

and mercy is a real thing and if that is not a value I don't know what is.

How mercy gets to exist where it comes from perhaps can be seen from the inner evidence and images of the poem—an act of self-realization, self-acceptance and the consequent and inevitable relaxation of protective anxiety and selfhood and the ability to see and love others in themselves as angels without stupid mental self deceiving moral categories selecting *who* it is safe to sympathize with and who is not safe.

See Dostoyevsky and Whitman.

* * *

Thus I fail to see why you characterize my work as destructive or negative. Only if you are thinking an outmoded dualistic puritanical academic theory ridden world of values can you fail to see I am talking about *realization* of love. LOVE.

The poems are religious and I meant them to be and the effect on audience is (surprising to me at first) a validation of this. It is like "I give the primeval sign" of Acceptance, as in Whitman.

* * *

But as to technique—[Ruth] Witt-Diamant said you were surprised I exhibited any interest in the "Line" etc.

What seems formless tho effective is really effective thru discovery or realization of rules and meanings of forms and experiments in them.

The "form" of the poem is an experiment. Experiment with uses of the catalogue, the ellipsis, the long line, the litany, repetition, etc.

The latter parts of the first section set forth a "formal" esthetic derived in part incidentally from my master who is Cezanne.

The poem is really built like a brick shithouse.

This is the general ground plan—all an accident, organic, but quite symmetrical surprisingly. It grew (part III) out of a desire to build up rhythm using a fixed base to respond to and elongating the response still however containing it within the elastic of one breath or one big streak of thought.

The Poem is really built
like a brick shithouse

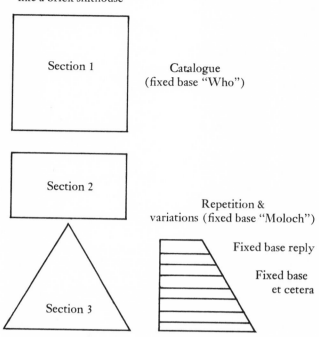

Catalogue
(fixed base "Who")

Repetition &
variations (fixed base "Moloch")

Fixed base reply

Fixed base
et cetera

This is the general ground plan—all an
accident, organic but quite symmetrical, surprisingly.

* * *

The Long Line I use came after 7 yrs. work with
fixed iambic rhyme, and 4 yrs. work with Williams' short
line free form—which as you must know has its own mad
rules—indefinable tho they be at present—

The long line, the prose poem, the spontaneous
sketch are XX century French forms which Academic
versifiers despite their continental interests (in XIX cen-
tury French "formal" forms, Baudelaire) have completely
ignored. Why?

This form of writing is very popular in S.A. and is
after all the most interesting thing happening in France.

Whitman
Apollinaire
Lorca

* * *

The long line—you need a good ear and an emotional
ground-swell and technical and syntactical ease facility
and a freedom "esprit" to deal with it and make of it any-
thing significant. And you need something to say, i.e.
clear realized feelings. Same as any free verse.

The lines are the result of long thought and experi-
ment as to what unit constitutes *one speech-breath-
thought.* . . .

We think and speak rhythmically all the time, each
phrasing, piece of speech, metrically equivalent to what
we have to say emotionally.

Given a mental release which is not mentally blocked,
the breath of verbal intercourse will come with excellent
rhythm, a rhythm which is perhaps unimprovable.

* * *

Since each wave of speech-thought needs to be mea-
sured (we speak and perhaps think in waves)—or what I
speak and think I have at any rate in *Howl* reduced to
waves of relatively equally heavy weight—and set next
to one another they are in a balance O.K.

The technique of writing both prose and poetry, the
technical problem of the present day, is the problem of
Transcription of the natural flow of the mind, the tran-
scription of the melody of actual thought or speech.

I have leaned more toward capturing the inside-
mind-thought rather than the verbalized speech. This
distinction I make because most poets see the problem
via Wordsworth as getting nearer to actual *speech*, verbal
speech.

I have noticed that the unspoken visual-verbal flow
inside the mind has great rhythm and have approached
the problem of Strophe, Line and stanza and measure by
listening and transcribing (to a great extent) the coherent
mental flow. Taking *that* for the model for Form as
Cezanne took Nature.

This is not surrealism—they made up an artificial
literary imitation.

I transcribe from my ordinary thoughts—waiting for
extra exciting or mystical moments or near mystical mo-
ments to transcribe.

This brings up problems of image, and transcription
of mental flow gives helpful knowledge because we think
in sort of surrealist (juxtaposed images) or haiku-like
form.

A haiku as the 1910–20's imagists did *not* know, con-
sists of 2 visual (or otherwise) images stripped down and
juxtaposed—the charge of electricity created by these 2
poles being greater when there is a greater distance be-
tween them—as in Yeats' phrase "murderous innocence
of the sea"—2 opposite poles reconciled in a flash of
recognition.

The mind in its flow creates such fantastic ellipses
thus the key phrase of method in *Howl* is "Hydrogen
Jukebox" which tho quite senseless makes in context
clear sense. . . .

* * *

. . . So anybody who wants to hang on to traditional
metrics and values will wind up stultified and self-
deceived anyway despite all the sincerity in the world.

Everybody thinks they should learn academically from "experience" and have their souls put down and destroyed and this has been raised to the status of "value" but to me it seems just the usual old fake death, caused by fear and lack of real experience. I suffered too much under Professor Trilling, whom I love, but who is a poor mental fanatic after all and not a free soul—I'm straying.

* * *

I've said nothing about the extraordinary influence of Bop music on rhythm and drugs on the observation of rhythm and mental processes—not enough time and out of paper.

* * *

Summary

I. VALUES

Howl is an "affirmation" of individual experience of God, sex, drugs, absurdity etc. Part I deals sympathetically with individual cases. Part II describes and rejects the Moloch of society which confounds and suppresses individual experience and forces the individual to consider himself mad if he does not reject his own deepest senses. Part III is an expression of sympathy and identification with C.S. who is in the madhouse—saying that his madness basically is rebellion against Moloch and I am with him, and extending my hand in union. This is an affirmative act of mercy and compassion, which are the basic emotions of the poem. The criticism of society is that "Society" is merciless. The alternative is private, individual acts of mercy. The poem is one such. It is therefore clearly and consciously built on a *liberation* of basic human virtues.

To call it work of nihilistic rebellion would be to mistake it completely. Its force comes from positive "religious" belief and experience. It offers no "constructive" program in sociological terms—no poem could. It does offer a constructive human value—basically the *experience*—of the enlightment of mystical experience—without which no society can long exist.

* * *

II. TECHNIQUE

A. These long lines or Strophes as I call them came spontaneously as a result of the kind of feelings I was trying to put down, and came as a surprise solution to a metrical problem that preoccupied me for a decade.

I have considerable experience writing both rhymed iambics and short line Post-W.C.W. free verse.

Howl's 3 parts consist of 3 different approaches to the use of the long line (longer than Whitman's, more French).

1. Repetition of the fixed base "Who" for a catalogue.

A. building up consecutive rhythm from strophe to strophe.

B. abandoning of fixed base "who" in certain lines but carrying weight and rhythm of strophic form continuously forward.

2. Break up of strophe into pieces within the strophe, thus having the strophe become a new usable form of stanza—Repetition of fixed base "Moloch" to provide cement for continuity. *Supermarket* uses strophe stanza and abandons need for fixed base. I was experimenting with the form.

3. Use of a fixed base, "I'm with you in Rockland," with a reply in which the strophe becomes a longer and longer streak of speech, in order to build up a *relatively* equal nonetheless free and variable structure. Each reply strophe is longer than the previous. I have measured by ear and speech-breath, there being no other measure for such a thing. Each strophe consists of a set of phrases that can be spoken in one breath and each carries relatively equal rhetorical weight. Penultimate strophe is an exception and was meant to be—a series of cries—"O skinny legions run outside O starry spangled shock of mercy O victory etc." You will not fail to observe that the cries are all in definite rhythm.

The technical problem raised and partially solved is the break-through begun by Whitman but never carried forward, from both iambic stultification and literary automatism, and unrhythmical short-line verse, which does not yet offer any kind of *base* cyclical flow for the build up of a powerful rhythm. The long line seems for the moment to free speech for emotional expression and give it a measure to work with. I hope to experiment with short-line free verse with what I have learned from exercise in long.

B. Imagery—is a result of the *kind* of line and the kind of emotions and the kind of speech-and-interior flow-of-the-mind transcription I am doing—the imagery often consists of 1920's W.C.W. imagistically observed detail collapsed together by interior associative logic—i.e., "hydrogen jukebox," Apollinaire, Whitman, Lorca. But *not* automatic surrealism. Knowledge of Haiku and ellipsis is crucial.

Yours
Allen Ginsberg

Richard Eberhart, from "West Coast Rhythms"

The West Coast is the liveliest spot in the country in poetry today. It is only here that there is a radical group movement of young poets. San Francisco teems with young poets.

Reprinted from *New York Times Book Review*, September 2, 1956.

Part of this activity is due to the establishment of the Poetry Center at San Francisco State College three years ago. Its originator and moving spirit is Ruth Witt-Diamant, who began by offering readings by local poets and progressed to importing older poets from the East. She hopes next to stimulate the writing of verse drama.

Part of the activity of the young group has been inspired by Kenneth Rexroth, whose presence in San Francisco over a long period of time, embodying his force and convictions, creates a rallying point of ideas, interest and informal occasions. The influence of Kenneth Patchen is also felt by this group. Robinson Jeffers looms as a timeless figure down the Coast. . . .

In the Bay region there are several poetry readings each week. They may be called at the drop of a hat. A card may read "Celebrated Good Time Poetry Night. Either you go home bugged or completely enlightened. Allen Ginsberg blowing hot; Gary Snyder blowing cool; Philip Whalen puffing the laconic tuba; Mike McClure his hip highnotes; Rexroth on the big bass drum. Small collection for wine and postcards . . . abandon, noise, strange pictures on walls, oriental music, lurid poetry. Extremely serious. Town Hall theatre. One and only final appearance of this apocalypse. Admission free."*

Hundreds from about 16 to 30 may show up and engage in an authentic, free-wheeling celebration of poetry, an analogue of which was jazz thirty years ago. The audience participates, shouting and stamping, interrupting and applauding. Poetry here has become a tangible social force, moving and unifying its auditors, releasing the energies of the audience through spoken, even shouted verse, in a way at present unique to this region. . . .

The most remarkable poem of the young group, written during the past year, is "Howl," by Allen Ginsberg, a 29-year-old poet who is the son of Louis Ginsberg, a poet known to newspaper readers in the East. Ginsberg comes from Brooklyn; he studied at Columbia; after years of apprenticeship to usual forms, he developed his brave new medium. This poem has created a furor of praise or abuse whenever read or heard. It is a powerful work, cutting through to dynamic meaning. Ginsberg thinks he is going forward by going back to the methods of Whitman.

My first reaction was that it is based on destructive violence. It is profoundly Jewish in temper. It is Biblical in its repetitive grammatical build-up. It is a howl against everything in our mechanistic civilization which kills the spirit, assuming that the louder you shout the more likely you are to be heard. It lays bare the nerves of suffering and spiritual struggle. Its positive force and energy come from a redemptive quality of love, although it destructively catalogues evils of our time from physical deprivation to madness.

In other poems, Ginsberg shows a crucial sense of humor. It shows up principally in his poem "America," which has lines "Asia is rising against me./ I haven't got

a Chinaman's chance." Humor is also present in "Supermarket in California." His "Sunflower Sutra" is a lyric poem marked by pathos.

Lawrence Ferlinghetti is the publisher of the Pocket Poet Series from his bookshop in San Francisco, the City Lights Pocket Bookshop. . . .

In this series Ferlinghetti's "Pictures of the Gone World" offers his own poetry in a flowing variety of open-running lines. He develops a personal, ritual anecdote as a fresh type of recognition, with acute visual perceptions. He seems to have learned something from James Laughlin. His work measures a racy young maturity of experience. . . .

Of the still bookless poets, Philip Whalen has somewhat Poundian poems and a highly successful refrain "Love You" in a direct and forceful poem entitled "3 Variations: All About Love." Gary Snyder's poetry is most like Rexroth's, not due so much to direct influence as to identity of sources. Both owe much to Far Eastern verse and philosophy, both are deeply bound into the natural world of stars, birds, mountains and flowers. Michael McClure writes with grace and charm on "For the Death of 100 Whales" and "Point Lobos: Animism," striving for "The rising, the exuberance, when the mystery is unveiled." . . .

It is certain that there is a new, vital group consciousness now among young poets in the Bay region. However unpublished they may be, many of these young poets have a numerous and enthusiastic audience. They acquire this audience by their own efforts. Through their many readings they have in some cases a larger audience than more cautiously presented poets in the East.

They are finely alive, they believe something new can be done with the art of poetry, they are hostile to gloomy critics, and the reader is invited to look into and enjoy their work as it appears. They have exuberance and a young will to kick down the doors of older consciousness and established practice in favor of what they think is vital and new.

Allen Ginsberg, on board USNS *Pvt. Joseph F. Merrell*, T-AKV-4 (c/o Fleet Post Office, San Francisco), to Lionel Trilling, in New York City

[May 1956]

Dear Lionel:

Enclosed find the ditto mss. of a pamphlet of poems I have being printed here. They are natural developments of the method & practice I was pursuing about 5 years ago. There seems to have been enuf mercy around to get me to heaven anyway, no?

Let me know what you think of them. I can't really imagine what your reaction should be, and I'm interested.

Though my tastes at school were not so, I'm reading a lot of Lorca, Apollinaire, Crane, Thomas—and Whitman. He is a mountain too vast to be seen. Nobody still

* This was text of postcard invitation to Berkeley encore of Six Gallery poetry reading, November 1955.

understands him despite the recent books which were just vain and inept, tho sincere.

I had the experience of teaching a term poetry writing at SF State Coll., guest gorilla, I am a really good teacher, naked half the time with big blue flashes of communication. I read them Whitman aloud. If you read him aloud with understanding and some personal passion he comes on what he's supposed to, near saint. Anybody can understand.

Charles Olson is a good poet, Black Mountain now an, the only, Eastern center of real poetic discipline, i.e. freedom. His poem the Death of Europe in a recent Origin Magazine issue is my specimen for this conclusion. If you get to see it, worth while.

I think what is coming is a romantic period (strangely tho everybody thinks that by being hard-up and classical they are going to make it like Eliot which is silly). Eliot & Pound are like Dryden & Pope. What gives now is much more personal—how could there be now anything but a reassertion of naked personal subjective truth—eternally real? Perhaps Whitman will be seen to have set the example and been bypassed for half a century.

There are several good unknown Zen poets out hear (here) two to be exact whose learning and wild accomplishment put to shame anything I heard of in the East. This is an amazing situation.

I'm leaving in two weeks to the Arctic to rhapsodize over icebergs & get $$ to visit Europe in the winter coming. Perhaps I'll see you in NYC then. Please write, let me know what you think of the poems. Mail will be forwarded north.

As ever,
Allen

Kerouac's here too, big genius.

If you like these poems see what you can do to have them reviewed because in normal run of things they likely will not be.

Lionel Trilling, in New York City, to Allen Ginsberg, on board USNS *Pvt. Joseph F. Merrell*

May 29, 1956

Dear Allen,

I'm afraid I have to tell you that I don't like the poems at all. I hesitate before saying that they seem to me quite dull, for to say of a work which undertakes to be violent and shocking that it is dull is, I am aware, a well known and all too easy device. But perhaps you will believe that I am being sincere when I say they are dull. They are not like Whitman—they are all prose, all rhetoric, without any music. What I used to like in your poems, whether I thought they were good or bad, was the *voice* I heard in them, true and natural and interesting. There is no real voice here. As for the doctrinal element of the poems, apart from the fact that I of course

reject it, it seems to me that I heard it very long ago and that you give it to me in all its orthodoxy, with nothing new added.

Sincerely yours,
Lionel Trilling

Naomi Ginsberg, in Pilgrim State Hospital, New York, to Allen Ginsberg, in Berkeley, California

[postmarked] *June 11, 1956**

Dear Allen,

I hope this reaches you. I sent one before which, maybe, they didn't send out!

Congratulations on your birthday!† Received your poetry‡ I'd like to send it to Louis for criticism. Now what does he think of it! It seemed to me your wording was a little too hard. Do tell me what father thinks of it. You know you have to have a job to get married. I wish you did have a good job. What did you specialise in when you went to college. This going to the North Pole, who supplies the wearing material? They say when you visit the Eskimos you need a double coat of fur. Are you fit for that flying job? Don't take chances with your life! I wish you get married. Do you like farming? Its as good a job as any.

I hope you behave well. Don't go in for too much drink and other things that are not good for you. Eugene and his wife visited me. They expected a child then. I suppose they have it by this time.

I do hope you can get a good job so you can get a girl to get married. Eugene's wife is beautiful.

As for myself. I still have the wire on my head. The doctors know about it. They are cutting the flesh and bone. They are giving me teethache. I do wish you were back east so I could see you. I met Max's§ daughter, she is charming and married. I am glad you are having your poetry published. I wish I were out of here and home at the time you were young; then I would be young. I'm in the prime of life now— Did you read about the two men who died at 139 & 149 yrs of age. I wonder how they lived. I'm looking for a good time.

I hope you are not taking drugs as suggested by your poetry. That would hurt me. Don't go in for ridiculous things. With love & good news (mother)

Naomi

---

* Naomi Ginsberg died on June 9, 1956, two days before the hospital mailed her letter, written on the eve of her death. The letter was received by Ginsberg days after the news of her death had reached him. See his account in "Kaddish," *Collected Poems*, p. 224.

† Allen Ginsberg was thirty on June 3, 1956.

‡ The poetry she referred to was the Ditto'd version of "Howl."

§ Max was Naomi's brother.

Allen Ginsberg, on board USNS *Pvt. Joseph F. Merrell*
(mailed San Francisco), to Ezra Pound,
in St. Elizabeths Hospital, Washington, D.C.

[Early June 1956]

Dear Mr. Pound:

Please READ at least 1 page of the enclosed mss. Or 1 line for that matter so long as you can judge the rhythm.

These are all l-o-n-g lines, used in various ways. I don't think nobody's tried this this way.

Williams wrote an introduction, it will be published by City Lights in SF sometime in July.

I know you are fatigued but I am sending you a gift. I am not a Greek. . . .

Please let me know how the poems strike or affect you.

> As ever,
> Allen Ginsberg

[Pound did not reply but instead forwarded Ginsberg's letter to William Carlos Williams with note typed on verso.]

Ezra Pound, in St. Elizabeths Hospital,
Washington, D.C., to William Carlos Williams,
in Rutherford, New Jersey

[June 1956]

You got more room in yr/ house than I hv/ in my
   cubicle
If he's yours why dont yu teach him the value of time
   to those who want to
read something that wil tell 'em wot they dont know

Allen Ginsberg, on board USNS *Pvt. Joseph F. Merrell*
(mailed San Francisco), to William Carlos Williams,
in Rutherford, New Jersey

[Early June 1956]

Dear Dr. Williams:

Thanks for your introduction. The book is over in England being printed, and will be out in July sometime. Your foreword is personal and compassionate and you see the point of what has happened. You should see what strength & gaiety there is beyond that though.

The book will contain 3 shorter poems too, written subsequent to Howl:

> Supermarket in California—a homage to Whitman
> Sunflower Sutra—declaration of the experience of
>   happy real mercy
> America—make of it what you can.

I have never been interested in writing except for the splendor of actual experience etc. bullshit, I mean I've never been really crazy, confused at times.

Here are these poems, more long lines, used in different ways, experiments. . . .

> Adios.
> Allen Ginsberg

IF YOU DONT HAVE TIME FOR ANYTHING ELSE PLEASE READ ENCLOSED SUNFLOWER SUTRA

[A much longer excerpt from this letter may be found incorporated by William Carlos Williams into Book Five, *Paterson*, with Ginsberg's signature reduced to initials.]

Allen Ginsberg, on board USNS *Sgt. Jack J. Pendleton*,
T-AKV-5, docked in Seattle, to Lawrence Ferlinghetti,
in San Francisco

June 22, 1956

Dear Larry:

Well what news? I am in Seattle, will be here over weekend and thru next Friday, will return to SF next weekend for a few days—arrive sometime Sunday I expect, around the 30th or 31st. If therefore you got or will get proofs hold on to them, I'll look them over myself.

Generally speaking the Greyhound poem* stinks on ice, at least the end does—that wont last no 1000 years—I had a night mare about it standing on the prow several days ago. I dunno what to do, havn't written anything better on it since leaving town. Maybe later. . . .

> As ever,
> Allen

* "In the Baggage Room at Greyhound."

Allen Ginsberg, on board USNS *Sgt. Jack J. Pendleton*
at sea (mail collected by tender),
to Lawrence Ferlinghetti, in San Francisco

July 3, 1956

Dear Larry:

This being my first book I want it right if I can. Therefore I thought and decided this, about the justifications, of margins. (The reason for my being particular is that the poems are actually sloppy enough written, without sloppiness made worse by typographical arrangement. The one element of order & prearrangement I did pay care to was arrangement into prose-paragraph strophes: each one definite unified long line. So any doubt about irregularity of right hand margin will be sure to confuse critical reader about intention of the prosody. Therefore I've got to change it so it's right.)

It looks like the whole book will have to be reset practically. Find out how much it costs to reset the first proofs we received, which is my fault for not having followed precisely thru and made sure in advance it was understood. I will pay that no matter how much up to $200.00, which I guess it may well cost. For the material they received subsequent to the first proofs, that's their look-to, I think. Can we get them to change that on their own? . . .

Allen

Allen Ginsberg, on board USNS *Sgt. Jack J. Pendleton* at sea, to Eugene Brooks, in New York City

July 10, 1956

Dear Gene,

. . . Got proofs of my book from England and they were set up all wrong, so there'll be a further delay till suppose after summer. The lines were printed wrong due to my negligence & publisher here negligence in instructing printer to line it up like prose, each long line, and make even margin on right hand. As result lines chopped off in middle. So decided it was worth my paying to get right. It will probably set me back $90.00 or so. I didn't want the City Lights man to have the burden, he's putting out as much as he can anyway to have it published without me being finicky about how it is set in type. I instructed him when the bill for the extra work comes to send it to you. He'll give you instructions where to send the money. Withdraw whatever is needed from the amounts I've been sending you. His name is Lawrence Ferlinghetti. He'll write you. Probably next month you'll get this. Letter then will explain what to do. Hate to put out gold like that but I want to get the book right, the writing is sloppy enough as it is without it being fouled up typographically too. There seems to have been room for a lot more writing than anticipated so (for 50 pages) I added a few earlier poems at the end as an appendix. It'll be quite a book. Williams introduction is weird. He don't remember much, talks about how he used to know me "after the first world war."* But he understands the poem and sympathizes. I mean I always thought of that piece of writing (Howl) as an energetic & healthy & rather affirmative & compassionate yell dispite the surface rusty machinery & suicides it is littered with, and he got that point immediately and dug it as the base of the poem. This was gratifying & somewhat of a relief as all I heard from Eberhart & Univ. types & Trilling by implication was a lot of selfsatisfied talk about how I seemed to dwell exclusively on negative protest. Williams is goodhearted and knows his way around the soul. . . .

Love to everybody, send this letter to Louis.

Allen

* "He was physically slight of build and mentally much disturbed by the life which he had encountered about him during those first years after the first world war as it was exhibited to him in and about New York City." Williams, in his introduction, clearly meant to say the Second World War.

Allen Ginsberg, on board USNS *Sgt. Jack J. Pendleton*, docked in Seattle, to Lawrence Ferlinghetti, in San Francisco

[July 1956, second visit to Seattle prior to Arctic voyage]

Dear Lawrence:

I have not yet had time to put together another copy of the mailing list I spoke of but will in a week or so after we sail, and will mail it then, you'll have it in time.

Enclosed please find a note to my brother,
Eugene Brooks
505 West 125 Street
New York City

When the bill comes for the changes I ordered and said I would pay for, send it on to him with instructions how and where to pay it, whether to send you a check or else to Villiers directly, whatever way is most convenient or efficient for you to handle it. In any case send him instructions what to do. He has my money in the bank. If any legal problems rise up to bug us also, consult him, as he is an attorney-at-law. I have already written him of this arrangement, about paying for changes, etc. so he will wait to hear from you.

. . . I leave here in 3 days (Friday or Saturday) (from here, is Seattle) finally for Arctic. Sorry I wasn't able to be around for final OK on proofs so I guess you'll have to read them. Please see that they are alright finally as to the margins.

. . . Drop me a line and let me know what's happening with the book—send me a card for sure when you see the proofs and tell me if it came out alright.

As ever,
Allen

Allen Ginsberg, on board USNS *Sgt. Jack J. Pendleton* at sea, to Lawrence Ferlinghetti, in San Francisco

August 9, 1956 [dated July 9, 1956]

Dear Larry,

Received the copy of the book you sent me promptly—and was excited to see it. Everything worked out fine with the typography—it looks much better this way & it seems to have been real cheap to do—$20. is nuthin. I shuddered when I read the poetry tho, it all seems so jerry-built sloppy and egocentric, most of it. *Greyhound* looks fine, I'm glad you told me to put it in. Reading it all through I'm not sure it deserves all the care & work you've put into it and the encouragement you've given me in fact to tell you the truth I am already embarrassed by half of it but what the hell, thankyou anyway for all your courtesy and I hope few people will see it with such jaded eyes as I do, tho I guess it's best the poems have a truthful fate than an oversympathetic one. I wonder if we will actually sell the thousand copies. . . .

Allen

Louis Ginsberg, in Paterson, New Jersey, to Allen Ginsberg, in Berkeley, California

September 13, 1956

Dear Allen,

. . . I was happy to see it.* Edith† keeps a copy in her purse and shows it to all and sundry. I have passed it around the Newark folks. I rejoice that your book is coming out. I predict it will make a name for you. You may wake up some morning and find yourself famous. I do hope so.

Love
Your father,
Louis

* "West Coast Rhythms," Richard Eberhart's article on the San Francisco Poetry Renaissance in *New York Times Book Review* (see p. 154).
† Edith Ginsberg, the author's stepmother.

Lucien Carr, in New York City, to Allen Ginsberg, in Berkeley, California

September 21, 1956

Dear Allen,

Received copy of Howl (Library of Congress Catalog Card Number: 56—8587) today and was most buoyed up by your fine success. I thought America was about the funniest poem I had ever read & quite penetratingly to the point.

It is very impressive to see the name of Ginsberg on the list with Ferlinghetti, Rexroth and Patchen (who the hell is Ferlinghetti?).

As you might expect I have one small gripe. I was touched at being included in your dedication.*But I value a certain anonymity in life and it always jars me when my friends, of all people, find it desirable to include mention of me in their works—dedication page as well as text. I hope you bear that idiosyncrasy in mind in your next book—"Moan"

It's a small matter
The book is very impressive.

Lucien

*   DEDICATION
To—
Jack Kerouac, new Buddha of American prose, who spit forth intelligence into eleven books written in half the number of years (1951-1956)—*On the Road, Visions of Neal, Dr Sax, Springtime Mary, The Subterraneans, San Francisco Blues, Some of the Dharma, Book of Dreams, Wake Up, Mexico City Blues,* and *Visions of Gerard*—creating a spontaneous bop prosody and original classic literature. Several phrases and the title of *Howl* are taken from him.
William Seward Burroughs, author of *Naked Lunch,* an endless novel which will drive everybody mad.
Neal Cassady, author of *The First Third,* an autobiography (1949) which enlightened Buddha. All these books are published in Heaven.
Lucien Carr, recently promoted to Night Bureau Manager of New York United Press.

Gary Snyder, in Kyoto, to Allen Ginsberg, in Berkeley, California

October 12, 1956

Dear Allen,

Four copies of *Howl* I ordered from Ferlinghetti came this week, I am carefully figgering where to plant these bombs. It looks real nice & I can't read it without yr voice ringing in my ears & a vision of your navy sweater & Levis & wine & frosty weather outside like in the Northwest. . . .

Gary

Allen Ginsberg, in San Francisco, to Jack Kerouac, in Mexico City

[Fall 1956]

Dear Jack,

. . . Beginning to get long admiring letters from starry-eyed Parkinson & N.Y. types about Howl. Did you see the N.Y. Times Sept 2 article—I don't remember. . . . Agh! I'm sick of the whole thing, that's all I think about, famous authorhood, like a happy empty dream. W.C.Williams wrote he dug it & read it to "young artists" in N.Y. & they were excited & "Up their alley" and ordered 5 copies extra to pass around to the young. How beautiful, tho. I guess I really feel good about it. It's assuming proportions of an "it" in my life. . . .

Allen

Allen Ginsberg, in Paterson, New Jersey, to Lawrence Ferlinghetti, in San Francisco

December 20, 1956

Dear Larry:

. . . Went to N.Y.Times and bearded them for a review, got interviewed by Harvey Breit, and will, I think, get Howl reviewed there. Few stores carry City Lights, generally unobtainable unless you know where, but one review in Times or Trib or Sat Review could break the ice maybe. . . .

Allen

Lawrence Ferlinghetti, in San Francisco, to Allen Ginsberg, in Tanger, Morocco

February 1957

dear allen . . . the hell with contracts. . . . we will just tell them you have standing agreement with me and you can give me anything you feel like giving me on reprints whenever you get back to States and sit in Poetry Chairs in hinterland CCNYs and are rich and famous and fat and fucking your admirers and getting reprinted in all of seldenrod-man's anthologias, until then, natch, the loot shud be yurs since as you say i am getting famous as your publisher anyway. . . . Do you want more HOWLs and other P[ocket]P[oets] sent now (which ones?) and charged against you? How many? . . . Am still reading Kerouac's poetry woiks and will be at it for some time yet. . . . Max Weiss at Fantasy here is already to do HOWL recording. . . . He is great and honest. He will probably want contract and will send. (Re contracts, you see whut happens after one week in NY—I am talking just like all the other literary detectives there before i leave—contractscontractscontracts . . . well fuckem and fuck the partisanreview whom i've never sent anything to and we'll make it here in sf* . . . OK? G'bye . . .

larry

* San Francisco.

Lucien Carr, in New York City, to Allen Ginsberg, in Tanger, Morocco

April 24, 1957

Dear Allen,
    . . . Trust you'll see to it that one little change will be made to delete self from front page.*

Lucien

* Ferlinghetti had already received an advance bound copy of the second edition. Unbound sheets containing the dedication page were replaced, with Carr's name deleted, at a cost to Ginsberg of $25.

Allen Ginsberg, in Tanger, Morocco, to Lawrence Ferlinghetti, in San Francisco

[June 1957]

. . . Received your letter today with clippings. I guess this is more serious than the customs seizure since you can lose real money on this deal if they find you guilty. What does it look like? I guess with the ACLU it should be possible to beat—except this is local law—does that give police complete discretion to decide what's obscene? If so, that may make it difficult. . . . Presumably a matter of local politics—therefore can anything be done to call off police through politicians at City Hall thru state college thru Poetry Center thru Witt Diamant? If it is a matter of purely local law & juvenile bureau, perhaps somebody at Berkeley & State Coll . . . but arrest and formal charges have been filed already, so I guess open showdown is inevitable.

Lawrence Ferlinghetti, in San Francisco, to Allen Ginsberg, in Paris

September 17, 1957

Dear Allen . . . Got your last and guess you are now in Paris. I am working on Gregory's book right now, and he agrees with me that you shud do Introduction. . . . I've just sent you, by surface mail, a copy of the Fourth Printing of HOWL. The LIFE article on Sept 9, with your pict, is causing the national distributor to take two or three hundred copies a week . . . though this probably won't keep up indefinitely! *Time* article, on general scene

Peter Orlovsky, Jack Kerouac & William S. Burroughs, Tanger Beach, Morocco, Summer 1957. J.K. & author typing *Naked Lunch* drafts, *Howl* trial had commenced in San Francisco.   *Photo by A.G.*

here, is due out in another week. . . . Have you seen any of the articles on the trial, except what I sent? Am saving clips so you can go over them when you hit town again. . . . On other matters, please let me know if Villiers ever sent HOWL to your father. . . . If not, I'll send them from here. . . . Trial is not over yet—we're in court again this Thursday. . . . Yes, wd like to see mss by Kerouac, Burroughs. . . . Typos in HOWL can't be changed now, without much expense, since photo offset plates are 16 pages to one plate, and one change means 16 pages redone. . . . (I found one typo—"solipisims"—which slipped thru all these printings)—Question of Fucked in the Ass not yet settled in court—so had to let that stand again. . . . Got to go. . . . when you gonna see gregory. . . . his book's going to be great. . . .

larry

Lawrence Ferlinghetti, in San Francisco, to Allen Ginsberg, in Paris

September 28, 1957

Dear Allen . . . Will send you clips on final action on HOWL trial next week, when judge brings in his written decision and opinion. I am writing it up for next issue of EVERGREEN, per request of Don Allen. . . .

LF

Carl Solomon, in New York City, to Allen Ginsberg, in Paris

December 29, 1957

Dear Allen,

. . . By the way, my profound thanks for the sentiments expressed in "Howl," an excellent piece of writing and just to my taste.

Your friend
Carl

John Hollander, Review of *Howl and Other Poems*

It is only fair to Allen Ginsberg . . . to remark on the utter lack of decorum of any kind in his dreadful little volume. I believe that the title of his long poem, "Howl," is meant to be a noun, but I can't help taking it as an imperative. The poem itself is a confession of the poet's faith, done into some 112 paragraphlike lines, in the ravings of a lunatic friend (to whom it is dedicated), and in the irregularities in the lives of those of his friends who populate his rather disturbed pantheon. Here is the poem's beginning:

Reprinted from *Partisan Review*, Spring 1957.

"I saw the best minds of my generation destroyed by
    madness, starving hysterical naked,
dragging themselves through the negro streets at dawn
    looking for an angry fix . . ."

This continues, sponging on one's toleration, for pages and pages. A kind of climax was reached, for me, in a long section of screams about "Moloch!", at a rare point of self-referential lucidity: "Dreams! adorations! illuminations! religions! the whole boatload of sensitive bullshit!" *Howl* seems to have emerged under the influence of a kind of literary *Festspiel* held at frequent intervals on the West Coast, in the course of which various poets, "with radiant cool eyes," undoubtedly, read their works before audiences of writhing and adoring youths. "Howl" and the other longer poems in this book, including "America," "Sunflower Sutra," "In the Baggage Room at Greyhound" and some dismal pastiches of William Carlos Williams (who wrote a brief reminiscence of the poet to introduce this volume), all proclaim, in a hopped-up and improvised tone, that nothing seems to be worth saying save in a hopped-up and improvised tone. There are also avowed post-Poundian pacts with Walt Whitman and Apollinaire, and perhaps an unacknowledged one with Lautréamont. I don't know; Mr. Ginsberg prefaces *Howl* with a long dedication to some of his fellow-writers that reads just like his poems ("To . . . William Seward Burroughs, author of *Naked Lunch*, an endless novel which will drive everybody mad"), and in the book he alludes to a "spontaneous bop prosody." Perhaps this is as good a characterization of his work as any.

I have spent this much time on a very short and very tiresome book for two reasons. The first of these is involved with the fact that Mr. Ginsberg and his circle are being given a certain amount of touting by those who disapprove of what Horace Gregory, writing in these pages last fall, christened "The Poetry of Suburbia." If it turns out to be to anybody's profit, I shouldn't be a bit surprised if *Howl* and its eventual progeny were accorded some milder version of the celebration Colin Wilson has received in England. This may not be a real danger, however. If it suddenly appeared that there were no possible worlds between suburbia and subterranea, I expect most of us would go underground. But this is not quite yet the case, and the publicity seems regrettable, in view of the fact (my second reason for dealing with him here) that Allen Ginsberg has a real talent and a marvelous ear. It shows up in some of the funniest and most grotesque lines of "Howl," and even without knowing his profound and carefully organized earlier writing (unpublished in book form), one might suspect a good poet lurking behind the modish facade of a frantic and *talentlos* avant-garde.

In *On the Poetry of Allen Ginsberg*,

ed. Lewis Hyde
(Ann Arbor: University of Michigan Press, 1984),
John Hollander attached a rider to the reprint
of his 1957 review.

Addendum (February 1984)

This review was written in my youth and in a sort of worked-up high dudgeon which echoed the high-camp-prophetic mode of *Howl*'s front matter, and which may have masked some of my disappointment in a turn I saw an old friend and poetic mentor to have taken. I only regret now that I hadn't given "America" and "In a Supermarket in California" time to register; I should have certainly commended them. As for not foreseeing that Allen Ginsberg would provide so much hymnody and doctrine to the counterculture which was soon to emerge, I have no regrets, having no stake in prophecy.

Allen Ginsberg, in New York City, to John Hollander [in Cambridge, Mass.?]

September 7, 1958

Dear John:

Got your letter, slow answering . . . It's just that I've tried to do too much explaining & get overwhelmed by the vastness of the task, & sometimes what seems to be all the accumulated ill-will & evil vibrations in America (Kerouac got beaten up at the San Remo for his trouble in coming down there & making himself available.) But to begin somewhere, I should might begin with one thing, simple (I hate to go back to it over & over, like revolving around my corpse, the construction of Howl.) This may be corny to you, my concern with that, but I've got to begin somewhere & perhaps differences of opinion between us can be resolved by looking at that. See, for years before that, thinking in Williams line, which I found very helpful & quite real for what it is doing, the balance by ear of short lines formed of relatively natural ordinary notebook or conversation speech. Xbalba* is fragments of mostly prose, written in a mexican school copybook, over half a year—then re-reading, picking out the purest thoughts, stringing them together, arranging them in lines suitably balanced—mostly measured by the phrase—, that is one phrase a line—you know it's hard to explain this because it's like painting and unless you do it like practicing a piano, you don't think in those terms & get the experience of trying to work that way, so you don't notice all the specific tricks—that anyone who works in that field gets to be familiar with—that's why I'm interested in Blackburn, Levertov, Creeley, Oppenheimer, all the Black Mt people—they work steadily consistently trying to develop this line of goods, and each has a different interesting approach—they all stem out of Williams—but I can tell their lines apart they really are different—just as you can tell the difference between styles & approaches of abstract painters. When you tell me it's [the work of above-named writers] just a bore to you, that just cuts off communication, I mean I don't know what to say, I get embarrassed I feel you're being arbitrary & stubborn, it's some sort of ploy, & I just want to retreat & go about my work and stop explanations. Of course you may not be interested in this field of experiment, but that doesn't mean it's uninteresting to others, that it's categorically a bore. I *also* believe it's the main "tradition," not that there is any tradition except what we make ourselves. But basically I'm not interested in tradition because I'm more interested in what I'm doing, what it's inevitable for me to do. This realization has given me perspective on what a vast sad camp the whole literary-critical approach of School [Columbia College] has been—basically no one has insight into poetry techniques except people who are exercising them. But I'm straying at random. But I'm now getting bugged at people setting themselves up as scholars and authorities and *getting in the way* of continued creative work or its understanding or circulation—there is not one article on the Beat or SF scene yet that has not been (pro or con) invalidated (including yours) by the basic fact that the author is just a big windbag not knowing what he's talking about—no technical background, no knowledge of the vast body of experimental work, published and unpublished (the unpublished is the best), no clear grasp of the various different schools of experiment all converging toward the same or similar end, all at once coming into intercommunication, no knowledge of the letters and conversations in between, not even the basic ability (like Podhoretz) to tell the difference between prosody and diction (as in his *PR** diatribes on spontaneous bop prosody confusing it with the use of hiptalk not realizing it refers to rhythmical construction of phrases & sentences.) I mean where am I going to begin a serious explanation if I have to deal with such unmitigated stupid ignorant ill willed inept vanity as that—someone like that wouldn't listen unless you hit him over the head with a totally new universe, but he's stuck in his own hideous world, I would try, but he scarcely has enough heart to hear)—etc etc—so all these objections about juvenile delinquency, vulgarity, lack of basic education, bad taste, etc etc, no form, etc I mean it's impossible to discuss things like that—finally I get to see them as so basically *wrong* (unscientific) so dependent on ridiculous provincial schoolboy ambitions & presuppositions and so lacking contact with practical fact—that it seems a sort of plot almost, a kind of organized mob stupidity—the final camp of its announcing itself as a representative of value or civilization or taste—I mean I give up, that's just too much fucking nasty brass. And you're guilty of that too John, you've just got to drop it, and take me seriously, and listen to what I have to say. It doesn't mean you have to agree, or change your career or your writing, or anything hideous, it just means you've got to

---

* "Siesta in Xbalba," *Collected Poems*, pp. 97–110.

* "The Know-Nothing Bohemians," *Partisan Review*, Spring 1958.

have the heart and decency to take people seriously and not depend *only* on your own university experience for arbitrary standards of value to judge others by. It doesn't mean you have to agree, that Free Verse is the Only Path of Prosodaic Experiment, or that Williams is a Saint, or I have some horrible magic secret (tho god knows I have enough, this week with that damned buddhist laughing gas, everybody has). Just enough to dig, you to dig, what others besides yourself are trying to do. And be interested in their work or not, but not get in the way, in fact even encourage where you can see some value. And you're in a position to encourage, you teach, you shouldn't hand down limited ideas to younger minds—that was the whole horror of Columbia, there just was nobody there (maybe except Weaver) who had a serious involvement with advanced work in poetry. Just a bunch of Dilettantes. And THEY have the nerve to set themselves up as guardians of culture?!!? Why it's such a piece of effrontery—enough to make anyone Paranoiac, it's a miracle Jack or myself or anybody independent survived—tho god knows the toll in paranoia been high enough. All these grievances I'm pouring out to you. Well why revise.

Back to Howl: construction. After sick & tired of shortline free verse as not expressionistic enough, not swinging enough, can't develop a powerful enough rhythm, I simply turned aside, accidentally to writing part I of "Howl," in solitude, diddling around with the form, thinking it couldn't be published anyway (queer content my parents shouldn't see etc) also it was out of my short-line line. But what I did taught my theory, I changed my mind about "measure" while writing it.* Part one uses repeated base *who*, as a sort of kithara† BLANG, homeric (in my imagination) to mark off each statement, each rhythmic unit.‡ So that's experiment with longer & shorter variations on a fixed base—the principle being, that each line has to be contained within the elastic of one breath—with suitable punctuatory expressions where the rhythm has built up enough so that I have to let off steam by building a longer climactic line in which there is a jazzy ride. All the ear I've ever developed goes into the balancing of those lines. The interesting moment's when the rhythm is sufficiently powerfully pushing ahead so I can ride out free and drop the *who* key that holds it together. The method of keeping a long line still all poetic & not prosey is the concentration & compression of basically imagistic notations into surrealist or cubist phrasing, like hydrogen jukeboxes. Ideally anyway. Good example of this is Gregory's§ great (I swear) Coit Tower ode. Lines have greater poetic density. But I tried to keep the language sufficiently dense in one way or another—use of primitive naive grammar (expelled for

crazy), elimination of prosy articles & syntactical sawdust, juxtaposition of cubist style images, of hot rhythm.

Well then Part II. Here the basic repeated word is Moloch. The long line is now broken up into component short phrases with ! rhythmical punctuation. The key repeat BLANG word is repeated internally in the line (basic rhythm sometimes emerging /—/—) but the rhythm depends mostly on the internal Moloch repeat. Lines here lengthened—a sort of free verse prose poetry STANZA form invented or used here. This builds up to climax (Visions! Omens! etc) and then falls off in coda. Part III, perhaps an original invention (I thought so then but this type of thinking is vain & shallow anyway) to handling of long line (for the whole poem is an experiment in what you can do with the long line—the whole book is)— ::: that is, a phrase base rhythm (I'm with you etc) followed as in litany by a response of the same length (Where you're madder etc), then repeat of base over and over with the response elongating itself slowly, still contained within the elastic of one breath—till the stanza (for it is a stanza form there, I've used variations of it since)* building up like a pyramid, an emotion crying siren sound, very appropriate to the expressive appeal emotion I felt (a good healthy emotion said my analyst at that time, to dispose once and for all of that idiotic objection)—anyway, building up to the climax where there's a long long long line, penultimate, too long for one breath, where I open out & give the answer (O starry spangled shock of Mercy the eternal war is here). All this rather like a jazz mass, I mean the conception of rhythm not derived from jazz directly but if you listen to jazz you get the idea (in fact specifically old trumpet solo on a *JATP* "Can't Get Started" side†)—well all this is built like a brick shithouse and anybody can't hear the music is as I told you I guess I meekly informed Trilling, who is absolutely lost in poetry, is got a tin ear, and that's so obviously true, I get sick and tired I read 50 reviews of Howl and not one of them written by anyone with enough technical interests to notice the fucking obvious construction of the poem, all the details besides (to say nothing of the various esoteric classical allusions built in like references to Cezanne's theory of composition etc etc)—that I GIVE UP and anybody henceforth comes up to me with a silly look in his eye & begins bullshitting about morals and sociology & tradition and technique & Juvenile Delinquency—I mean I je ne sais plus parler‡—the horrible irony of all these jerks who can't *read* trying to lecture me (us) on FORM. . . .

Footnote to Howl is too lovely & serious a joke to try to explain. The built-in rhythmic exercise should be clear, it's basically a repeat of the Moloch section. It's dedicated to my mother who died in the madhouse and its says I loved her anyway & that even in worst conditions life is holy. The exaggeratedness of the statements

---

* From W. C. Williams' triadic ladder line to extended-breath verse.
† Ancient instrument supposedly used for recitation of tragedy among Greeks, seven or eleven strings, related to lyre.
‡ Anaphora.
§ Gregory Corso, "Ode to Coit Tower," in *Gasoline* (San Francisco: City Lights Books, 1958).

* "Kaddish," Part IV.
† Illinois Jacquet's solo, *Jazz at the Philharmonic*, Vol. II, ed. Norman Granz; a series of live jazz albums.
‡ Arthur Rimbaud, "Matin," in *A Season in Hell*, trans. Louise Varese (New York: New Directions, 1961), p. 80.

is appropriate, and anybody who doesnt understand the specific exaggerations will never understand Rejoice in the Lamb or Lorca's Ode to Whitman or Mayakovsky's At the Top of My Voice or Artaud's Pour En Finir Avec le Judgement de Dieu or Apollinaire's "inspired bullshit" or Whitman's madder passages or anything, anything, anything about the international modern spirit in poesy* to say nothing about the international tradition in prosody which has grown up nor the tradition of open prophetic bardic poetry which 50 years has sung like an angel over the poor soul of the world while all sorts of snippy castrates pursue their good manners and sell out their own souls and the spirit of god who now DEMANDS sincerity and hell fire take him who denies the voice in his soul—except that it's all a kindly joke & the universe disappears after you die so nobody gets hurt no matter how little they allow themselves to live & blow on this Earth. . . .

Latter's unclear I'll start over. Tho poetry in

* See Appendix IV.

Williams has depended a lot on little breath groups for its typographical organization, and in *Howl* an extension into longer breaths (which are more natural to me than Williams short simple talks)—there is another way you would *say* it, a thought, but the way you would think it—i.e. we think rapidly, in visual images as well as words, and if each successive thought were transcribed in its confusion (really its ramification) you get a slightly different prosody than if you were talking slowly. . . .

yours in the kingdom of music
Nella Grebsnig
Allen

[A much fuller version of this thirty-page letter, discussing the work of poets who read at Six Gallery, as well as Kerouac and Corso, the social and literary context of the 1950s, with A.G.'s reaction to contemporaneous reviews of *Howl*, including John Hollander's, was printed in Jane Kramer's *Allen Ginsberg in America* (New York: Random House, 1968), pp. 163–77.]

Appendix II
First Reading at the Six Gallery, October 7, 1955

FROM *The Literary Revolution in America*   *Allen Ginsberg and Gregory Corso*

In the fall of 1955 a group of six unknown poets in San Francisco, in a moment of drunken enthusiasm, decided to defy the system of academic poetry, official reviews, New York publishing machinery, national sobriety and generally accepted standards to good taste, by giving a free reading of their poetry in a run down secondrate experimental art gallery in the Negro section of San Francisco. They sent out a hundred postcards, put up signs in North Beach (Latin Quarter) bars, bought a lot of wine to get the audience drunk, and invited the well known Frisco Anarchist resident poet Kenneth Rexroth to act as Master of Ceremonies. Their approach was purely amateur and goofy, but it should be noted that they represented a remarkable lineup of experience and character—it was an assemblage of really good poets who knew what they were writing and didn't care about anything else. They got drunk, the audience got drunk, all that was missing was the orgy. This was no ordinary poetry reading. Indeed, it resembled anything but a poetry reading. The reading was such a violent and beautiful expression of their revolutionary individuality (a quality bypassed in American poetry since the formulations of Whitman), conducted with such surprising abandon and delight by the poets themselves, and presenting such a high mass of beautiful unanticipated poetry, that the audience, expecting some Bohemian stupidity, was left stunned, and the poets were left with the realization that they were fated to make a permanent change in the literary firmament of the States.

The poets participating were a curious group. First, Philip Lamantia, a surrealist blood poet, former member of San Francisco Anarchist group, who at the age of 13 had in imitation of Rimbaud written surrealist poetry, come to New York, consulted Breton and other surrealists, renounced surrealism, lived with Indians and priests in Mexico, took drugs, underwent visions, became Catholic, became silent, and reappeared at age of 28 in native town to take part in the reading.

The second poet, the youngest, was representative of the Black Mountain School—which derives in influence from Pound and W. C. Williams. Michael McClure read some of his own work and some of [Robert Duncan's. McClure] writes relatively sober mystical poetry. . . .

The next poet, Philip Whalen, a strange fat young man from Oregon—in appearance a Zen Buddhist Bodhisattva—read a series of very personal relaxed, learned mystical-anarchic poems. His obvious carelessness for his reputation as a poet, his delicacy and strange American sanctity is evident in his poetry, written in rare post-

Poundian assemblages of blocks of hard images set in juxtapositions, like haikus.

The most brilliant shock of the evening was the declamation of the now-famous rhapsody, *Howl*, by Allen Ginsberg. . . . The poem initiates a new style in composition in the U.S., returning to the bardic-strophic tradition, till now neglected in the U.S., of Apollinaire, Whitman, Artaud, Lorca, Mayakovsky—and improving on the tradition to the extent of combining the long lines and coherence of Whitman, with the cubist imagery of the French and Spanish traditions, and adding to that a fantastic rhythmic structure which begins on a relatively flat base of repetition, and builds up to the rhythmic crisis of a Bach fugue, and ends on a high peak of ecstatic elongation of the line structure. . . . The poem is built like a pyramid, in three parts, and ends in fantastic merciful tears—the protest against the dehumanizing mechanization of American culture, and an affirmation of individual particular compassion in the midst of a great chant.

The reading was delivered by the poet, rather surprised at his own power, drunk on the platform, becoming increasingly sober as he read, driving forward with a strange ecstatic intensity, delivering a spiritual confession to an astounded audience—ending in tears which restored to American poetry the prophetic consciousness it had lost since the conclusion of Hart Crane's *The Bridge*, another celebrated mystical work.

But this was not all! The last poet to appear on the platform was perhaps more remarkable than any of the others: Gary Snyder, a bearded youth of 26, also from the Northwest, formerly a lumberjack and seaman, student of literature and anthropology who had lived with American Indians and taken the religious drug Peyote with them, and who is now occupied in the study of Chinese and Japanese preparatory to the drunken silence of a Zen Monastery in Japan. He read parts of a hundred page poem he had been composing for 5 years, Myths and Texts—composition of fragments of all his experiences forming an anarchic and mystical pattern of individual revelation.

Reprinted abridged from *Litterair Paspoort* 100 (Amsterdam), November 1957.

```
            6 POETS AT 6 GALLERY

   Philip Lamantia reading mss. of late John
   Hoffman-- Mike McClure, Allen Ginsberg.
   Gary Snyder & Phil Whalen--all sharp new
   straightforward writing-- remarkable coll-
   ection of angels on one stage reading
   their poetry. No charge, small collection
   for wine and postcards. Charming event.

            Kenneth Rexroth, M.C.

   8 PM Friday Night October 7,1955

       6 Gallery 3119 Fillmore St.
       San Fran
```

Perhaps the most strange poet in the room was not on the platform—he sat on the edge of it, back to the poets, eyes closed, nodding at good lines, swigging a bottle of California red wine—at times shouting encouragement or responding with spontaneous images—jazz style—to the long zig-zag rhythms chanted in *Howl*. This was Jack Kerouac, then unknown also, now perhaps the most celebrated novelist in America. . . . Mr. Kerouac is also a superb poet, his poems are automatic, pure, brilliant, awesome, gentle, and unpublished as of yet. . . .

I should, at this point, remark that William Carlos Williams, of all the great older poets, has remained in closest touch with these young poets, and he, if anyone, supplies the link with the democratic experimental tradition of the poet.

Mention should also be given Mr. Lawrence Ferlinghetti, publisher of Mr. Ginsberg's *Howl*, and himself poet of a book of verse, *Pictures of the Gone World*. Ferlinghetti is the most advanced publisher in America in that he publishes "suspect" literature, literature usually rejected by other publishing houses because of their wild neo-bop prosody, non-commercial value, extreme expression of soul, and the pure adventure of publishing it. For his pains Mr. Ferlinghetti is now on trial in the American courts for having published Mr. Ginsberg.

This article should properly end with the announcement of the completion of *Naked Lunch*, a long epic prose-poem by William Seward Burroughs. Burroughs is the shadowy unknown genius behind the more publicized figures of Kerouac and Ginsberg, and the completion and editing of his work was the occasion of a transatlantic reunion of the three early this year in Tangiers. The book seems destined to have great difficulties in finding a publisher—its style, almost surrealistic, its structure, its automaticism, its theme, the desecration of the unity, the human image desecrated by a mad society, its images, sex, drugs, dreams, riots, hangings, secret narcotic phantasmal police—in short, *Naked Lunch* is a prose-poetic novel in the tradition of Rimbaud, Artaud, Genet, but the treatment of the work is too *naked* to be admitted into American consciousness past the barrier of commercial publishing, customs inspection, and legal censorship of its "obscenity."

In America, apart from the Little Rock stagnant sign of doom, apart from money-wild cultureless majority of humans that inhabit it, apart from the wealth and woe and fear and sorrow and false joy and guilt, there is, out of all this, in America, a new forceful stir of young poets, and they have taken it upon themselves, with angelic clarions in hand, to announce their discontent, their demands, their hope, their final wondrous unimaginable dream.

From *The Dharma Bums*

Jack Kerouac

. . . It was a great night, a historic night in more ways than one. Japhy Ryder and some other poets (he also wrote poetry and translated Chinese and Japanese poetry into English) were scheduled to give a poetry reading at the Gallery Six in town. They were all meeting in the bar and getting high. But as they stood and sat around I saw that he was the only one who didn't look like a poet, though poet he was indeed. The other poets were either hornrimmed intellectual hepcats with wild black hair like Alvah Goldbook, or delicate pale handsome poets like Ike O'Shay (in a suit), or out-of-this-world genteel-looking Renaissance Italians like Francis DaPavia (who looks like a young priest), or bow-tied wild-haired old anarchist fuds like Rheinhold Cacoethes, or big fat bespectacled quiet booboos like Warren Coughlin. And all the other hopeful poets were standing around, in various costumes, worn-at-the-sleeves corduroy jackets, scuffly shoes, books sticking out of their pockets. . . .

Anyway I followed the whole gang of howling poets to the reading at Gallery Six that night, which was, among other important things, the night of the birth of the San Francisco Poetry Renaissance. Everyone was there. It was a mad night. And I was the one who got things jumping by going around collecting dimes and quarters from the rather stiff audience standing around in the gallery and coming back with three huge gallon jugs of California Burgundy and getting them all piffed so that by eleven o'clock when Alvah Goldbook was reading his, wailing his poem "Wail" drunk with arms outspread everybody was yelling "Go! Go! Go!" (like a jam session) and old Rheinhold Cacoethes the father of the Frisco poetry scene was wiping his tears in gladness. Japhy himself read his fine poems about Coyote the God of the North American Plateau Indians (I think), at least the God of the Northwest Indians, Kwakiutl and whatall. "Fuck you! sang Coyote, and ran away!" read Japhy to the distinguished audience, making them all howl with joy, it was so pure, fuck being a dirty word that comes out clean. And he had his tender lyrical lines, like the ones about bears eating berries, showing his love of animals, and great mystery lines about oxen on the Mongolian road showing his knowledge of Oriental literature even on to Hsuan Tsung the great Chinese monk who walked from China to Tibet, Lanchow to Kashgar and Mongolia carrying a stick of incense in his hand. Then Japhy showed his sudden barroom humor with lines about Coyote bringing goodies. And his anarchistic ideas about how Americans don't know how to live, with lines about commuters being trapped in living rooms that come from poor trees felled by chainsaws (showing here, also, his background as a logger up north). This voice was deep and resonant and somehow brave, like the voice of oldtime American heroes and orators. Something earnest and strong and humanly hopeful I liked about him, while the other poets were either too dainty in their aestheticism, or too hysterically cynical to hope for anything, or too abstract and indoorsy, or too political, or like Coughlin too incomprehensible to understand (big Coughlin saying things about "unclarified processes" though where Coughlin did say that revelation was a personal thing I noticed the strong Buddhist and idealistic feeling of Japhy, which he'd shared with goodhearted Coughlin in their buddy days at college, as I had shared mine with Alvah in the Eastern scene and with others less apocalyptical and straighter but in no sense more sympathetic and tearful).

Meanwhile scores of people stood around in the darkened gallery straining to hear every word of the amazing poetry reading as I wandered from group to group, facing them and facing away from the stage, urging them to glug a slug from the jug, or wandered back and sat on the right side of the stage giving out little wows and yesses of approval and even whole sentences of comment with nobody's invitation but in the general gaiety nobody's disapproval either. It was a great night. Delicate Francis DaPavia read, from delicate onionskin yellow pages, or pink, which he kept flipping carefully with long white fingers, the poems of his dead chum Altman who'd eaten too much peyote in Chihuahua (or died of polio, one) but read none of his own poems—a charming elegy in itself to the memory of the dead young poet, enough to draw tears from the Cervantes of Chapter Seven, and read them in a delicate Englishy voice that had me crying with inside laughter though I later got to know Francis and liked him. . . .

Between poets, Rheinhold Cacoethes, in his bow tie and shabby old coat, would get up and make a little funny speech in his snide funny voice and introduce the next reader; but as I say come eleven-thirty when all the poems were read and everybody was milling around wondering what had happened and what would come next in American poetry, he was wiping his eyes with his handkerchief.

From Chap. 2 (New York: Viking Press, 1958).
KEY: Japhy Rider = Gary Snyder; Alvah Goldbook = Allen Ginsberg; Rheinhold Cacoethes = Kenneth Rexroth; Warren Coughlin = Philip Whalen; Francis DaPavia = Philip Lamantia; Ike O'Shea = Michael McClure; Altman = John Hoffman.

FROM *Peter Orlovsky and Allen Ginsberg interview, 1975*

James McKenzie

PETER ORLOVSKY: I was with Neal Cassady at the Six Gallery reading, and Neal said to me, "Come over here, Peter, come stand next to me." I said, "Why? Why, Neal?" and he said, "Well, I don't know anybody here." So I was standing next to Neal but then I moved over and stood next to someone else because, you know, I was a little embarrassed. I was very, very bashful and embarrassed—very self-conscious, you know, in those days. And Neal was there, dressed in his brakeman's uniform. He had his vest on—his watch and his vest. . . . He was very proud, smiling, very happy, full of smiles and bowing. . . .

ALLEN GINSBERG: He came up to me and he said, "Allen, my boy. I'm proud of you." [Laughter] It was really nice—it was the nicest thing I heard that night. It was completely, unabashedly, friendly, happy approval.

Interview in North Dakota, 1975. In *Unspeakable Visions of the Individual*, ed. Arthur and Glee Knight (California, Pa., 1979).

FROM *Jack's Book*

Barry Gifford and Lawrence Lee

ALLEN GINSBERG: The Six Gallery reading had come about when Wally Hedrick, who was a painter and one of the major people there, asked Rexroth if he knew any poets that would put on a reading. Maybe Rexroth asked McClure to organize it and McClure didn't know how or didn't have time. Rexroth asked me, so I met McClure and Rexroth suggested I go visit another poet who was living in Berkeley, which was Gary. So I went right over to Gary's house and immediately had a meeting of minds with him over William Carlos Williams, 'cause I had written *Empty Mirror* at that time and he had begun *Myths and Texts*, or *The Berry Feast*, or something, and he told me about his friend Philip Whalen who was due in town the next day. And I told him about my friend Kerouac who was in town that day, and within three or four days we all met. . . .

Jack and I were coming from Berkeley, and had just arrived in San Francisco at the Key System Terminal, the bus terminal there, and we met right out on First and Mission, by accident. Gary was with Phil and I was with Jack, and we all went off immediately and started talking. And then Philip Lamantia was in town, whom I'd known from '48 in New York, and then there was Michael McClure. So there was a whole complement of poets. Then Gary and I decided we ought to invite Rexroth to be the sixth—sixth poet—to introduce at the Six Gallery, be the elder, since he had linked us up.

New York: St. Martin's Press, 1978.

FROM *Ferlinghetti: A Biography*

Neeli Cherkovski

On the night of the reading the Ferlinghettis invited some of the poets to ride with them. Ginsberg, Kerouac, Kirby, and one or two others managed to get into the car and off they sped. About seventy-five people had crowded into the small gallery. After Ginsberg read the first part of *Howl*, the audience reaction was amazing. They seemed to know that they had heard a great poem, demonstrating that fact by their applause. A party was held after the reading, and most of the poets attended. The Ferlinghettis were tired and went home. Ferlinghetti immediately sat down at his typewriter and composed a telegram that he sent to Ginsberg. The message paraphrased one that Ralph Waldo Emerson had sent to Walt Whitman upon receiving a copy of the 1855 edition of *Leaves of Grass*. The telegram to Ginsberg read: "I greet you at the beginning of a great career. When do I get the manuscript?"

Garden City, N.Y.: Doubleday, 1979.

FROM *Scratching the Beat Surface*

Michael McClure

Three years before the peyote experience just described, I had given my first poetry reading with Allen Ginsberg, the Zen poet Philip Whalen, Gary Snyder, and the American Surrealist poet Philip Lamantia. The reading was in October 1955, at the Six Gallery in San Francisco. The Six Gallery was a cooperative art gallery run by young artists who centered around the San Francisco Art Institute. They were fiery artists who had either studied with Clyfford Still and Mark Rothko or with the newly emerging figurative painters. Their works ranged from huge drip and slash to minute precision smudges turning into faces. Earlier in the year poet Robert Duncan had given a staged reading of his play *Faust Foutu* (Faust Fucked) at the Six Gallery and, with the audacious purity of an Anarchist poet, he had stripped off his clothes at the end of the play.

On this night Kenneth Rexroth was master of ceremonies. This was the first time that Allen Ginsberg read *Howl*. Though I had known Allen for some months preceding, it was my first meeting with Gary Snyder and Philip Whalen. Lamantia did not read his poetry that night but instead recited works of the recently deceased John Hoffman—beautiful prose poems that left orange stripes and colored visions in the air. . . .

The Six Gallery was a huge room that had been converted from an automobile repair shop into an art gallery. Someone had knocked together a little dais and was exhibiting sculptures by Fred Martin at the back of it— pieces of orange crates that had been swathed in muslin and dipped in plaster of paris to make splintered, sweeping shapes like pieces of surrealist furniture. A hundred and fifty enthusiastic people had come to hear us. Money was collected and jugs of wine were brought back for the audience. I hadn't seen Allen in a few weeks and I had not heard *Howl*—it was new to me. Allen began in a small and intensely lucid voice. At some point Jack Kerouac began shouting "GO" in cadence as Allen read it. In all of our memories no one had been so outspoken in poetry before—we had gone beyond a point of no return—and we were ready for it, for a point of no return. None of us wanted to go back to the gray, chill, militaristic silence, to the intellective void—to the land without poetry—to the spiritual drabness. We wanted to make it new and we wanted to invent it and the process of it as we went into it. We wanted voice and we wanted vision. . . .

Ginsberg read on to the end of the poem, which left us standing in wonder, or cheering and wondering, but knowing at the deepest level that a barrier had been broken, that a human voice and body had been hurled against the harsh wall of America and its supporting armies and navies and academies and institutions and ownership systems and power-support bases. . . .

San Francisco: North Point Press, 1982.

Also that night Gary Snyder, bearded and neat, a rugged young man of nature at age twenty-five, read his scholarly and ebullient nature poem, *A Berry Feast.* . . .

Snyder's gloss on the poem reads: "The berry feast is a first-fruits celebration that consumes a week of mid-August on the Warm Springs Indian Reservation in Oregon. Coyote is the name of the Trickster-Hero of the mythology of that region." . . .

Even in those days Philip Whalen was a big man. As I watched him read, the meaning of his metamorphic poem gradually began to sink in. We laughed as the poem's intent clarified. Here was a poem by a poet-scholar (who is now a Zen priest as well as a major American poet) with a multiple thrust. Whalen was using the American speech that William Carlos Williams instructed us to use, but he put it to a different use. Whalen's poems were not only naturalistic portrayals of objects and persons transformed by poetry—they also used American speech for the naked joy of portraying metamorphosis and of exemplifying and aiding change in the universe. They manifested a positive Whiteheadian joy in shifting and in processes. Whalen read this poem ["Plus Ça Change"] with a mock seriousness that was at once biting, casual, and good natured. . . .

The Six Gallery reading was open to the world and the world was welcome. There were poets and Anarchists and Stalinists and professors and painters and bohemians and visionaries and idealists and grinning cynics.

I had been fascinated by the thought and the poetry of the French maudite, antiphysical, mystic poet Antonin Artaud, who had died toothless and, it is said, mad in Paris in 1948, only seven years before our Six Gallery reading. One of my first exchanges with Philip Lamantia on meeting him in 1954 was to ask where I could find more works by Artaud. I was fascinated by Artaud's visionary gnosticism. . . .

One phrase of Artaud's fascinated me: "It is not possible that in the end the miracle willl not occur." I replied with a poem I read at the Six Gallery ["Point Lobos: Animism"]. . . .

At the Six Gallery I also read a poem that sprang from an article in *Time* magazine (April 1954). Excerpts from the article used to preface the poem say:

Killer whales. . . . Savage sea cannibals up to thirty feet long with teeth like bayonets . . . one was caught with fourteen seals and thirteen porpoises in its belly . . . often tear at boats and nets . . . destroyed thousands of dollars' worth of fishing tackle. . . . Icelandic government appealed to the U.S., which has thousands of men stationed at a lonely NATO airbase on the subarctic island. Seventy-nine bored G.I.'s responded with enthusiasm. Armed with rifles and machine guns one posse of Americans climbed into four small boats and in one morning wiped out a pack of 100 killers. . . .

I was horrified and angry when I read about the slaughter and I wrote: "For the Death of 100 Whales." . . .

Appendix III
Legal History of HOWL

From Horn on *Howl* (with interleaved communications) by Lawrence Ferlinghetti

When William Carlos Williams, in his Introduction to *Howl*, said that Ginsberg had come up with "an arresting poem" he hardly knew what he was saying. The first edition of *Howl*, Number Four in the Pocket Poet Series, was printed in England by Villiers, passed thru customs without incident, and was published at the City Lights bookstore here in the fall of 1956. Part of a second printing was stopped by customs on March 25, 1957, not long after an earlier issue of *The Miscellaneous Man* (published in Berkeley by William Margolis) had been seized coming from the same printer. Section 305 of the Tariff Act of 1930 was cited. The San Francisco *Chronicle* (which alone among the local press put up a real howl about censorship) reported, in part:

> Collector of Customs Chester MacPhee continued his campaign yesterday to keep what he considers obscene literature away from the children of the Bay Area. He confiscated 520 copies of a paperbound volume of poetry entitled *Howl and Other Poems*. . . . "The words and the sense of the writing is obscene," MacPhee declared. "You wouldn't want your children to come across it."

[I had submitted the ms. of *Howl* to the ACLU *before* sending it to the printer in England, to see if they would defend us *if* the book was busted, and a good thing too, since without the ACLU, City Lights would no doubt have gone broke and out of business. We were barely breaking even those years, and living on very little, and the expense of a court trial would have been disastrous.]*

On April 3 [1957] the American Civil Liberties Union . . . informed Mr. MacPhee that it would contest the legality of the seizure, since it did not consider the book obscene. We announced in the meantime that an entire new edition of *Howl* was being printed within the United States, thereby removing it from customs jurisdiction. No changes were made in the original text, and a photo-offset edition was placed on sale at City Lights bookstore and distributed nationally while the customs continued to sit on the copies from Britain. . . .

[San Francisco Collector of Customs deserves a word of thanks for seizing Allen Ginsberg's *Howl and Other Poems* thereby rendering it famous. Perhaps we could have a medal made. It would have taken years for critics to accomplish what the good collector did in a day, merely by calling the book obscene. City Lights Books now has had an entirely new edition printed locally and thereby removed it from customs jurisdiction. I should like to justify this action by defending *Howl* as a poetic work leaving moral argument to others. I consider *Howl* to be the most significant long poem to be published in this country since World War II, perhaps since Eliot's *Four Quartets*. In some sense it's a gestalt and archetypical configuration of the mass culture which produced it. The results are a condemnation of our culture. If it is an obscene voice of dissent, perhaps this is really why officials object to it. Condemning it, however, they are condemning our world for it is what he observes that is the great voice of *Howl*. . . .]†

Notes on the obscenity trial of *Howl*, from *Evergreen Review* (Winter 1957). Copyright © 1957 by Lawrence Ferlinghetti. Reprinted by permission of City Lights Books.

* Lawrence Ferlinghetti to Allen Ginsberg, San Francisco, April 27, 1986.
† Lawrence Ferlinghetti, *San Francisco Chronicle*, May 19, 1957; "This World" section, p. 35: William Hogan's "Between the Lines" column.

Lawrence Ferlinghetti & Shigeyoshi Murao, front bench left, *Howl* trial courtroom, San Francisco Hall of Justice, Summer 1957.   *Photo Courtesy City Lights.*

On May 29 customs released the books it had been holding, since the United States Attorney at San Francisco refused to institute condemnation proceedings against *Howl*.

Then the police took over and arrested us, Captain William Hanrahan of the juvenile department (well named, in this case) reporting that the books were not fit for children to read. Thus during the first week in June I found myself being booked and fingerprinted in San Francisco's Hall of Justice. The city jail occupies the upper floors of it, and a charming sight it is, a picturesque return to the early Middle Ages. And my enforced tour of it was a dandy way for the city officially to recognize the flowering of poetry in San Francisco. As one paper reported, "The Cops Don't Allow No Renaissance Here."

The ACLU posted bail. Our trial went on all summer, with a couple of weeks between each day in court. The prosecution soon admitted it had no case against either Shig Murao or myself as far as *The Miscellaneous Man* was concerned, since we were not the publisher of it, in which case there was no proof we knew what was inside the magazine when it was sold at our store. And, under the California Penal Code, the willful and lewd *intent* of the accused had to be established. Thus the trial was narrowed down to *Howl*.

The so-called People's Case (I say so-called, since the People seemed mostly on our side) was presented by Deputy District Attorney Ralph McIntosh whose heart seemed not in it nor his mind on it. He was opposed by some of the most formidable legal talent to be found, in the persons of Mr. Jake ("Never Plead Guilty") Ehrlich, Lawrence Speiser (former counsel for the ACLU), and Albert Bendich (present counsel for the ACLU)—all of whom defended us without expense to us.

The critical support for *Howl* (or the protest against censorship on principle) was enormous. . . . [Letters and written statements were received from Henry Rago, editor of *Poetry* (Chicago); Robert Duncan and Director Ruth Witt-Diamant of the San Francisco (State College) Poetry Center; Thomas Parkinson (University of California); James Laughlin (New Directions); Kenneth Patchen; Northern California Booksellers Association; and Barney Rosset and Donald Allen, editors of the *Evergreen Review* (in which "Howl" was reprinted during the trial).]*

At the trial itself, nine expert witnesses testified in behalf of *Howl*. They were eloquent witnesses, together furnishing as good a one-sided critical survey of *Howl* as could possibly be got up in any literary magazine. These witnesses were: Mark Schorer and Leo Lowenthal (of the University of California faculty), Walter Van Tilburg Clark, Herbert Blau, Arthur Foff, and Mark Linenthal (all of the San Francisco State College faculty), Kenneth Rexroth, Vincent McHugh (poet and novelist), and Luther Nichols (book editor of the San Francisco *Examiner*). . . .

Legally, a layman could see that an important principle was certainly in the line drawn between "hard core pornography" and writing judged to be "social

* L. F. text summarized by A. G.

speech." But more important still was the court's acceptance of the principle that if a work is determined to be "social speech" the question of obscenity may not even be raised. Or, in the words of Counsel Bendich's argument:

> The first amendment to the Constitution of the United States protecting the fundamental freedoms of speech and press prohibits the suppression of literature by the application of obscenity formulae unless the trial court first determines that the literature in question is utterly without social importance." (*Roth* v. *U.S.*)
>
> . . . What is being urged here is that the majority opinion in *Roth* requires a trial court to make the constitutional determination; to decide in the first instance whether a work is utterly without redeeming social importance, *before* it permits the test of obscenity to be applied. . . .
>
> . . . The record is clear that all of the experts for the defense identified the main theme of *Howl* as social criticism. And the prosecution concedes that it does not understand the work, much less what its dominant theme is.

Judge Horn agreed, in his opinion. . . . Under banner headlines, the *Chronicle* reported that "the Judge's decision was hailed with applause and cheers from a packed audience that offered the most fantastic collection of beards, turtlenecked shirts and Italian hairdos ever to grace the grimy precincts of the Hall of Justice." The decision was hailed editorially as a "landmark of law." Judge Horn has since been reelected to office, which I like to think means that the People agree it was the police who here committed an obscene action.

Footnotes to My Arrest for Selling *Howl*

Shigeyoshi Murao

Imagine being arrested for selling poetry! Two police officers from the juvenile squad arrested me. Obscenity was under their purview as a way of protecting the children. They had a "John Doe" warrant for my arrest. I kidded the police officers that I, Shigeyoshi Murao, a Japanese-American, was being arrested as a "John Doe" white man. They smiled, but did not laugh. It was a quotidian arrest. They never even handcuffed me. I was taken by patrol car to the Hall of Justice, three blocks from the store. In the basement, I was fingerprinted, posed for mug shots and locked in the drunk tank. The cell smelled of piss. There was a piss-stained mattress on the floor. For lunch, they served me wieners, very red. The trusty told me that the sausages were full of saltpeter so that the prisoners would not get hard-ons. I didn't eat lunch. The trusty ate my lunch.

In jail, I had no noble thoughts of fighting for freedom of the press and censorship. I had planned to live a quiet life of reading, listening to music and playing chess the rest of my life. Yet here I was involved in a case for selling obscenity.

Two hours later, I was bailed out of jail by the ACLU lawyers. In the jail cell, there was a penal code posted on the wall. Over the penal code, there was graffiti—"cocksuckers." The officers near the police desk talked in the American jocular manner. One said, "The judge must have gotten laid last night; he's so easy on these fuckin' assholes." Another answered, "Nah, the judge must have jacked off last night. His wife is dead."

The week *Life* magazine featured the trial, I flew to Chicago to see my parents. My father, whose English was limited, read *Life*. My spoken Japanese was also limited. I could not explain to them why I was arrested for obscenity. They were just satisfied I did not have to go to jail.

For the trial, I wore a cheap, light-blue summer suit with a white buttoned shirt and a black knit tie. In those days, you had to dress properly or you were held in contempt of court. Jake Ehrlich, our famous criminal lawyer, never said a word to me during the trial, except to make sure that I permitted the press to take pictures of me. After a few sessions, I was dismissed from the case. Section B of the penal code states, ". . . did knowingly sell . . ." The prosecutors could not prove that I had read the book. Eventually we won the case.

Sometime during the trial, someone from the JACL (Japanese American Citizens League) called to ask how I was. After the trial, Ernie Bessig, the ACLU director, talked to me about how his Northern California chapter fought for Japanese-American rights during World War II, the only ACLU chapter to do so.

I went on to a twenty-four-year career of selling books. I became famous for selling bad poetry; but I sold some good ones too. *Howl* was one of them.

March 1986

From How Captain Hanrahan Made *Howl* a Best-Seller

David Perlman

. . . The preparations for the trial produced a certain amount of concern in both legal and literary circles. Captain William Hanrahan, chief of the department's Juvenile Bureau, announced, "We will await the outcome of this case before we go ahead with other books." He did not reveal what books he had in mind, but he made it clear he had quite a list. He also disclosed that his men had been taking a look around the shelves of the city's bookstores—of which there are far more per capita than in any other metropolis outside New York.

When Captain Hanrahan was asked what standards he used to judge a book, his reply was brief but vague: "When I say filthy I don't mean suggestive, I mean filthy words that are very vulgar." He was also asked whether he was planning to send his men out to confiscate the

The Reporter, December 12, 1957.

Bible. His denial was vehement. "Let me tell you, though," the captain added, "what King Solomon was doing with all those women wouldn't be tolerated in San Francisco!"

The City Lights Pocket Bookshop, where Captain Hanrahan's men had dragged their net for filth, is not an ordinary emporium of literature. Its owner, and the principal defendant in the case, is Lawrence Ferlinghetti, a poet himself, a painter, and a canny and relatively affluent citizen of a San Francisco district called North Beach, which is a largely Italian neighborhood near the waterfront, between Telegraph and Russian Hills. Ferlinghetti's store is right in the center of the district . . .

Ferlinghetti's bookshop sells no hard covers,* but it does stock all the quarterlies, all the soft-cover prestige lines of the major publishers, a lot of foreign imprints and periodicals, and just about every other sort of pocket book except the kind whose bosomy covers leer from the racks of drugstores and bus terminals.

His store also contains a lively bulletin board, on which appear notices of art exhibits, beer blasts, little-theater castings, ceramic sales, and odd jobs wanted. The City Lights is tiny and crowded, but it is open far into the night. Many residents in the quarter find it an ideal place for browsing, meeting friends, catching up on North Beach gossip, and even buying books. It is, in a way, the intellectual center of North Beach.

Ferlinghetti is also a publisher. He has issued, under the City Lights imprint, a "Pocket Poets" series, retailing for seventy-five cents each. The first three works offered were Ferlinghetti's own *Pictures of the Gone World*, Rexroth's *Thirty Spanish Poems of Love and Exile*, and Patchen's *Poems of Humor and Protest*. The fourth was a forty-four-page volume called *Howl and Other Poems* by Allen Ginsberg . . .

This was the poem that aroused the San Francisco Police Department and was the actual defendant in the case of *People* vs. *Ferlinghetti*. Ginsberg himself was far away on a trip to Europe, and the owner of the book-store never took the stand, nor was any evidence presented against him beyond the fact that he had published "Howl." His clerk, Shigeyoshi Murao, was even less involved. The prosecutor conceded that there was no evidence to show the clerk even knew what was in the book, and it was quickly agreed that Murao should be acquitted. It was also agreed that the trial would be held without a jury.

The judge was Clayton W. Horn of the San Francisco Municipal Court, who functions primarily as one of the city's four police magistrates. Judge Horn, who regularly teaches Bible class at a Sunday school, was under something of a cloud when he mounted the bench for the "Howl" case. He had just been raked over by the local press for a decision in which he had sentenced five lady shoplifters to attend *The Ten Commandments* and write penitential essays on the supercolossal epic's moral lesson.

The chief defense counsel was J. W. Ehrlich, known

* It was the first all-paperback bookstore in the U.S., inspired by French custom.

for thirty years in San Francisco as "Jake The Master." . . .

Ehrlich's opponent was Ralph McIntosh, an elderly assistant district attorney . . . something of a specialist in smut cases. Pornographic movies, nudist magazines, and Jane Russell's appearance in *The Outlaw* have all been targets of his zeal. . . .

The first major encounter of the trial came when Ehrlich carefully pitted McIntosh against the defense's principal witness, Mark Schorer. Schorer is professor of English and chairman of graduate studies at the University of California; he is one of America's leading critics, is a textbook consultant to the U.S. Army, has published three novels and seventy-five short stories, and has been awarded a Fulbright and three Guggenheim fellowships.

In his characteristically imperturbable drawl, Schorer testified on direct examination by Ehrlich: "I think that 'Howl,' like any work of literature, attempts and intends to make a significant comment on or interpretation of human experience as the author knows it."

He said the theme and structure "create the impression of a nightmare world in which the 'best minds of our generation' are wandering like damned souls in hell." Much of the content, Schorer said, is "a series of what one might call surrealistic images."

Judge Horn, having carefully read the evolving common law on the subject, ruled that while Schorer and other experts could not testify whether or not they thought the poem obscene, they could state whether they thought the controversial language contained in the poem was "relevant" to the intent and theme of the poet.

"Ginsberg uses the rhythms of ordinary speech and also the diction of ordinary speech," Schorer said. "I would say the poem uses necessarily the language of vulgarity."

Then came the cross-examination. For an hour McIntosh pecked at Schorer, stormed at him, and read him nearly every questionable line in the book. The prosecutor railed at the poem too, and it was sometimes difficult to tell which he objected to more, its dirt or its incomprehensibility.

"I presume you understand the whole thing, is that right?" McIntosh asked Schorer at one point, a dare in his voice.

Schorer smiled. "I hope so," he said. "It's not always easy to know that one understands exactly what a contemporary poet is saying, but I think I do."

"McIntosh flourished the book triumphantly. "Do you understand," he demanded, "what 'angelheaded hipsters burning for the ancient heavenly connection to the starry dynamo in the machinery of night' means?"

"Sir, you can't translate poetry into prose," Schorer answered. "That's why it's poetry."

The audience, among whom were North Beach writers, downtown booksellers, and a few criminal-courts regulars, roared. The judge smiled tolerantly, but McIntosh would not give up.

"In other words," he asked, "you don't have to understand the words?"

"You don't understand the individual words taken out of their context," Schorer explained patiently. "You can no more translate it back into logical prose English than you can say what a surrealistic painting means in words because it's *not* prose."

This still didn't satisfy McIntosh, who kept reading the poem's opening lines and demanding a literal explanation. Finally Schorer said: "I can't possibly translate, nor, I am sure, can anyone in this room translate the opening part of this poem into rational prose."

For some reason, this testimony set McIntosh up immensely. "That's just what I wanted to find out," he declared with the air of one who has just clinched his case.

Having established the impossibility of translation, the prosecutor then read aloud one line of "Howl" after another, each with its quota of Anglo-Saxon words or vivid sexual images, and demanded more translations.

Schorer patiently declined to give them, and McIntosh finally turned to Judge Horn to complain: "Your Honor, frankly I have only got a batch of law degrees. I don't know anything about literature. But I would like to find out what this is all about. It's like this modern painting nowadays, surrealism or whatever they call it, where they have a monkey come in and do some finger painting."

The judge declined to instruct the witness to enlighten McIntosh on the poem's meaning, so the prosecutor tried another tack. He read a few more vivid phrases into the record and then asked Schorer: "Now couldn't that have been worded some other way? Do they have to put words like that in there?"

But Judge Horn disallowed the question, and offered a bit of literary criticism himself: "I think it is obvious," he said, "that the author could have used another term; whether or not it would have served the same purpose is another thing; that's up to the author."

By this time McIntosh was about ready to give up on Schorer. But he decided to have one final go at him. Turning to some of the poems that followed "Howl" in the volume, he asked Schorer to characterize them.

"Those are what one would call lyric poems," Schorer explained, "and the earlier ones are hortatory poems."

McIntosh pricked up his ears.

"Are what?" he demanded.

"Hortatory, Mr. McIntosh."

"That's all," said the prosecutor, and sat down. Schorer bowed gracefully towards McIntosh, and withdrew amid applause.

The defense placed nine expert witnesses on the stand in all, and with each one of them McIntosh went through the same maneuvers: bewilderment at the poem, contempt for the expert on the stand, and glee at the extraction of four-letter words. But no jury was present to see his act.

From Luther Nichols, book critic of the San Francisco *Examiner*, he learned that "Ginsberg's life is a vagabond one; it's colored by exposure to jazz, to Columbia University, to a liberal and Bohemian education, to a certain amount of bumming around. The words he has used are valid and necessary if he's to be honest with his purpose. I think to use euphemisms in describing this would be considered dishonest by Mr. Ginsberg."

From Walter Van Tilburg Clark, author of *The Ox-Bow Incident*, came this statement: "They seem to me, all of the poems in the volume, to be the work of a thoroughly honest poet, who is also a highly competent technician."

"Do you classify yourself as a liberal?" McIntosh asked Clark. But that was as far as he got. Judge Horn barred the question the instant it was uttered.

It was from Kenneth Rexroth—who described himself as a "recognized American poet of recognized competence, and a poetry critic of recognized competence"—that Ehrlich drew the highest qualitative judgment on "Howl." "Its merit is extraordinarily high," Rexroth said. "It is probably the most remarkable single poem published by a young man since the second war."

McIntosh made an effort to discredit the poem by bringing in two expert witnesses of his own to testify in rebuttal.

One was David Kirk, assistant professor of English at the University of San Francisco, a Catholic school. Kirk condemned "Howl" as a "poem apparently dedicated to a long-dead movement called Dadaism. And therefore the opportunity is long past for any significant literary contribution of this poem," and as a "weak imitation of a form that was used eighty or ninety years ago by Walt Whitman."

The second was a blonde named Gail Potter who passed out little printed brochures announcing that she gives private lessons in speech and diction, and who offered a formidable array of qualifications as an expert. She had, she said, rewritten *Faust* from its forty original versions; she had written thirty-five feature articles; she had written a pageant for what she called "one of the big affairs in Florida"; and she had taught at a business college, a church school for girls, and the College of Southern Florida at Lakeland.

"You feel like you are going through the gutter when you have to read that stuff," Miss Potter said of "Howl." Then she shuddered in distaste and added: "I didn't linger on it too long, I assure you."

Jake Ehrlich bowed Miss Potter off the stand without a question, and that was the prosecution's case.

In the arguments of opposing counsel as the trial wound up, the debate ran true to form. McIntosh cried aloud that San Francisco was in dire danger:

"I would like you to ask yourself, Your Honor, in determining whether or not these books are obscene, would you like to see this sort of poetry printed in your local newspaper? Or would you like to have this poetry read to you over the radio as a diet? In other words, Your Honor, how far are we going to license the use of filthy, vulgar, obscene, and disgusting language? How far can we go?"

For Jake Ehrlich, "Howl" was honest poetry, written by an honest poet, and dirty only to the dirty-minded. As for its potential tendency to arouse lustful thoughts

in readers, "The Master" dismissed that key question in a sentence. "You can't think common, rotten things just because you read something in a book unless it is your purpose to read common, rotten things and apply a common, rotten purpose to what you read."

Judge Horn took two weeks to deliberate before reaching a verdict. He took the trouble to read *Ulysses* and the famous court decisions that are part of its publishing history. He read other works that were once attacked as obscene. He read the law, both statute and common.

He found "Howl" not obscene and Ferlinghetti not guilty. His written opinion, although it comes from the state's lowest-ranking bench, must now stand as a major codification of obscenity law in California. . . .

**The People of the State of California
vs. Lawrence Ferlinghetti,
Excerpts from the Decision (October 3, 1957)**

Horn, Clayton W., J. The defendant is charged with a violation of Section 311.3 of the Penal Code of the State of California. Defendant pleads Not Guilty. The complaint alleged that the defendant did willfully and lewdly print, publish and sell obscene and indecent writings, papers and books, to wit: "Howl and Other Poems." . . .

Unless the words used take the form of dirt for dirt's sake and can be traced to criminal behavior, either actual or demonstrably imminent, they are not in violation of the statute. Indecent as used in the Penal Code is synonymous with obscene, and there is no merit in the contention of the prosecution that the word indecent means something less than obscene. . . .

In determining whether a book is obscene it must be construed as a whole. The courts are agreed that in making this determination, the book must be construed as a whole and that regard shall be had for its place in the arts.

The freedoms of speech and press are inherent in a nation of free people. These freedoms must be protected if we are to remain free, both individually and as a nation. The protection for this freedom is found in the First and Fourteenth Amendments to the United States Constitution, and in the Constitution of California, Art. I, sec. 9 which provides in part:

> Every citizen may freely speak, write, and publish his sentiments on all subjects, being responsible for the abuse of that right; and no law shall be passed to restrain or abridge the liberty of speech or of the press . . .

The Fourteenth Amendment to the Federal Constitution prohibits any State from encroaching upon freedom of speech and freedom of the press to the same extent that the First Amendment prevents the Federal Congress from doing so.

These guarantees occupy a preferred position under our law to such an extent that the courts, when considering whether legislation infringes upon them, neutralize the presumption usually indulged in favor of constitutionality.

Thomas Jefferson in his bill for establishing religious freedom wrote that "to suffer the Civil Magistrate to intrude his powers into the field of opinion, and to restrain the profession or propagation of principles on supposition of their ill tendency, is a dangerous fallacy which at once destroys all religious liberty . . . it is time enough for the rightful purposes of civil government for its officers to interfere when principles break out into overt acts against peace and good order." . . .

The authors of the First Amendment knew that novel and unconventional ideas might disturb the complacent, but they chose to encourage a freedom which they believed essential if vigorous enlightenment was ever to triumph over slothful ignorance.

I agree with the words of Macaulay who finds it difficult to believe that in a world so full of temptations as this, any gentleman, whose life would have been virtuous if he had not read Aristophanes and Juvenal, will be made vicious by reading them.

I do not believe that "Howl" is without redeeming social importance. The first part of "Howl" presents a picture of a nightmare world; the second part is an indictment of those elements in modern society destructive of the best qualities of human nature; such elements are predominantly identified as materialism, conformity, and mechanization leading toward war. The third part presents a picture of an individual who is a specific representation of what the author conceives as a general condition.

"Footnote to Howl" seems to be a declamation that everything in the world is holy, including parts of the body by name. It ends in a plea for holy living. . . .

The theme of "Howl" presents "unorthodox and controversial ideas." Coarse and vulgar language is used in treatment and sex acts are mentioned, but unless the book is entirely lacking in "Social importance" it cannot be held obscene. . . .

There are a number of words used in "Howl" that are presently considered coarse and vulgar in some circles of the community; in other circles such words are in everyday use. It would be unrealistic to deny these facts. The author of "Howl" has used those words because he believed that his portrayal required them as being in character. The People state that it is not necessary to use such words and that others would be more palatable to good taste. The answer is that life is not encased in one formula whereby everyone acts the same or conforms to a particular pattern. No two persons think alike; we were all made from the same mold but in different patterns. Would there be any freedom of press or speech if one must reduce his vocabulary to vapid innocuous euphemism? An author should be real in treating his subject and be allowed to express his thoughts and ideas in his own words. . . .

While the publishing of "smut" or "hard core pornography" is without any social importance and obscene by present-day standards, and should be punished for the good of the community, since there is no straight and unwavering line to act as a guide, censorship by Government should be held in tight reign. To act otherwise would destroy our freedoms of free speech and press. Even religion can be censored by the medium of taxation. The best method of censorship is by the people as self-guardians of public opinion and not by government. So we come back, once more, to Jefferson's advice that the only completely democratic way to control publications which arouse mere thoughts or feelings is through non-governmental censorship by public opinion.

From the foregoing certain rules can be set up, but as has been noted, they are not inflexible and are subject to changing conditions, and above all each case must be judged individually.

1. If the material has the slightest redeeming social importance it is not obscene because it is protected by the First and Fourteenth Amendments of the United States Constitution, and the California Constitution.

2. If it does not have the slightest redeeming social importance it may be obscene.

3. The test of obscenity in California is that the material must have a tendency to deprave or corrupt readers by exciting lascivious thoughts or arousing lustful desire to the point that it presents a clear and present danger of inciting to anti-social or immoral action.

4. The book or material must be judged as a whole by its effect on the *average adult* in the community.

5. If the material is objectionable only because of coarse and vulgar language which is not erotic or aphrodisiac in character it is not obscene.

6. Scienter must be proved.

7. Book reviews may be received in evidence if properly authenticated.

8. Evidence of expert witnesses in the literary field is proper.

9. Comparison of the material with other similar material previously adjudicated is proper.

10. The people owe a duty to themselves and to each other to preserve and protect their constitutional freedoms from any encroachment by government unless it appears that the allowable limits of such protection have been breached, and then to take only such action as will heal the breach.

11. I agree with Mr. Justice Douglas: I have the same confidence in the ability of our people to reject noxious literature as I have in their capacity to sort out the true from the false in theology, economics, politics, or any other field.

12. In considering material claimed to be obscene it is well to remember the motto: "*Honi soit qui mal y pense.*" (Evil to him who evil thinks.)

Therefore, I conclude the book "Howl and Other Poems" does have some redeeming social importance, and I find the book is not obscene.

The defendant is found not guilty.

Appendix IV
Model Texts: Inspirations Precursor to HOWL

Commentary on Poems

These poems were familiar to me by summer 1955. They're arranged in chronological order, a mini-anthology drawn from *Anthology XX Century Expansive Poetry & Heroic Precursors*, composed for my Poetics classes at Naropa Institute.* The principle is expansion of breath, inspiration as in unobstructed breath, "unchecked original impulse" expressed by Walt Whitman. Memory of these verse rhythms superimposed on my own breath passed into the inspiration of "Howl."

The elasticity of the long verse line of Christopher Smart is the immediate inspiration *by ear*. No other English verse plays with humorous quantitative delicacy of line, variably long or short, counterpointed to its neighbors in such accurate balance. Smart's aural intelligence tends to the appropriate syncopated whip crack of a definite self-enclosed rhythm. Here a "variable measure" differs from the powerful ten-syllable balances of Milton. Blake's prophetic verse has similar integrity derived from Hebrew Biblic prosody.

With Shelley we have the buildup of mighty rhythm to ecstatic consciousness: the consciousness of Inspiration, or Breath itself (life as breathing, *spīritus*) as the pivotal self-contemplative subject of the poem. Theme and Word are one.

> The breath whose might I have invoked in song
> Descends on me; my spirit's bark is driven . . .
> ("Adonais")
> . . . be thou, Spirit fierce,
> My spirit!   ("Ode to the West Wind")

This symphonic Hallelujah-like chorale of romantic absolutism, reaching its apogee in Shelley's breakthru to unobstructed Spirit, heard from my poet father's breath in childhood, determines the physical spirit of my own poetry.

In Apollinaire's "Zone" we have the variable breath-stop line of Smart, with the superimposition of the Modern: XX Century automobiles, hangars at the airfield, posters, newspapers, billboards, an industrial street, the world's altitude record, a dirty bar, milkmen. Apollinaire introduces the jump cut, as from "Coblenz at the Hotel of the Giant" to "Rome sitting under a Japanese medlar tree": montage of time & space, surrealist juxtaposition of opposites, compression of images, mind gaps or dissociations, "hydrogen jukeboxes."

Kurt Schwitters' "Priimiitittiii" provided a model

---

* A contemplative college founded 1974 by Chögyam Trungpa, Rinpoche, in Boulder, Colorado, with its Jack Kerouac School of Disembodied Poetics; formally accredited 1986. It is the first such Buddhist college in the Western World.

structure for pure sound. Despite mystical and sociologic preoccupations, the practical base for poetry is aesthetics of mouth & ear. This "art for art's sake" requires humorous dispassionate inquisitiveness into word materials, in this case sound-forms. How make logical measures & symmetric structures out of the variable breath of long verse? Specifically, Schwitters' little pyramid of sound, the anaphoric fugue-like structure of "Priimiitittiii," provided shape for the graduated litany used in Part III of "Howl" (and later "Kaddish," Part IV).

Frank O'Hara first showed me Marshall's translation of Mayakovsky's penultimate suicide death rattle, "At the Top of My Voice": "My verse / with labour / thrusts through weighted years . . ." Eternal voice claims mortal majesty, self-created or self-born, thus equal to the universe itself, of same stuff as universe. Shakespeare scribes this universal public voice, "That in black ink my love may still shine bright . . . / You still shall live—such virtue hath my pen— / Where breath most breathes, even in the mouths of men." As it breathes "by the incantation of this verse" in Shelley's "West Wind," it sings through Bob Dylan's "Hard Rain": "And I'll tell it and think it and speak it and breathe it / And reflect from the mountain where all souls can see it."

Though in Shelley's terza rima and Spencerian stanzas, Apollinaire's Cubist associations and Mayakovsky's rhymed ladders we have artful means of prophetic proclamation, Antonin Artaud's holy despair breaks all old verse forms and arrives at breath identical to the concentrated spontaneous utterance of besieged spirit burning & "signalling through the flames" of historical or personal crisis. Artaud's physical breath has inevitable propulsion toward specific inviolable insight on "Moloch whose name is the Mind!" My familiarity with this text comes from Carl Solomon, 1948.

Lorca's spirit transcending the concrete prison of megalopolis is articulated with montage of concrete attributes: "New York of wires and death: / What angel do you carry hidden in your cheek? / . . . beard full of butterflies / . . . corduroy shoulders worn down by the moon . . ." Here the variable verse line of Whitman gets "hopped up" to hyperbole, intensified by inclusion of mind-jump-cut facts put together in a flash, surrealist agility.

Hart Crane's "Atlantis" harks back to "Adonais"' mighty rhyme. His blank verse builds an ecstatic expostulation of spirit similar to Shelley's abandon. Crane provides an American bench mark of spiritual breath, updated with industrial landscape & futurist vision. He tries for breakthrough to eternal consciousness: the will is there, the heart passion, the physical ear, the human means for such a pillar of air or whirlwind of inspiration. Although the visual object is fragmented or composite, the breath is precise, practical, grounded, and so it does attain its object—the release of devotional generosity.

In William Carlos Williams' more moderate analysis, "The pure products of America go crazy," we have a breakthrough parallel to Crane's. W.C.W.'s insight is focused in pictures, the world is appreciated sanely, visually objectified. An extensive breath is maintained in a long sentence encompassing not only our hell of despair ("excrement of some sky") but also a version of real paradise ("deer going by fields of goldenrod"), as well as our everyday maneuverings—"no one to drive the car."

Whitman as innovator of many of these breaths and visions remains a mountain too vast to be seen. Natural ecstasy, surrealist juxtaposition ("seas of bright juice suffuse heaven"), long line including startling raw observation of ordinary mind (amounting to surrealism), breakthrough out of the crust of hyper-industrialized consciousness, majestic proclamation of presence, consciousness of the mortal ground of immortality—these the good gray Bard has in abundance.

Unscrew the locks from the doors!
Unscrew the doors themselves from their jambs!
                                                    A. G.

Christopher Smart (b. 1722): from *Jubilate Agno*

Let Elizur rejoice with the Partridge, who is a prisoner of state and is proud of his keepers.

Let Shedeur rejoice with Pyrausta, who dwelleth in a medium of fire, which God hath adapted for him.

Let Shelumiel rejoice with Olor, who is of a goodly savour, and the very look of him harmonizes the mind.

Let Jael rejoice with the Plover, who whistles for his live, and foils the marksmen and their guns.

Let Raguel rejoice with the Cock of Portugal—God send good Angels to the allies of England!

Let Hobab rejoice with Necydalus, who is the Greek of a Grub.

Let Zurishaddai with the Polish Cock rejoice—The Lord restore peace to Europe.

Let Zuar rejoice with the Guinea Hen—The Lord add to his mercies in the WEST!

Let Chesed rejoice with Strepsiceros, whose weapons are the ornaments of his peace.

Let Hagar rejoice with Gnesion, who is the right sort of eagle, and towers the highest.

Let Libni rejoice with the Redshank, who migrates not but is translated to the upper regions.

Let Nahshon rejoice with the Seabreese, the Lord give the sailors of his Spirit.

Let Helon rejoice with the Woodpecker—the Lord encourage the propagation of trees!

Let Amos rejoice with the Coote—prepare to meet thy God, O Israel.

Let Ephah rejoice with Buprestis, the Lord endue us with temperance & humanity, till every cow have her mate!

For I am not without authority in my jeopardy, which I derive inevitably from the glory of the name of the Lord.

For I bless God whose name in Jealous—and there is a zeal to deliver us from everlasting burnings.

For my existimation is good even amongst the slanderers and my memory shall arise for a sweet savour unto the Lord.

For I bless the PRINCE of PEACE and pray that all the guns may be nail'd up, save such as are for the rejoicing days.

For I have abstained from the blood of the grape and that even at the Lord's table.

For I have glorified God in GREEK and LATIN, the consecrated languages spoken by the Lord on earth.

For I meditate the peace of Europe amongst family bickerings and domestic jars.

For the HOST is in the WEST—the Lord make us thankful unto salvation.

For I preach the very GOSPEL of CHRIST without comment & with this weapon shall I slay envy.

For I bless God in the rising generation, which is on my side.

For I have translated in the charity, which makes things better & I shall be translated myself at the last.

For he that walked upon the sea, hath prepared the floods with the Gospel of peace.

For the merciful man is merciful to his beast, and to the trees that give them shelter.

For he hath turned the shadow of death into the morning, the Lord is his name.

For I am come home again, but there is nobody to kill the calf or to pay the musick.

Fragment "B1," Stanzas 3–44. *Jubilate Agno*, ed. W. H. Bond (New York: Greenwood Press, 1969).

Let Sarah rejoice with the Redwing, whose harvest is in the frost and snow.

Let Rebekah rejoice with Iynx, who holds his head on one side to deceive the adversary.

Let Shuah rejoice with Boa, which is the vocal serpent.

Let Ehud rejoice with Onocrotalus, whose braying is for the glory of God, because he makes the best musick in his power.

Let Shamgar rejoice with Otis, who looks about him for the glory of God, & sees the horizon compleat at once.

Let Bohan rejoice with the Scythian Stag—he is beef and breeches against want & nakedness.

Let Achsah rejoice with the Pigeon who is an antidote to malignity and will carry a letter.

Let Tohu rejoice with the Grouse—the Lord further the cultivating of heaths & the peopling of deserts.

Let Hillel rejoice with Ammodytes, whose colour is deceitful and he plots against the pilgrim's feet.

Let Eli rejoice with Leucon —he is an honest fellow, which is a rarity.

Let Jemuel rejoice with Charadrius, who is from the HEIGHT & the sight of him is good for the jaundice.

Let Pharaoh rejoice with Anataria, whom God permits to prey upon the ducks to check their increase.

Let Lotan rejoice with Sauterelle. Blessed be the name of the Lord from the Lote-tree to the Palm.

Let Dishon rejoice with the Landrail, God give his grace to the society for preserving the game.

Let Hushim rejoice with the King's Fisher, who is of royal beauty, tho' plebeian size.

Let Machir rejoice with Convolvulus, from him to the ring of Saturn, which is the girth of Job; to the signet of God from Job & his daughters BLESSED BE JESUS.

Let Atad bless with Eleos, the nightly Memorialist ε λεησον χυριε.

Let Jamin rejoice with the Bittern blessed be the name of Jesus for Denver Sluice, Ruston, & the draining of the fens.

Let Ohad rejoice with Byturos who eateth the vine and is a minister of temperance.

Let Zohar rejoice with Cychramus who cometh with the quails on a particular affair.

Let Serah, the daughter of Asher, rejoice with Ceyx, who maketh his cabin in the Halcyon's hold.

Let Magdiel rejoice with Ascarides, which is the life of the bowels—the worm hath a part in our frame.

For the hour of my felicity, like the womb of Sarah, shall come at the latter end.

For I shou'd have avail'd myself of waggery, had not malice been multitudinous.

For there are still serpents that can speak—God bless my head, my heart & my heel.

For I bless God that I am of the same seed as Ehud, Mutius Scævola, and Colonel Draper.

For the word of God is a sword on my side—no matter what other weapon a stick or a straw.

For I have adventured myself in the name of the Lord, and he hath mark'd me for his own.

For I bless God for the Postmaster general & all conveyancers of letters under his care especially Allen & Shelvock.

For my grounds in New Canaan shall infinitely compensate for the flats & maynes of Staindrop Moor.

For the praise of God can give to a mute fish the notes of a nightingale.

For I have seen the White Raven & Thomas Hall of Willingham & am myself a greater curiosity than both.

For I look up to heaven which is my prospect to escape envy by surmounting it.

For if Pharaoh had known Joseph, he woud have blessed God & me for the illumination of the people.

For I pray God to bless improvements in gardening till London be a city of palm-trees.

For I pray to give his grace to the poor of England, that Charity be not offended & that benevolence may increase.

For in my nature I quested for beauty, but God, God hath sent me to sea for pearls.

For there is a blessing from the STONE of Jesus which is founded upon hell to the precious jewell on the right hand of God.

For the nightly Visitor is at the window of the impenitent, while I sing a psalm of my own composing.

For there is a note added to the scale, which the Lord hath made fuller, stronger & more glorious.

For I offer my goat as he browses the vine, bless the Lord from chambering & drunkeness.

For there is a traveling for the glory of God without going to Italy or France.

For I bless the children of Asher for the evil I did them & the good I might have received at their hands.

For I rejoice like a worm in the rain in him that cherishes and from him that tramples.

Let Becher rejoice with Oscen who terrifies the wicked, as trumpet and alarm the coward.

Let Shaul rejoice with Circos, who hath clumsy legs, but he can wheel it the better with his wings.

Let Hamul rejoice with the Crystal, who is pure and translucent.

Let Ziphion rejoice with the Tit-Lark who is a groundling, but he raises the spirits.

Let Mibzar rejoice with the Cadess, as is their number, so are their names, blessed be the Lord Jesus for them all.

Let Jubal rejoice with Cæcilia, the woman and the slow-worm praise the name of the Lord.

Let Arodi rejoice with the Royston Crow, there is a society of them at Trumpington & Cambridge.

For I am ready for the trumpet & alarm to fight, to die & to rise again.

For the banish'd of the Lord shall come about again, for so he hath prepared for them.

For sincerity is a jewel which is pure & transparent, eternal & inestimable.

For my hands and my feet are perfect as the sublimity of Naphtali and the felicity of Asher.

For the names and number of animals are as the names and number of the stars.

For I pray the Lord Jesus to translate my MAGNIFICAT into verse and represent it.

For I bless the Lord Jesus from the bottom of Royston Cave to the top of King's Chapel.

Percy Bysshe Shelley (b. 1791): from *Adonais*

Who mourns for Adonais? Oh, come forth,
Fond wretch! and know thyself and him aright.
Clasp with thy panting soul the pendulous Earth;
As from a center, dart thy spirit's light
Beyond all worlds, until its spacious might
Satiate the void circumference: then shrink
Even to a point within our day and night;
And keep thy heart light lest it make thee sink
When hope has kindled hope, and lured thee to the brink.

Or go to Rome, which is the sepulcher,
Oh, not of him, but of our joy: 'tis naught
That ages, empires, and religions there
Lie buried in the ravage they have wrought;
For such as he can lend—they borrow not
Glory from those who made the world their prey;
And he is gathered to the kings of thought
Who waged contention with their time's decay,
And of the past are all that cannot pass away.

Go thou to Rome—at once the Paradise,
The grave, the city, and the wilderness;
And where its wrecks like shattered mountains rise,
And flowering weeds, and fragrant copses dress
The bones of Desolation's nakedness
Pass, till the spirit of the spot shall lead
Thy footsteps to a slope of green access
Where, like an infant's smile, over the dead
A light of laughing flowers along the grass is spread;

And gray walls molder round, on which dull Time
Feeds, like slow fire upon a hoary brand;
And one keen pyramid with wedge sublime,
Pavilioning the dust of him who planned

Final stanzas, 47–55.

This refuge for his memory, doth stand
Like flame transformed to marble; and beneath,
A field is spread, on which a newer band
Have pitched in Heaven's smile their camp of death,
Welcoming him we lose with scarce extinguished breath.

Here pause: these graves are all too young as yet
To have outgrown the sorrow which consigned
Its charge to each; and if the seal is set,
Here, on one fountain of a mourning mind,
Break it not thou! too surely shalt thou find
Thine own well full, if thou returnest home,
Of tears and gall. From the world's bitter wind
Seek shelter in the shadow of the tomb.
What Adonais is, why fear we to become?

The One remains, the many change and pass;
Heaven's light forever shines, Earth's shadows fly;
Life, like a dome of many-colored glass,
Stains the white radiance of Eternity,
Until Death tramples it to fragments.—Die,
If thou wouldst be with that which thou dost seek!
Follow where all is fled!—Rome's azure sky,
Flowers, ruins, statues, music, words, are weak
The glory they transfuse with fitting truth to speak.

Why linger, why turn back, why shrink, my Heart?
Thy hopes are gone before: from all things here
They have departed; thou shouldst now depart!
A light is passed from the revolving year,
And man, and woman; and what still is dear
Attracts to crush, repels to make thee wither.
The soft sky smiles—the low wind whispers near:
'Tis Adonais calls! oh, hasten thither,
No more let Life divide what Death can join together.

That Light whose smile kindles the Universe,
That Beauty in which all things work and move,
That Benediction which the eclipsing Curse

Of birth can quench not, that sustaining Love
Which through the web of being blindly wove
By man and beast and earth and air and sea,
Burns bright or dim, as each are mirrors of
The fire for which all thirst; now beams on me,
Consuming the last clouds of cold mortality.

The breath whose might I have invoked in song
Descends on me; my spirit's bark is driven,
Far from the shore, far from the trembling throng
Whose sails were never to the tempest given;
The massy earth and spherèd skies are riven!
I am borne darkly, fearfully, afar;
Whilst, burning through the inmost veil of Heaven,
The soul of Adonais, like a star,
Beacons from the abode where the Eternal are.

Percy Bysshe Shelley: *Ode to the West Wind*

I

O wild West Wind, thou breath of Autumn's being,
Thou, from whose unseen presence the leaves dead
Are driven, like ghosts from an enchanter fleeing,

Yellow, and black, and pale, and hectic red,
Pestilence-stricken multitudes: O thou,
Who chariotest to their dark wintry bed

The wingèd seeds, where they lie cold and low,
Each like a corpse within its grave, until
Thine azure sister of the Spring shall blow

Her clarion o'er the dreaming earth, and fill
(Driving sweet buds like flocks to feed in air)
With living hues and odors plain and hill:

Wild Spirit, which art moving everywhere;
Destroyer and preserver; hear, oh, hear!

II

Thou on whose stream, mid the steep sky's commotion,
Loose clouds like earth's decaying leaves are shed,
Shook from the tangled boughs of Heaven and Ocean,

Angels of rain and lightning: there are spread
On the blue surface of thine aery surge,
Like the bright hair uplifted from the head

Of some fierce Maenad, even from the dim verge
Of the horizon to the zenith's height,
The locks of the approaching storm. Thou dirge

Of the dying year, to which this closing night
Will be the dome of a vast sepulcher,
Vaulted with all thy congregated might

Of vapors, from whose solid atmosphere
Black rain, and fire, and hail will burst: oh, hear!

III

Thou who didst waken from his summer dreams
The blue Mediterranean, where he lay,
Lulled by the coil of his crystàlline streams,

Beside a pumice isle in Baiae's bay,
And saw in sleep old palaces and towers
Quivering within the wave's intenser day,

All overgrown with azure moss and flowers
So sweet, the sense faints picturing them! Thou
For whose path the Atlantic's level powers

Cleave themselves into chasms, while far below
The sea-blooms and the oozy woods which wear
The sapless foliage of the ocean, know

Thy voice, and suddenly grow gray with fear,
And tremble and despoil themselves: oh, hear!

IV

If I were a dead leaf thou mightest bear;
If I were a swift cloud to fly with thee;
A wave to pant beneath thy power, and share

The impulse of thy strength, only less free
Than thou, O uncontrollable! If even
I were as in my boyhood, and could be

The comrade of thy wanderings over Heaven,
As then, when to outstrip thy skiey speed
Scarce seemed a vision; I would ne'er have striven

As thus with thee in prayer in my sore need.
Oh, lift me as a wave, a leaf, a cloud!
I fall upon the thorns of life! I bleed!

A heavy weight of hours has chained and bowed
One too like thee: tameless, and swift, and proud.

V

Make me thy lyre, even as the forest is:
What if my leaves are falling like its own!
The tumult of thy mighty harmonies

Will take from both a deep, autumnal tone,
Sweet though in sadness. Be thou, Spirit fierce,
My spirit! Be thou me, impetuous one!

Drive my dead thoughts over the universe
Like withered leaves to quicken a new birth!
And, by the incantation of this verse,

Scatter, as from an unextinguished hearth
Ashes and sparks, my words among mankind!
Be through my lips to unwakened earth

The trumpet of a prophecy! O, Wind,
If Winter comes, can Spring be far behind?

Guillaume Apollinaire (b. 1880): *Zone*

You are tired at last of this old world

O shepherd Eiffel Tower the flock of bridges bleats at the
morning

You have had enough of life in this Greek and Roman
antiquity

Even the automobiles here seem to be ancient
Religion alone has remained entirely fresh religion
Has remained simple like the hangars at the airfield

You alone in all Europe are not antique O Christian faith
The most modern European is you Pope Pius X
And you whom the windows look down at shame pre-
vents you
From entering a church and confessing this morning
You read prospectuses catalogues and posters which shout
aloud
Here is poetry this morning and for prose there are the
newspapers
There are volumes for 25 centimes full of detective stories
Portraits of famous men and a thousand assorted titles

This morning I saw a pretty street whose name I have
forgotten
Shining and clean it was the sun's bugle
Executives and workers and lovely secretaries
From Monday morning to Saturday evening pass here
four times a day
In the morning the siren wails three times
A surly bell barks around noon
Lettering on signs and walls
Announcements and billboards shriek like parrots
I love the charm of this industrial street
Located in Paris somewhere between the rue Aumont-
Thiéville and the avenue des Ternes
Here is the young street and you are once again a little
child
Your mother dresses you only in blue and white
You are very pious and with your oldest friend René
Dalize
You like nothing so well as the ceremonies of church
It is nine o'clock the gas is down to the blue you come
secretly out of the dormitory
You pray the whole night in the college chapel
While eternal and adorable an amethyst profundity
The flaming glory of Christ turns for ever
It is the beautiful lily we all cultivate
It is the red-headed torch which the wind cannot blow
out
It is the pale and ruddy son of a sorrowful mother
It is the tree always thick with prayers
It is the double gallows of honor and of eternity
It is a six-pointed star
It is God who died on Friday and rose again on Sunday

Selected Writings, trans. Roger Shattuck (New York: New
Directions, 1971).

It is Christ who soars in the sky better than any aviator
He breaks the world's altitude record
Christ the pupil of the eye
Twentieth pupil of the centuries he knows how
And turned into a bird this century rises in the air like
Jesus
The devils in their abysses lift their heads to look at it
They say it is imitating Simon Magus in Judea
They shout that if it knows how to fly it should be called
a flyer
Angels hover about the lovely aerialist
Icarus Enoch Elijah Apollonius of Tyana
Flutter around the original airplane
They separate occasionally to give passage to those whom
the Holy Eucharist carries up
Those priests who rise eternally in lifting the host
The airplane lands at last without folding its wings
The sky fills up then with millions of swallows
In a flash crows falcons and owls arrive
Ibis flamingoes and marabous arrive from Africa
The great Roc celebrated by story tellers and poets
Glides down holding in its claws Adam's scull the first
head
The eagle rushes out of the horizon giving a great cry
From America comes the tiny humming-bird
From China have come long supple pihis
Which only have one wing and fly tandem
Then the dove immaculate spirit
Escorted by the lyre bird and the ocellated peacock
The phoenix that pyre which recreates itself
Veils everything for an instant with its glowing coals
Sirens leaving their perilous straits
Arrive all three of them singing beautifully
And everything eagle phoenix and Chinese pihis
Fraternize with the flying machine

Now you walk through Paris all alone in the crowd
Herds of bellowing busses roll by near you
The agony of love tightens your throat
As if you could never be loved again
If you were living in olden days you would enter a
monastery
You are ashamed when you catch yourself saying a
prayer
You ridicule yourself and your laughter bursts out like
hell fire
The sparks of your laughter gild the depths of your life
It is a picture hung in a somber museum
And sometimes you go to look at it closely

Today you walk through Paris the women are blood-
stained
It was and I would prefer not to remember it was during
beauty's decline

Surrounded by fervent flames Notre Dame looked at me
in Chartres
The blood of your Sacred Heart flooded me in the
Montmartre
I am ill from hearing happy words

The love from which I suffer is a shameful sickness
And the image which possesses you makes you survive in
  sleeplessness and anguish
It is always near you this passing image

Now you are on the shore of the Mediterranean
Under the lemon trees which blossom all year
With your friends you take a boat ride
One from Nice one from Menton and two from Turbie
We look down in fear at the octopodes on the bottom
And amid the algae swim fish images of our Saviour
You are in the garden of an inn on the outskirts of Prague
You feel completely happy a rose is on the table
And instead of writing your story in prose you watch
The rosebug which is sleeping in the heart of the rose
Astonished you see yourself outlined in the agates of St.
  Vitus
You were sad enough to die the day you saw yourself in
  them
You looked like Lazarus bewildered by the light
The hands of the clock in the Jewish quarter turn back-
  wards
And you go slowly backwards in your life
Climbing up to Hradchin and listening at night
In taverns to the singing of Czech songs

Here you are in Marseilles amid the watermelons

Here you are in Coblenz at the Hotel of the Giant

Here you are in Rome sitting under a Japanese medlar
  tree

Here you are in Amsterdam with a girl you find pretty
  and who is ugly
She is to marry a student from Leyden
There are rooms for rent in Latin Cubicula locanda
I remember I stayed three days there and as many at
  Gouda

You are in Paris at the *juge d'instruction*
Like a criminal you are placed under arrest
You have made sorrowful and happy trips
Before noticing that the world lies and grows old
You suffered from love at twenty and thirty
I have lived like a fool and wasted my time
You no longer dare look at your hands and at every
  moment I want to burst out sobbing
For you for her I love for everything that has frightened
  you

With tear-filled eyes you look at those poor emigrants
They believe in God they pray the women nurse their
  children
Their odor fills the waiting room of the gare Saint-Lazare
They have faith in their star like the Magi
They hope to make money in Argentina
And come back to their countries having made their
  fortunes
One family carries a red quilt as one carries one's heart

That quilt and our dream are both unreal
Some of these emigrants stay here and find lodging
In hovels in the rue des Rosiers or the rue des Écouffes
I have often seen them in the evening they take a stroll
  in the street
And rarely travel far like men on a checker board
There are mostly Jews their wives wear wigs
They sit bloodlessly in the backs of little shops

You are standing at the counter of a dirty bar
You have a cheap coffee with the rest of the riffraff

At night you are in a big restaurant

These women are not wicked still they have their worries
All of them even the ugliest has made her lover suffer
She is the daughter of a policeman on the Isle of Jersey

Her hands which I have not seen are hard and chapped
I have an immense pity for the scars on her belly

I humble my mouth by offering it to a poor slut with a
  horrible laugh

You are alone the morning is almost here
The milkmen rattle their cans in the street

The night departs like a beautiful half-caste
False Ferdine or waiting Leah

And you drink this burning liquor like your life
Your life which you drink like an eau-de-vie

You walk toward Auteuil you want to walk home on foot
To sleep among your fetishes from Oceania and Guinea
They are all Christ in another form and of another faith
They are inferior Christs obscure hopes

Adieu adieu

The sun a severed neck

Kurt Schwitters (b. 1887): *Priimiitittiii*

priimiitittiii	tisch
tesch	
priimiitittiii	tesh
tusch	
priimiitittiii	tischa
tescho	
priimiitittiii	tescho
tuschi	
priimiitittiii	
priimiitittiii	
priimiitittiii	too
priimiitittiii	taa
priimiitittiii	too
priimiitittiii	taa
priimiitittiii	tootaa
priimiitittiii	tootaa
priimiitittiii	tuutaa
priimiitittiii	tuutaa
priimiitittiii	tuutaatoo
priimiitittiii	tuutaatoo
priimiitittiii	tuutaatoo
priimiitittiii	tuutaatoo

Dada Painters and Poets: An Anthology, ed. Robert Motherwell (New York: George Wittenborn, 1947).

Vladimir Mayakovsky (b. 1893): *At the Top of My Voice*—First Prelude to a Poem of the Five Year Plan

Most respected
    comrades heirs and descendants:
Excavating
    our contemporary
        petrified muck
studying our days through dark dead centuries,
you'll,
    maybe,
        ask about me, Mayakovsky.
And, maybe,

your scholars will then reveal—
swamping with erudition
    questions that swarm—
there lived once a singer
    blood all-a-boil,
who hated most cold-water raw.
Professor,
    take off those optical-bicycles!
I'll myself relate
    about the times
        about myself.
I'm a sanitary inspector
    and water-carrier,

Mayakovsky and His Poetry, trans. Herbert Marshall (Bombay: Current Book House, 1955).

mobilised to the front
    by revolution,
        I came
from the seignorial horticulture
of poetry
    a most capricious dame,
precious Muse that grows, like Mary,
roses
    round
        a bungalow.
"Mary, Mary, quite contrary,
    how does your garden grow?"
Some pour verses from a sprinkler,
some just splutter
    from their lips—
curly-headed Mitraikies,
    muddle-headed Kudraikies—
who the devil knows which from which:
No quarantine will take them in—
there's those mandolines again:
"Tara-tina tara-tina
    t.......e.......n.......n..."
Not much of an honour,
    that from such roses
my very own statue will rise
over squares,
with gobs of tuberculosis,
where whores with hooligans
    and—syphilis . . .
I'm fed
    to the teeth
        with agit-prop,
I'd like
    to scribble for you
        love-ballads—
they're charming
    and pay quite a lot.
But I
    mastered myself,
        and crushed under foot
the throat
    of my very own songs.
Hi listen!
    Comrades heirs and descendants,
to an agitator,
    loud-speaker-in-chief:
Deafening
    poetic deluge,
I stride to you
    through lyrical volumes,
as the live
    with the living speaks.
I'll come to you
    in the distant communist far-off,
but not
    like Yessenin's rhymed knight-errants.
My verse will reach
    over the peaks of eras
far over the heads
    of poets and governments.

My verse will come,
but will come not ornate—
not like an arrow's
    lyrical love-flight from Eros,
not like a worn-out coin
    comes to the numismat
and not like the light of long-dead stars arrives.

My verse
    with labour
        thrusts through weighted years
emerging,
    ponderous,
        rock-rough,
            age-grim,
as when to-day
    an aqueduct appears,
firm-grounded once
    by the branded slaves of Rome.
You'll accidentally find
    in barrows of books,
wrought-iron lines of long-buried poems,
handle them
    with the care that respects
ancient
    but terrible weapons.
My words
    are not used
        to caressing ears;
nor titillate
    with semi-obscenities
maiden ears
    hidden in hair so innocent.
I open on parade
    my pages of fighters,
pass in review
    their lineal front.
My verses stand
    in lead-heavy letters,
ready for death
    and for deathless glory.
Stock-still stand my poems
    muzzle to muzzle set,
their gaping titles aimed
    and at the ready!
And weapons most beloved yet,
ever ready to
    charge with a cheer,
rear all alert
    my cavalry of wit,

tilting their rhymes,
    sharp-pointed spears.
And every single one
    armed to the teeth,
that swept through twenty years
    victorious,
every single one,
    to the very last leaf

I give to you,
    planet-proletariat.
The foe
    of the working class colossal—
is my own foe,
    dead-poisonous and ancient.
We marched behind the blood-red flag—
    impelled
by years of work
    and days of sheer starvation.
We opened
    Marx and Engels
            every tome,
as in our home
    we open wide the shutters,
but without reading
    we understood alone,
whose side we're on
    and in which camp we're fighters.
And not from Hegel
    did we learn
            our dialectics.
That burst
    through interclashing conflict
            into verse,
when under fire
    the bourgeois
            ran from our attacks,
as we
    once also
        ran from theirs.
Let glory,
    disconsolate widow frail,
trudge after genius
    in funeral anthems.
Die, my verse,
    die, like the rank and file,
as our unknown, unnumbered, fell
    in storming heaven.
To hell
    with many-tonned bronzes,
To the devil
    with sleek marble slime!
We'll square up with glory—
    why, we're mates and brothers—
So let there be
    a common monument for us
built up in battles—
            socialism.
Descendants,
    in your lexicons
            look up the flotsam
that floats down from Lethe,
    odd remnant-words
like "prostitution,"
            "tuberculosis,"
                    "blockades."

For you,
    who're so healthy and nimble,
a poet
    licked up
        consumptive spittle
with the crude rough tongue of placards.
From the tail of the years
    I must resemble
a long-tailed monster
    from a fossilized age.
So come,
    Comrade Life,
        let's step hard on the throttle,
and roar out
    the Five-Year-Plan's,
        remnant days.
I haven't got
    a ruble
        left from my verse,
the cabinet-makers
    didn't send the furniture home.
But my only need's
    a clean-laundered shirt,
for the rest
    I honestly
        don't give a damn.
When I appear
    in Tsi-Ka-Ka
        of coming
            bright decades,
above the band
    of skin-flint grafters
        in rhymes,
I'll lift up high,
    like a Bolshevik party-card,
all the hundred books
    of my
        ComParty poems!

Antonin Artaud (b. 1895): from *Van Gogh—The Man Suicided by Society*

introduction

You can say all you want about the mental health of Van Gogh who, during his lifetime, cooked only one of his hands, and other than that did no more than cut off his left ear,

in a world in which every day they eat vagina cooked in green sauce or the genitals of a newborn child whipped into a rage

    plucked as it came out of the maternal sex.

Artaud Anthology, trans. Jack Hirschman (San Francisco: City Lights, 1965).

And this is not an image, but a fact abundantly and daily repeated and cultivated throughout the world.

And thus, demented as this assertion may seem, present-day life goes on in its old atmosphere of prurience, of anarchy, of disorder, of delirium, of dementia, of chronic lunacy, of bourgeois inertia, of psychic anomaly (for it isn't man but the world that has become abnormal), of deliberate dishonesty and downright hypocrisy, of a mean contempt for anything that shows breeding,

of the claim of an entire order based on the fulfillment of a primitive injustice,

in short, of organized crime.

Things are bad because the sick conscience now has a vital interest in not getting over its sickness.

So a sick society invented psychiatry to defend itself against the investigations of certain visionaries whose faculties of divination disturbed it.

· ·

Faced with Van Gogh's lucidity, always active, psychiatry becomes nothing but a den of gorillas, so obsessed and persecuted that it can only use a ridiculous terminology to palliate the most frightful anxiety and human suffocation

· ·

And what is a genuine lunatic?

He is a man who prefers to go mad, in the social sense of the word, rather than forfeit a certain higher idea of human honor.

That's how society strangled all those it wanted to get rid of, or wanted to protect itself from, and put them in asylums, because they refused to be accomplices to a kind of lofty swill.

For a lunatic is a man that society does not wish to hear but wants to prevent from uttering certain unbearable truths.

But in that case, internment is not the only weapon, and the concerted assemblage of men has other ways of undermining the wills of those it wants to break.

· ·

That is why there was a collective spell cast on Baudelaire, Edgar Allan Poe, Gérard de Nerval, Nietzsche, Kierkegaard, Hölderlin and Coleridge.

There was a spell cast on Van Gogh also.

It can happen during the day but preferably, and generally, it happens at night.

· ·

Confronted by this concerted swill, which deals with sex on the one hand and the masses of some other psychic rites on the other as a base or point of support, there is nothing unbalanced in walking around at night with 12 candles attached to your hat to paint a landscape from nature;

how else could Van Gogh have had light, as our friend the actor Roger Blin so rightly pointed out the other day?

As for the cooked hand, that was heroism pure and
simple;
   as for the severed ear, that was direct logic,
   and I repeat,
   a world that, day and night and more and more eats
the uneatable
   in order to bring its evil will around to its own ends,
   has nothing else to do at this point
   but to shut up.

. . . .

post-scriptum

And it happened to Van Gogh as it usually happens,
during an orgy, a mass, an absolution or any other rite of
consecration, possession, succubation or incubation.
   So it introduced itself into his body,
   this society
   absolved
   consecrated
   sanctified
   and possessed of the devil
   effaced the supernatural consciousness that he had
just acquired, and like a flood of black crows in the
fibers of his internal tree,
   submerged him in a last swell
   and, taking his place,
   killed him. . . .
   For it is the anatomical logic of modern man to
never have been able to live nor think of living except
as one possessed.

Federico García Lorca (b. 1898): *Ode to Walt Whitman*

Along the East River and the Bronx
the boys were singing showing their waists,
with the wheel, the oil, the leather and the hammer.
Ninety thousand miners extracted silver from rocks
and children drew stairs and perspectives.

But none would sleep,
none wanted to be a river,
none loved the great leaves,
none, the blue tongue of the beach.

Along the East River and the Queensborough
the boys were fighting with Industry,
and the Jews were selling to the faun of the river
the rose of the Circumcision,
and the sky rushed through bridges and roofs
herds of bison pushed by the wind.

The Selected Poems of Federico García Lorca, trans.
Stephen Spender and J. L. Gili (New York: New Directions,
1955).

But none would pause,
none wanted to be a cloud,
none searched for the ferns
nor the yellow wheel of the tambourine.

When the moon rises,
the pulleys will turn to disturb the sky:
a boundary of needles will fence in the memory
and the coffins will carry away those who do not work.

New York of slime,
New York of wires and death:
What angel do you carry hidden in your cheek?
What perfect voice will tell the truths of the wheat?
Who, the terrible dream of your stained anemones?

Not for one moment, beautiful aged Walt Whitman,
have I failed to see your beard full of butterflies,
nor your shoulders of corduroy worn out by the moon,
nor your thighs of virginal Apollo,
nor your voice like a pillar of ashes:
ancient and beautiful as the mist,
you moaned like a bird
with the sex transfixed by a needle,
enemy of the satyr,
enemy of the vine,
and lover of bodies under the rough cloth.
Not for one moment; virile beauty,
who in mountains of coal, posters and railways,
dreamed of being a river and sleeping like a river
with that comrade who would place in your breast
the small pain of an ignorant leopard.

Not for one moment, Adam of blood, male,
lone man in the sea, beautiful aged Walt Whitman,
because through the terraces,
clustered around the bars,
pouring out of sewers in bunches,
trembling between the legs of chauffeurs
or revolving on the platforms of absinthe,
the pansies, Walt Whitman, dreamed of you.

This one also! This one! And they fall
on your chaste and luminous beard,
Northern blonds, Negroes of the sands,
multitudes of shrieks and gestures,
like cats or like snakes,
the pansies, Walt Whitman, the pansies,
muddy with tears, flesh for the whip,
boot or bite of subduers.

This one also! This one! Tainted fingers
appear on the shore of your dreams
when the friend eats your apple
with a faint taste of petrol
and the sun sings along the navels
of boys that play under bridges.

But you did not search for the scratched eyes,
or the very dark swamp where children are submerged,
or the frozen saliva,
or the wounded curves resembling toad's bellies
which the pansies carry in cars and terraces
while the moon strikes at them along the corners of fear.

You searched for a nude who was like a river.
Bull and dream that would join the wheel with the
    seaweed,
father of your agony, camelia of your death,
and would moan in the flames of your hidden Equator.

Because it is just that man does not search for his delight
in the jungle of blood of the following morning.
The sky has shores where to avoid life,
and certain bodies must not repeat themselves in the
    dawn.

Agony, agony, dream, ferment and dream.
This is the world, my friend, agony, agony.
The corpses decompose under the clock of the cities.
War passes weeping with a million grey rats,
the rich give to their mistresses
small illuminated moribunds,
and Life is not noble, nor good, nor sacred.

Man can, if he wishes, lead his desire
through vein of coral or celestial nude:
tomorrow love will be rocks, and Time
a breeze which comes sleeping through the branches.

That is why I do not raise my voice, aged Walt Whitman,
against the little boy who writes
a girl's name on his pillow,
nor the boy who dresses himself in the bride's trousseau
in the darkness of the wardrobe,
nor the solitary men in clubs
who drink the water of prostitution with nausea,
nor the men with a green stare
who love man and burn their lips in silence.
But against you, yes, pansies of the cities,
of tumescent flesh and unclean mind,
mud of drains, harpies, unsleeping enemies
of Love which distributes crowns of joy.

Against you always, you who give boys
drops of soiled death with bitter poison.
Against you always,
Fairies of North America,
Pájaros of Havana,
Jotos of Mexico,
Sarasas of Cadiz,
Apios of Seville,
Cancos of Madrid,
Floras of Alicante,
Adelaidas of Portugal.

Pansies of the world, murderers of doves!
Women's slaves, bitches of their boudoirs,
opened with the fever of fans in public squares
or ambushed in frigid landscapes of hemlock.

Let there be no quarter! Death
flows from your eyes
and clusters grey flowers on the shores.
Let there be no quarter! Take heed!
Let the perplexed, the pure,
the classicists, the noted, the supplicants,
close the gates of the Bacchanalia.

And you, beautiful Walt Whitman, sleep on the Hudson's
    banks,
with your beard toward the Pole and your hands open.
Bland clay or snow, your tongue is calling for
comrades that keep watch on your gazelle without a
    body.
Sleep; nothing remains.
A dance of walls agitates the meadows
and America drowns itself in machines and lament.
I want the strong air of the most profound night
to remove flowers and words from the arch where you
    sleep,
and a black boy to announce to the gold-minded whites
the arrival of the reign of the ear of corn.

Hart Crane (b. 1899): *Atlantis*

Through the bound cable strands, the arching path
Upward, veering with light, the flight of strings,—
Taut miles of shuttling moonlight syncopate
The whispered rush, telepathy of wires.
Up the index of night, granite and steel—
Transparent meshes—fleckless the gleaming staves—
Sibylline voices flicker, waveringly stream
As though a god were issue of the strings. . . .

And through that cordage, threading with its call
One arc synoptic of all tides below—
Their labyrinthine mouths of history
Pouring reply as though all ships at sea
Complighted in one vibrant breath made cry,—
"Make thy love sure—to weave whose song we ply!"
—From black embankments, moveless soundings hailed,
So seven oceans answer from their dream.

And on, obliquely up bright carrier bars
New octaves trestle the twin monoliths
Beyond whose frosted capes the moon bequeaths
Two worlds of sleep (O arching strands of song!)—
Onward and up the crystal-flooded aisle
White tempest nets file upward, upward ring
With silver terraces the humming spars,
The loft of vision, palladium helm of stars.

Sheerly the eyes, like seagulls stung with rime—
Slit and propelled by glistening fins of light—
Pick biting way up towering looms that press
Sidelong with flight of blade on tendon blade
—Tomorrows into yesteryear—and link
What cipher-script of time no traveller reads
But who, through smoking pyres of love and death,
Searches the timeless laugh of mythic spears.

Like hails, farewells—up planet-sequined heights
Some trillion whispering hammers glimmer Tyre:
Serenely, sharply up the long anvil cry
Of inchling æons silence rivets Troy.
And you, aloft there—Jason! hesting Shout!
Still wrapping harness to the swarming air!
Silvery the rushing wake, surpassing call,
Beams yelling Æolus! splintered in the straits!

The Bridge (New York: Liveright, 1933).

From gulfs unfolding, terrible of drums,
Tall Vision-of-the-Voyage, tensely spare—
Bridge, lifting night to cycloramic crest
Of deepest day—O Choir, translating time
Into what multitudinous Verb the suns
And synergy of waters ever fuse, recast
In myriad syllables—Psalm of Cathay!
O Love, thy white, pervasive Paradigm . . . !

We left the haven hanging in the night—
Sheened harbor lanterns backward fled the keel.
Pacific here at time's end, bearing corn.—
Eyes stammer through the pangs of dust and steel.
And still the circular, indubitable frieze
Of heaven's meditation, yoking wave
To kneeling wave, one song devoutly binds—
The vernal strophe chimes from deathless strings!

O Thou steeled Cognizance whose leap commits
The agile precincts of the lark's return;
Within whose lariat sweep encinctured sing
In single chrysalis the many twain,—
Of stars Thou art the stitch and stallion glow
And like an organ, Thou, with sound of doom—
Sight, sound and flesh Thou leadest from time's realm
As love strikes clear direction for the helm.

Swift peal of secular light, intrinsic Myth
Whose fell unshadow is death's utter wound,—
O River-throated—iridescently upborne
Through the bright drench and fabric of our veins;
With white escarpments swinging into light,
Sustained in tears the cities are endowed
And justified conclamant with ripe fields
Revolving through their harvests in sweet torment.

Forever Deity's glittering Pledge, O Thou
Whose canticle fresh chemistry assigns
To wrapt inception and beatitude,—
Always through blinding cables, to our joy,
Of thy white seizure springs the prophecy:
Always through spiring cordage, pyramids
Of silver sequel, Deity's young name
Kinetic of white choiring wings . . . ascends.

Migrations that must needs void memory,
Inventions that cobblestone the heart,—
Unspeakable Thou Bridge to Thee, O Love.
Thy pardon for this history, whitest Flower,
O Anwerer of all—Anemone,—
Now while thy petals spend the suns about us, hold—
(O Thou whose radiance doth inherit me)
Atlantis,—hold thy floating singer late!

So to thine Everpresence, beyond time,
Like spears ensanguined of one tolling star
That bleeds infinity—the orphic strings,
Sidereal phalanxes, leap and converge:
—One Song, one Bridge of Fire! Is it Cathay,
Now pity steeps the grass and rainbows ring
The serpent with the eagle in the leaves . . . ?
Whispers antiphonal in azure swing.

William Carlos Williams (b. 1883): *To Elsie*

The pure products of America
go crazy—
mountain folk from Kentucky

or the ribbed north end of
Jersey
with its isolate lakes and

valleys, its deaf-mutes, thieves
old names
and promiscuity between

devil-may-care men who have taken
to railroading
out of sheer lust of adventure—

and young slatterns, bathed
in filth
from Monday to Saturday

to be tricked out that night
with gauds
from imaginations which have no

peasant traditions to give them
character
but flutter and flaunt

sheer rags—succumbing without
emotion
save numbed terror

under some hedge of choke-cherry
or viburnum—
which they cannot express—

Unless it be that marriage
perhaps
with a dash of Indian blood

will throw up a girl so desolate
so hemmed round
with disease or murder

that she'll be rescued by an
agent—
reared by the state and

sent out at fifteen to work in
some hard-pressed
house in the suburbs—

some doctor's family, some Elsie—
voluptuous water
expressing with broken

Collected Earlier Poems (New York: New Directions, 1966).

brain the truth about us—
her great
ungainly hips and flopping breast

addressed to cheap
jewelry
and rich young men with fine eyes

as if the earth under our feet
were
an excrement of some sky

and we degraded prisoners
destined
to hunger until we eat filth

while the imagination strains
after deer
going by fields of goldenrod in

the stifling heat of September
Somehow
it seems to destroy us

It is only in isolate flecks that
something
is given off

No one
to witness
and adjust, no one to drive the car

Appendix V
Bibliography of HOWL by Bill Morgan

HOWL Editions

Howl for Carl Solomon. San Francisco: Ditto mimeograph, May 16, 1956 (25–50 copies).

Howl and Other Poems. San Francisco: City Lights Books, November 1, 1956. Reprinted 33 times; unexpurgated edition beginning with 8th printing.

The Pocket Poets Series, Vol. 1. Millwood, N.Y.: Kraus Reprint Co., 1973.

Howl for Carl Solomon. San Francisco: Grabhorn-Hoyem, 1971 (275 copies).

Moloch. Lincoln, Mass.: Penmaen Press, 1978 (300 copies, broadside).

HOWL Translations

Albanian

Howl, Jeta E Re, Skopje, Yugoslavia, 1986. Translated by Fadil Bajraj.

Chinese

Modern American Poetry 2. Beijing: Foreign Literature Publishing House, 1985. Translated by Yihen H. Zhao.

Su Que Bu [*Poetry Gazette*]. Hefei, Anhwei, 1986.

Czech

"Kvileni," in *Sesity* 30 (April 1969). Translated by Jan Zabrana.

Danish

A.G. "Hyl," in *Nyt fra Jorden.* Arhus, Denmark: Rhodos, 1969. Translated by Erik Thygesen.

Thygesen, Erik, ed. *San Francisco Renaissancen.* Odense, Denmark: Sirius Forlagt, 1964. Translated by Erik Thygesen and Ib Ørnoskov.

"Hylen" in *Vindrosen* 6, no. 4 (May 1959). Translated by Poul Sørensen.

Dutch

A.G. "Howl," in *Proef m'n tong in je oor.* Amsterdam: De Bezige Bij, 1966. Translated by Simon Vinkenoog.

Van Son, Jacques. "Howl," in *The Beat Generation/Bob Dylan.* Utrecht, Netherlands: Spektakel/Walhalla, 1979.

Finnish

A.G. "Huuto," in *Huuto Ja Muita Runoja.* Turku, Finland: Kustannusliike Tajo, 1963. Translated by Anselm Hollo.

"Huuto," in *Parnasso* 2 (1961). Translated by Anselm Hollo.

French

A.G. *Howl and Other Poems.* Paris: Christian Bourgois, 1977. Translated by Robert Cordier and Jean-Jacques Lebel.

A. G. *Howl and Other Poems/Kaddish.* Paris: Christian Bourgois, 1980. Translated by Robert Cordier and Jean-Jacques Lebel.

Lebel, Jean-Jacques. *La Poésie de la Beat Generation.* Paris: Denoël, 1965. Translated by Jean-Jacques Lebel.

Ellipse 8–9. Montreal, 1971. Translated by Jean-Jacques Lebel.

German

A.G. "Geheul," in *Das Geheul und andere Gedichte.* Wiesbaden: Limes Verlag, 1959. Translated by Wolfgang Fleischmann and Rudolf Wittkopf.

A.G. "Geheul," in *Das Geheul und andere Gedichte.* Wiesbaden: Limes Verlag, 1979. Translated by Carl Weissner.

"Geheul," in *Akzente* 1 (1959). Translated by Walter Höllerer.

"Geheul," in *Exempla* 3, no. 1 (1977). Translated by Jörg Ross.

Greek

A.G. "ΟΤΡΛΙΑΧΡΟ," in *Sugkhroné Poiésé.* Athens: Boukoumanis, 1974. Translated by Jennie Mastorski.

A.G. "ΟΤΡΛΙΑΧΡΟ," in *Poiémata.* Athens: AKMON, 1978. Translated by Aris Berlis.

Hebrew

Omer, Dan, ed. *An Anthology of American Beat Poetry.* Jersualem, Israel: I. Marcus, 1967. Translated by Dan Omer.

Iked 2 (July 1960). Translated by Isumor Yeiuz Kest.

Hungarian

A.G. "Üvöltés," in *Nagyáruház Kaliforniában.* Budapest: Európa Könyvkiadó, 1973. Translated by Orbán Ottó.

A.G. "Üvöltés," in *A leples bitang.* Budapest: Európa Könyvkiadó, 1984. Translated by Orbán Ottó.

"Üvöltés," in *Üvöltés.* Budapest: Európa Könyvkiadó, 1967. Translated by Orbán Ottó.

"Üvöltés," in *Nagyvilág* 8, no. 6 (June 1963). Translated by Somlyó György.

Italian

A.G. "Urlo," in *Jukebox All'Idrogeno.* Milan: Arnoldo Mondadori Editore, 1965. Translated by Fernanda Pivano.

JAPANESE

A.G. *Howl.* Tokyo, 1963. Translated by Yu Suwa. *Eureka* 47 (1960).

LITHUANIAN

"Kauksmas," trans. Antanas Danielius, in *Tiesa* (Vilna) 269 (November 22, 1985).

MACEDONIAN

A.G. Poems, Skopje, Yugoslavia, 1986: Makedonska Kniga. Translated by Savo Cvetanovski.

NORWEGIAN

A.G. "Hyl," in *Hyl*. Oslo: Pax Forlag, n.d. Translated by Olav Angell.

POLISH

A.G. "Skowyt," in *Skowyt i inne wiersze*. Bydgoszcz, Poland: Pomorze, 1984. Translated by Grzegorz Musiał.

A.G. "Skowyt," in *Utwory Poetyckie*. Krakow: Wydawnictwo Literackie, 1984. Translated by Bogdan Baran.

Truszkowska, Teresa, ed. "Skowyt," in *Wizjonerzy i Buntownicy*. Krakow: Wydawnictwo Literackie, 1976. Translated by Teresa Truszkowska.

"Skowyt," in *Jazz* 9, no. 7/8 (August 1964). Translated by Waclaw Iwaniuk.

"Skowyt" in *Puls*, No. 4–5 (Autumn–Winter 1978–1979). Warsaw (Samizdat edition). Translated by Piotra Allena (pseudonym for Piotr Bikont).

"Skowyt," in *Tematy* 9 (Winter 1964). Translated by Waclaw Iwaniuk.

"Skowyt," in *Literatura na Świecie* 42 (October 1974). Translated by Teresa Truszkowska and Leszek Elektorowicz.

Schäffer, Boguslaw. *Howl* (musical setting). Warsaw: Polskie Wydawnictwo Muzyczne, 1974. Translated by Leszek Elektorowicz.

PORTUGUESE

A.G. "Uivo," in *Uivo*. Lisbon: Publicações dom Quixote, 1973. Translated by José Palla e Carmo.

RUMANIAN

Caraion, Ion, ed. "Urlet de Minie," in *Antologia Poeziei Americane*. Bucharest: Editura "Univers," 1979. Translated by Ion Caraion.

SERBO-CROATIAN

A.G. "Urlik," in *Hidrogenski Džuboks*. Belgrade: Narodna Knjiga, 1983. Translated by Zoran Petković and Mihailo Ristić.

A.G. "Urlik," in *Urlik Uma*. Belgrade: DOB, 1983. Translated by Vojo Sindolić.

"ТРІІН," in *Antologiji moderne američke poezije*. Belgrade: Prosveta, 1972. Translated by Ivan V. Lalić.

"Urlik," in *Vidici* 24, no. 5–6 (September–October 1978). Translated by Ljiljana Kojić-Bogdanović and Branko Aleksić.

SPANISH

A.G. "Aullido," in *Aullido*. Santiago, Chile: Editorial del Pacífico, 1957? Translated by Fernando Alegría.

A.G. "Aullido," in *Aullido y otros poemas*. Montevideo, Uruguay: Los Huevos del Plata, 1969. Translated by Andres Boulton Figueira de Mello.

A.G. "Aullido," in *Aullido, Kaddish y Otros Poemas*. Toluca, México: Universidad Autónoma del Estado de México, 1981. Translated by José Vicente Anaya.

Barnatán, Marcos Ricardo, ed. "Aullido," in *Antología de la "Beat Generation."* Barcelona, Spain: Plaza and Janes, 1970. Translated by Marcos Ricardo Barnatán.

"Aullido," in *Revista Literaria de la Sociedad de Escritores de Chile* 1, no. 3 (November 1957). Translated by Fernando Alegría.

"Moloch," in *El Comercio*, May 15, 1960. Translated by José Miguel Oviedo and Carlos Zavaleta.

"Aullido," in *Airón* 1, no. 3–4 (May 1961). Translated by Madela Ezcurra and Leandro Katz.

"Aullido," in *El Corno Emplumado/Plumed Horn* 2 (April 1962). Translated by Agustí Bartra.

"Aullido," in *Ventana* 3, no. 14, ser. 3 (August 1962). Translated by Roberto Cuadra.

"Aullido," in *Haoma* 1, no. 3 (April 1968). Translated by Andres Boulton Figueira de Mello.

SWEDISH

A.G. "Howl," in *Tårgas & Solrosor*. Stockholm: FIBs Lyrikklubb, 1971. Translated by Gösta Friberg and Gunnar Harding.

TURKISH

A.G. and Ferlinghetti, Lawrence. "Uluma," in *Amerika*. Istanbul: Ada Yayinlari, 1976. Translated by Orhan Duru and Ferit Edgü.

RECORDINGS

San Francisco Poets. New York: Evergreen Records, 1958. LP no. EVR–1, 33⅓ rpm, 12″ mono.

San Francisco Poets. New York: Hanover Records, 1959. LP no. M–5001, 33⅓ rpm, 12″ mono. Matrix: HMG 117.

Allen Ginsberg Reads Howl and Other Poems. Berkeley, Cal.: Fantasy Records, 1959. LP no. 7013, 33⅓ rpm, 12″ mono. Matrix: V–5998–1854/1855.

Beauty and the Beast, by Anne Waldman and Allen Ginsberg. Boulder, Colo.: Naropa Recordings, 1976. 1 cassette.

Howl and Other Poems. Wuppertal, West Germany: S Press Tapes, 1981. 1 cassette.

Acknowledgments

Compilation of the manuscripts, documentation and information in this edition of *Howl* was made possible by kindhearted John Clellon Holmes' retrieval and return of original draft to author.

Editor & biographer Barry Miles examined Columbia archives for additional drafts and the mass of material in appendixes, sat with author through annotations, and typed & qualified transcripts and notes, mapping and editing the entire book.

Bibliographer Bill Morgan sorted thru Columbia archives for several years, cataloguing & indexing the entire deposit for retrievability.

Prof. Gordon Ball, editing author's *Journals Early Fifties Early Sixties*, helped fix chronology and found relevant entries. Early annotations evolved through Fernanda Pivano's meticulous Italian translations.

Raymond Foye curated author's three-decade-old photographs, Juanita Lieberman indexed and guarded them, Brian Graham made prints; Robert Frank advised the project.

Wood engraving by Lynd Ward (with Moloch text) was hand printed as poetry broadside by Michael McCurdy, 1978, in limited edition of 300, with 150 signed & numbered: Penmaen Press, RD 2, Box 145, Great Barrington, MA 01230.

Kenneth A. Lohf, Director of Manuscripts and Rare Books at Special Collections Division, Butler Library, Columbia University, preserved author's papers since 1968.

The following granted permission for print or reprint of letters, critiques, commentaries & images, often with great magnanimity: Eugene Brooks, Lucien Carr, Neeli Cherkovsky, Francesco Clementi, Gregory Corso, Richard Eberhart, Lawrence Ferlinghetti, Barry Gifford, John Hollander, Lewis Hyde, Tuli Kupferberg, Larry Lee, Michael McClure, James McKenzie, Shigeyoshi Murao, Peter Orlovsky, David Perlman, Louis Simpson, Gary Snyder, Diana Trilling, May Ward.

Bob Rosenthal, patient poet, coordinated and collaborated in all activities, established & kept track of household archives, and conducted research with Juanita Lieberman & Greg Masters.

Vicki Stanbury & Reid Fossey contributed neighborly typing. Archetype cover pattern invented by Harry Smith.

Author is indebted to others for supportive scholarship, encouragement and advice: Daniel Allman, Gabriel Austin, Ann Charters, Edith Ginsberg, James Laughlin, Michael McCurdy, Rosemary Bailey, Gerald Nicosia, Ed Sanders, Bob Sharrard & Nancy Peters of City Lights Books, and Craig Broadly, their *Subterraneans* distributor.

Andrew Wylie conceived the project; Harper & Row's Aaron Asher and Terry Karten edited the book; Marge Horvitz as copy editor integrated massive designs with late amendments; William Monroe contained all in head and hand; Sidney Feinberg designed the artifact; Julie Metz executed cover.

Carl Solomon's much-tried patience, friendship & commentary generously confirmed the possibility of this tome.

Index

page numbers in *italic* denote illustrations